# White Scholars / African American Texts

# White Scholars / African American Texts

EDITED BY LISA A. LONG

RUTGERS UNIVERSITY PRESS
NEW BRUNSWICK, NEW JERSEY, AND LONDON

Library of Congress Cataloging-in-Publication Data

White scholars / African American texts / edited by Lisa A. Long.

p. cm.

Includes bbliographical references and index.

ISBN 0-8135-3598-0 (hardcover : alk. paper) – ISBN 0-8135-3599-9 (pbk. : alk. paper)

1. African Americans-Study and teaching (Higher) 2. African Americans–Historiography. 3. American literature–African American authors–Study and teaching. 4. African Americans–Intellectual life. 5. Whites–United States–Intellectual life. 6. Teachers, White–United States. 7. Education, Higher–Social aspects–United States. 8. Education, Higher–Political aspects–United States. 9. United States–Race relations. I. Long, Lisa A.

E184.7.W48 2005

305.896'073'00711–dc22

2004023480

A British Cataloging-in-Publication record for this book is available from the British Library



Manufactured in the United States of America

# CONTENTS

## PART TWO
## Training and Working in the Field



## PART THREE
## Beyond Black and White



## PART FOUR
## Case Studies

# ACKNOWLEDGMENTS

When I told friends and colleagues that I was going to be editing a collection of essays, I received all of the usual warnings about the unique difficulties of such work. Nevertheless, I have found this to be one of the most edifying experiences of my professional life. Through this project I have discovered a diverse, fiercely dedicated, and generous community of scholars—both those who have offered up their writing to the collection and the many who have contributed in less tangible but no less influential ways. David LaCroix, Karla Simcikova, Montye Fuse, Margret Grebowicz, Amritjit Singh, and Kali Tal are among those who have shared their insights and shaped the common work in profound ways. Those who appear as contributors are all deeply committed to African American studies and to imagining productive and congenial communities of scholars and students—I have learned something from each and every one of them. To a person they have responded efficiently to the demands made upon them, despite the mounting workloads, family dramas, and health crises that are bound to circulate among a group of nineteen over the course of a few years. In particular, I acknowledge Sabine Meyer and Bill Andrews for delivering papers at the MLA special session that was the impetus for this collection. Subsequently, Bill has been particularly generous with his advice. My friend Dale Bauer has also continued to offer counsel and encouragement. John Ernest's early contribution to this collection is a part of his long-term support of my work in the field. And I thank especially Nellie McKay for the scholarship that has inspired so many of us and for her commitment to this project when so many other important tasks called her.

I have been lucky to find such a congenial home for this collection at Rutgers University Press. Leslie Mitchner recognized and embraced the seriousness of this work early on and has been a guiding force throughout the evolution of the project. The editorial staff members at Rutgers have been similarly professional and enthusiastic, particularly Melanie Halkias, Elizabeth Gratch, Nicole Manganaro, and Donna Liese. Venetria K. Patton and Maureen T. Reddy provided encouraging and probing readings of the entire manuscript, and I hope that the work is better for their attentions. I owe a great debt to Bill Hodges for allowing me to reproduce Norman Lewis's compelling painting *Journey to the End* on the cover of this book. And I thank the *PMLA* for granting me permission to reprint Nellie McKay's seminal guest column.

Finally, I acknowledge those close to home. North Central College has generously supported this work with summer research grant funding. I am grateful to Lisa Rashley, Sara Eaton, and Anna Leahy, good friends who are always willing to listen, read, cheer, calm, and advise. And James Amundson's love and quiet confidence continue to sustain me through all of life's challenges.

# FOREWORD

## Who Shall Teach African American Literature? Twenty-First-Century Reflections on a Problem of the Twentieth-Century Wheatley Court

Seven years ago, in 1997, my friend Martha Banta, then editor of the *Publication of the Modern Language Association* (*PMLA*), asked if I would write an essay for that journal on the question that *White Scholars / African American Texts* addresses. The topic intrigued me even as it seemed somewhat bold of me to attempt to engage this problem in such a public way. But I also felt complimented by my colleague's evident trust in my ability to respond thoughtfully to one of the most vexing issues for black and white scholars in the field at the end of the twentieth century. I accepted the challenge. When I mentioned my decision to a colleague at my home institution, he suggested (not unkindly) that I might well be suicidal. The essay appeared in the May 1998 issue of *PMLA*.

I began my career in 1978, and by the fall of 1998 I had been a professor in African American literature for twenty years, during a time when excitement was extraordinarily high among practitioners in the area, marking an important era in American cultural history. Most of those involved had high hopes that their efforts would be one aspect of a new time when the institutionalized conscious and unconscious racism that had relegated African Americans to second-class status since the 1870s appeared to be coming to an end. The story of how, when the pendulum swung in their direction, the apostles of African American literature successfully moved that field from the margins of American literature to its center is already well-known and need not be repeated here. As for me, by 1998 I had lived through both the pain and the joy of the mission that many black literature scholars undertook in those mid- to late 1970s and early 1980s years and at which they had succeeded splendidly. The momentum was fueled by the many discoveries of long out-of-print black texts from the eighteenth to the mid-twentieth centuries and by the new and outstanding scholarship that quickly followed. In addition, the rise of black women writers in the 1980s and

1990s played a meaningful role in expanding general interest in the literature as a whole. Inside of classrooms students across racial lines became intrigued by the new literature that introduced them to previously unknown worlds of experiences. The publication of *The Norton Anthology of African American Literature* in 1997 provides a fitting capstone to the efforts of the many well-known and not-so-well-known scholars and teachers who during this time devoted their careers to efforts to ensure the place of African American literature in the academy and in history.

Their successes, however, were not altogether trouble-free. Not surprisingly, beginning in the 1980s, many white professors, some already well established in their fields and some just entering, responded to the pied piper's call to black literature. Their numbers, particularly graduate students, increased steadily as the 1990s advanced. This situation led to serious concerns among many African Americans, especially those just beginning careers in black literature. Joined by other minority group scholars, these young aspiring scholars felt that as job seekers such a development put them at a disadvantage because the number of white job candidates exceeded those of their minority group cohorts, and race was not an inconsequential factor in the marketplace of college and university hiring practices. Others questioned the ability of white scholars, even those with the best intentions, to comprehend the nature of the black experience sufficiently well to qualify them to teach and engage in research in an area so far removed from their life experiences.

In my 1998 essay I attempted to respond to the concerns in this way. There was, I noted, a lot of blame to go around, with much of it belonging to the organizational structures and the individual concerns of institutions of higher education. When many institutions decided to diversify their faculties and student bodies by making African American faculty appointments and enrolling more African American students, their efforts fell short both in producing and employing sufficient black faculty to achieve the goal to which many paid little more than lip service. By the late 1990s, with white graduate student interest in black literature rising and insufficient positions for employment available to meet the needs of whites and blacks who desired those jobs (whose numbers had grown with the inclusion of other minority group students among them), the difficulties that ensued were inevitable. Thus, a number of young black and minority scholars saw themselves, once again, victims of race.

I fully agree that the terrible legacy of racism remains a cancer buried deep in the psyche of Western culture. The reality of its influence is ever present in the lives of some members of our society across all walks of life. But, although we are still far behind in creating a level playing field for all those who were previously not so privileged, there has been movement in that direction, and we need to find ways to work toward a common end. For example, English Departments may once again have to reconceptualize and expand the American literature component of their programs to permit more crossings-over during the training of graduate students. We have to believe that people of goodwill on all sides of the racial divide are sufficiently concerned about working toward fairness and justice for all in deciding how we carry out the business of our profession and that their efforts will eventually bear valuable rewards. We have only one of two ways to face the issue: we can live in hope and persist in engaging the struggle against racism and other barriers that exclude portions of our population from others wherever we find it, or we can die in despair.

In addition, I pointed out to those who believe that African Americans and other minority group peoples have proprietary claims to African American and other minority literatures that from my experiences the use of race as the major criterion qualifying individuals to teach African American literature makes a weak case. There is little question that between the 1970s and 1980s some white scholars took advantage of the new field's needs and produced bad work. But some black scholars did the same, believing that biology was all that was necessary to qualify them as experts in black studies. It is impossible for me not to acknowledge my debt and gratitude to the work of a number of serious white scholars who began mining the field before it became popular prior to the advent of cohort groups of well-trained black scholars in the arena. Some of that work (as well as that of a number of black scholars of that time, most of whom had toiled for many years in the historical black colleges and universities for small rewards), laid the foundations on which my work stands, and solid foundations they were! And, while I admit that experiencing a culture can be useful to understanding its expressive aspects, I don't believe it is the only measure by which to determine the qualifications of teachers and scholars in any field. There is also something of value in having the perspectives of outsiders to a culture as participants in the critical discourse evaluating its productions. I argued for more deliberate and aggressive efforts to open up American literary studies across the many racial and ethnic differences that separate the populations in this nation, for vigilance in making sure that the scholarship adheres to rigorous standards, and for graduate education that is as exacting in black and other minority literatures as in all others. Those of us in the academy, especially in the new areas of such minority studies, have the responsibility to uphold these criteria toward building a more robust and authentic American literary studies than now exists.

I was not surprised by the responses to my essay. Many minority scholars, but not all by any means, angrily disagreed with me on my positions. I took their concerns as seriously as I did those of the scholars who agreed with me. I recognized that theirs were not empty complaints made without cause. We disagree on how to achieve our common goal without further separations within the body of our profession. I had not expected to gain instant converts to my way of thinking; one of my hopes for the piece had been that it would open up a dialogue that would serve as a point of departure from which others could thoughtfully debate the merits of both sides of the issues. In this multiracial, multiethnic nation I stand firmly on the position that we all have the right to cross the boundaries that separate racial and ethnic groups from one another, for, if we do not, we will continue to perpetuate conditions that are likely to bring us to the divisive impasse of reinforcing a hierarchy of value within the collective. Such an eventuality would only move us backward and eliminate already hard-won gains.

In thinking about such matters as I put together these brief reflections, I cannot avoid wondering how the issues raised here might be addressed across the profession as a whole. I recognize that there are no easy solutions, and any steps we take are likely to be risky and may even fail. But I believe the new century calls us to this task. That the subject is of sufficient interest to as many scholars as contributed to *White Scholars / African American Texts* suggests it deserves serious thought toward a solution because it will not disappear on its own. And, while I hope that individual institutions will be moved in this direction, it is not a problem that any single faculty can resolve. The conversation needs to begin at the top levels of the profession. Could this be one that the officers of organizations such as the Modern Language Association in consultation with department chairs might be requested to take on as an item for their discussion and possible action as a first step toward engaging the membership? In short, I think it needs to move beyond the printed pages of this volume, which owes its existence to the presence of uncomfortable feelings and questions that are still as much with us today as they were nearly a decade ago. We have yet to disband the Wheatley Court, and that idea should give us cause for pause. I conclude my thoughts on who shall teach African American literature with my thanks and deep appreciation to Professor Lisa Long (a Wisconsin graduate but not my former student) for liberating my essay from the pages of *PMLA* and thus moving the conversation in the direction I originally hoped it would take. My fervent wish is that others of like mind to those of us included in this volume can be brought together to take these ideas beyond the realms of thinking and writing to the place where action can begin.

NELLIE Y. McKAY
10 November 2004

# White Scholars / African American Texts

# Introduction

## White Scholars / African American Texts

LISA A. LONG

In May 1998 Nellie Y. McKay published a provocative and timely guest column in *PMLA* in which she reminded readers of the appalling paucity of African American scholars in literary studies and expressed concern about the fates of the white scholars who end up studying African American literature. This collection of essays takes up one of the pressing implications of McKay's powerful argument, focusing particularly on the reality of a world in which the study and teaching of African American literature is done so often by white scholars and framed in terms of an exclusive black/white racial divide. In highlighting the "whiteness" of some African Americanists, this collection does not intend to imply that the teaching of African American literature by white scholars is definitively impossible. Indeed, such work is not only possible but imperative—we all have a responsibility to know this literature. That said, while the study of African American literature is possible for white scholars, there also are real and pressing impossibilities in that work, particularly given our nation's still unprocessed racial history. In short, this collection seeks to open up a public conversation about the vexatious, widely acknowledged, and yet rarely spoken ideological, pedagogical, and historical complexities faced by many white scholars who teach and research in African American literature. Those working in feminist and multicultural pedagogies more broadly have already begun to tease out the challenges of "teaching what you're not" (to borrow from the title of Katherine Mayberry's fine anthology). Yet the history of black/white racial formations in the United States remains particular, powerful, and in some ways paradigmatic and deserves extended treatment of its own.

Rather than arguing that some see white teachers and scholars solely as inauthentic, contributors to this collection seek to explore how the classroom and the academic world at large are ghosted by a history that snarls racial, pedagogical, and scholarly authorities. In the process many wrestle with how we can (or should) reconcile the tensions between humanist positions that assert we can know one another's experiences because we are all "human" and a more skeptical stance that insists that racial difference creates unbridgeable gaps in knowledge. To this end contributors fruitfully meld the theoretical and the experiential, engaging and synthesizing recent debates about the construction of race and the daily realities of functioning in an insistently raced academic world. Some draw largely on their personal experiences as or with white scholars to explore these tensions. Others look to African American texts themselves, noticing both invitations to and prohibitions against the white scholar and teacher. And still others have taken on the critical work of previous scholars in their efforts to tease out, as Elizabeth Abel following Toni Morrison's lead suggests, the whiteness that "gains materiality through the desires and fantasies played out in its interpretations of blackness" (498). It is my hope that this collection will contribute to the project Abel delineates.

In part this book emerged from a desire to simply "out" the anecdotes and innuendo that so often shape widespread assumptions about the current business of African American studies: the idea that white folks can't or shouldn't do African American studies; conversely, the idea that race shouldn't matter and that in a supposed academic meritocracy "good work" will be recognized and rewarded; that white students and scholars shouldn't go into African American literature because they aren't getting jobs in the field—and that, by implication, African American job candidates have a distinct advantage over white candidates and colleagues; that African American scholars have vexed feelings about their work training a generation of mostly white students and that some young white scholars feel unprepared to take on this complicated work; that many white scholars lack training or interest in African American literature or, conversely, that they might speak ignorantly and yet authoritatively about it; that African American scholars have experiential superiority that makes their academic work more authentic; and, concomitantly, that African American scholars need to approve or validate the efforts of white scholars.

I have initiated this project in full cognizance of Ann duCille's warnings about the pitfalls of such work, what she calls the move to "guilty conscience rhetoric." That is, duCille finds that the sort of navel gazing that white scholars can engage in as they recount finding their way to African American literature can "demean" the field rather than enrich it (45). Michael Awkward adds that the self-referential moments of white scholars can make white scholars themselves the focus of African American literature, in the worst-case scenarios signaling "a posture antithetical to Afro-Americanist interests" ("Negotiations" 592, 583). Yet without examinations of white scholars, as many of the contributors claim, we are unlikely to shape an educational community that will appeal to the interests of diverse scholars and serve African American texts. For many decades African American scholars have taken on most of the responsibility for leading discussions about the complexity of race in our reading practices, our classrooms, and our scholarly communities. Indeed, some white scholars, particularly those early on in their careers, subconsciously rely on African American scholars as racial arbiters. As I was corresponding with colleagues across the country while organizing this volume, prominent African American scholar Carla L. Peterson, graciously explaining her decision to decline my invitation to contribute, wrote: "I think this is a place for white scholars—not African-Americans—to engage in a conversation with each other and the broader public about such issues. I am just not sure that African Americans should have a role here; in fact, I think that their intervention might just muddy the waters" (e-mail). Peterson has been outnumbered by interested parties, who have argued that there are not enough African American scholars weighing in here. Who can or should speak about the politics of African American literary study is still clearly a vexed issue in and of itself. Nevertheless, I have included essays by African American scholars in hopes that they can help clarify rather than muddy the waters. On the other hand, I don't find "muddied waters" particularly problematic; this metaphor aptly suggests the opacities of the subject at hand. Thus, readers will discover a diversity of voices not only in terms of racial identity but also in terms of gender, geography, nationality, sexual orientation, and rank. Obviously, this text does not seek to wrest authority away from African American scholars; I do think, however, that it is high time that white scholars entered these difficult discussions in a lengthy format such as this.

In choosing the contributors, I have remained attuned to the many different types of scholars who have shown their interest in this topic. Given the sensitivity of these issues and the great range of powerful opinions they can elicit, an edited collection seemed the most judicious way of treating this material in order to present and authorize as many opinions as possible. I have deliberately crafted a book at odds with itself to this end—one that is meant to provoke readers but not necessarily to insist upon consensus or offer simple solutions. Contributors range from some of the most prominent scholars in African American literature to graduate students; from those who teach at large universities to those who might be the only African Americanist at their small colleges; from those who face classes filled with white faces to those who teach in racially diverse contexts. Then, too, the geographical and institutional environment in which each operates dictates the form of his or her work. This collection also makes it clear that studying African American literature today is a quite different enterprise than it was a generation ago. As Mayberry has suggested, "an identity-based definition of *credibility*" within academic settings is a historically specific phenomenon, one that has produced "an entirely new precondition of professional authority"—and one that has produced the conditions that have fueled this collection and others like it ("Introduction" 3). There is still no monolithic "white scholar," no one way of coming to the field, no singular set of problems and possibilities.

Nevertheless, as McKay points out, the fact that we have so few African American scholars in literary studies today is one of the realities that complicates the study of African American literature and culture by white scholars. Matters do seem to be improving—but at a glacial pace. The 2002 National Survey of Earned Doctorates reveals that 47 students who identified themselves as "black / African American" received Ph.D. degrees in English and American Language and Literature, in comparison to 705 students who identified themselves as white (Hoffer et al. 86).[1] These numbers indicate a slight shift from 1997, when the Modern Language Association (MLA) reported that 40 African American and 1,070 white students received Ph.D. degrees ("Findings"). And they demonstrate improvement over the 1992–1995 numbers McKay cites, which suggest that anywhere between 18 and 25 African American students received doctorates during each of those years (McKay 22). In the breakdown of the 2002s numbers, however, we discover that only 28 of the 47 students self-identified as black / African American specialized in American literature, while 270 white students became Americanists; we can only speculate about how many of these scholars are trained specifically in African American literature. The assumption that African American scholars will or should study African American literature is a limiting one—though anecdotal evidence offered here suggests that persistent hiring practices speciously insist upon such a simplistic conflation as jobs in African American studies are still used to hold the place for minority hires. All the same, if there were even more African Americans and other scholars of color entering and working in African American literature, I suspect, the presence of white scholars—though still complicated—would not seem *as* problematic.

In the past two decades there have been a number of excellent essays that have begun to tackle the issues taken on here. DuCille, Abel, Awkward, bell hooks, Charmaine Eddy, David Bleich, Gail B. Griffin, Kimberly Rae Connor, Minrose C. Gwin, Barbara T. Christian ("Response"), and, of course, Nellie McKay, among others, have begun to probe the interracial communities in which we all operate. Some of the books in the "MLA Teaching" series have touched briefly but tantalizingly on the complexities of white scholars / African American texts. For example, Kathryn Earle's and Toni McNaron's pieces on teaching *Sula* and *Beloved*, respectively, in McKay and Earle's *Approaches to Teaching the Novels of Toni Morrison*, offer strategies for addressing gaps in cultural knowledge. Finally, a number of provocative essays have appeared in recent anthologies treating multicultural literature on race more broadly. Mayberry's collection, *Teaching What You're Not: Identity Politics in Higher Education*, contains articles by Christie Farnham, Jacqueline Jones, and Donna J.

Watson that all, in one way or another, interrogate how the seemingly objective academic authority of scholars of African American studies can be challenged when a scholar's whiteness is revealed. Bonnie TuSmith and Maureen T. Reddy's recent collection, *Race in the Classroom: Pedagogy and Politics*, contains nearly a dozen excellent essays on issues of authority and evaluation and the development of transformative pedagogies in the field.[2] This is by no means an exhaustive review of all of the work that has been done on this subject; I leave it to the contributors and refer readers to our common works cited to round out this list. I do want to emphasize, however, the scattered but consistent attention the white scholar / African American text dynamic has elicited.

Much of the work in multicultural education has revolved around pedagogy and race. Because this book is more narrowly focused, it is able to address not only pedagogical challenges but also professional issues ranging from graduate training to canonization to probing considerations of personal attractions to particular African American authors within a specific and fundamental racial dyad. The scholarship on multicultural literature and pedagogy often addresses identity quite broadly in its efforts, as Mayberry phrases it, to consider a "wide variety of identity interfaces" (7). I argue that it is no coincidence that the specific intricacies of African American studies are so often featured in such texts. For example, Mayberry writes that multiculturalism has been driven by the politicization of "African Americans and other minorities"; elsewhere, she offers the example of "whites teaching black studies" to stand in for the complexities of racial politics in American classrooms (2, 4). These common rhetorical figures (deployed again and again in writing on multicultural literature) make African Americans the paradigmatic minority and whites the perennial interlopers. Thus, the black/white racial matrix is stubbornly trenchant and particular and deserving of our attentions here. This is not to suggest that the white scholar / African American text dynamic is simplistically binary in its nature. One whole section of this book is devoted to essays that complicate the deceptive racial "divide." Nor is it meant to diminish the realities or the histories of other ethnic and racial minorities in the United States as they have encountered or engaged with white culture or with one another. Slavery and the persistence of subsequent racism against African Americans, however, have taken their own forms. Whiteness is still the invisible, mythical norm, yet the black/white matrix often remains unremarked as the reliable signifier for other racial configurations in the United States.

One might argue that it is obvious that the history of African American enslavement makes the black/white racial matrix particular—slavery is the institutionalized racial lightning rod that has galvanized and, to a certain extent, organized subsequent discussions of race in the United States. Thus, it is through contemporary engagements with this history that I suggest we come to the topic at hand. I have taken on this project as a way of completing business left unfinished in my recent explorations of Octavia Butler's *Kindred* and Phyllis Alesia Perry's *Stigmata*, contemporary novels that imagine the persistence of slavery in the lives of modern African Americans. Butler's and Perry's female, African American protagonists "live" slavery, either through the psychic invasions of their enslaved ancestors or through fantastic time travels to slave times. Most significant, their bodies bear the wounds of their slave experiences: bleeding whip marks, manacle wounds, and even amputations attest to the reality of slavery in contemporary lives. Thus, Butler and Perry suggest that in order truly to apprehend American history, modern Americans must "feel" it in their bodies. Indeed, it is African American women who have blood ties to a traumatic past in the novels and are, then, authorized to speak about it because of that corporeal knowledge (though clearly special access to the past comes at a cost). In the article treating these novels, I also examine how students—both white and African American—sometimes perceive that they, too, are traumatically invaded by African American texts that deal with slavery.

Yet I just barely touched on the force of that history for white academics like me, particularly in our classrooms, our scholarly practices, and our professional communities. This oversight haunted me, and I subsequently became convinced of the need to see modern white bodies within this temporal dynamic as well. Thus, in the winter of 2002 I organized a special session entitled "White Scholars / African American Texts" for the annual meeting of the Modern Language Association. This is clearly an urgent topic for many, for the response to the call for papers that initiated the panel was overwhelming. Dozens of scholars from all over the country—indeed, all over the world—responded enthusiastically to the hard questions this project seeks to tackle. Many of the scholars who attended the panel, as well as the dozens more whom I've come to know subsequently through this book, wanted to talk about these fraught issues further; the brief conference meeting, with its constraints of time and form, simply did not suffice. And so this book emerged as a truly grassroots project. The graduate students who have written to me have been perhaps the most vociferous in their desire to see scholarly work on this topic, and I have been committed to representing some of their unique concerns here. Although most of the contributors to this book are employed primarily by English departments, the racial politics they address pertain to the coverage of African American texts in any number of disciplines.

One cannot take on the complexities of the white scholar / African American text dynamic without acknowledging at some level the fundamentally vexed nature of academic authority. Education itself mimics the power structures of domination and subordination, for to "master" any material historically has implied, in part, the imposition of one's self upon it, its subjugation to one's authority. No matter how well meaning white scholars are, how respectful of the material and cognizant of the ways that they cannot know it, the tenets of scholarly work demand that the scholar take command of it to a certain degree. In *Loose Canons: Notes on the Culture Wars* Henry Louis Gates Jr. has explained at length how the precepts of Western knowledge have been used by white folks as instruments of racist domination in U.S. history—how the belief in the "humanity" of Africans was contingent upon their "master[y]" of the "'arts and sciences'" (53). And Awkward points out the ways that some white critics still promulgate the notion of "whiteness as a normative intellectual state" ("Negotiations" 597). Debates about the purported whiteness of academic endeavors—particularly those that are theoretically engaged—are well worn. Yet recent scholars have begun to notice, as Judith Roof and Robyn Wiegman do in *Who Can Speak? Authority and Critical Identity*, that, "by exposing the way that objective and neutral methodologies repress the precise locations from which the speaker comes, academic discourses have begun to interrogate themselves from within, calling scholars to account, so to speak, for their own inescapable epistemic contingencies" ("Introduction" ix). And yet academic protocols have not been abandoned; indeed, they continue to thrive and to shape conversations about the study of African American literature in powerful ways. For example, duCille ascribes to "the white patriarchal society that has reared us and the white Eurocentric educational system that has trained us" the alternating defensiveness and aggression with which the current generation of scholars contends in making claims to African American women's literature (50). In racializing the discursive systems that form our disciplinary practices, duCille suggests that all academic endeavors can be racially suspect. As a result, book learning and contemporary experiences can sometimes be at odds in African American literary classrooms.

In highlighting the challenges of teaching and scholarly work by white schclars in the field rather than the many agreeable classes and discussions that take place between students and scholars about African American literature, I do not mean to misrepresent the important work that white folks do in teaching and studying African American literature. To focus for a moment on the classroom, however, I think that those students who resist white mastery in some ways "get it," get what the literature is teaching them, better than those who happily take the words of white scholars at face value and who say they "enjoy" the class and the literature they read. As Gail B. Griffin has recently argued, "our job is to *cause* trouble in the classroom," and very positive student evaluations in these contexts can be a sign of student comfort (3). And Maureen T. Reddy bemoans her students' continuing "social investment in white authority, which sticks like flypaper regardless of [her] efforts to get it off" in her courses ("Smashing" 59). Wresting away our students' racial-historical "innocence" is bound to cause pain and even anger. And much African American literature teaches that students should be distinctly uncomfortable with a white teacher's handling of racial situations and, by extension, of African American texts.

Many of the most commonly taught African American texts reinforce a history of dominating or ineffective white schoolteachers. There is Janie's absent father in *Their Eyes Were Watching God*; the distant, drug-addicted tutor in *The Oxherding Tale*; the controlling principal in *Black Boy*. But perhaps the most infamous white teacher in the most celebrated and widely taught African American novel of the last two decades is the character of schoolteacher in Toni Morrison's *Beloved*. I believe that the very ubiquity of *Beloved*—our shared fascination with this beautiful, horrifying novel, and its already overdetermined place in the African American literary canon—attests to the claims of history upon our contemporary scholarly communities. More to the point, the novel offers a pedagogy not only of but also *about* the white teacher-scholar.

Schoolteacher, a man initially distinguished by his fine manners and "book learning," arrives at Sweet Home to "put things in order" after the death of Sethe's relatively kind master, Mr. Garner. Although his main task is to oversee the running of the plantation, the small classes he conducts with his white pupils, the "sons or nephews" he brought with him (*Beloved* 36), merge with his work tutoring the enslaved, creating a pedagogy that affiliates the work of slave master and schoolmaster. What links both projects is schoolteacher's efforts to "know" the enslaved intimately so that he can teach them and teach about them. Morrison, for example, writes that he "developed a variety of corrections (which he recorded in his notebook) to reeducate" the enslaved when they back-talked (220). Sethe discovers that he is using his notes to tutor his white pupils in the phrenological differences between the human whites and beastly Africans (193). He measures the bodies of the enslaved and asks incessant, probing questions in order to control them through his knowledge of them (37). He is both scholar and pedagogue.[3] Thus, when Sethe kills Beloved, she ultimately defies the knowledge and the teaching of schoolteacher, insisting that he does not know her. Schoolteacher ascribes the incident to poor learning on the part of his nephew and of Sethe; he chastises his nephew for "mishandling" Sethe by beating her "beyond the point of education" (149).

Of course, contemporary white teachers and scholars of African American literature are not doing racist anthropological studies of authors or students, nor do they "own" their students; Morrison, however, insistently links school teaching, book learning, and colonial force. Mr. Garner had often deferred to the opinions of the enslaved, feeling that their expertise "did not deprive him of authority or power. It was schoolteacher who taught them otherwise" (*Beloved* 125). Thus, the narrator implies that those who garner their power from the knowledge industry are threatened by those who proffer their own ways of knowing. Schoolteacher beats an enslaved man named Sixo not for stealing but for telling an elegant lie, "to show him that definitions belonged to the definers—not the defined" (190). While this power dynamic may hold, at least in part, for schoolteachers of all races, ethnicities, and genders, the history of black/

white relations in this country nuances teaching in particular ways. Even the well-intentioned desires of white folks to gain knowledge of African American literature and culture can be seen as a co-optive move when placed in the context of a history in which African Americans have not been authorized to speak for themselves (see Griffin 7; Abel 484). Because there are so few African American scholars in the field, this history still resonates profoundly through our academic communities.

Morrison's last mention of education in *Beloved* shifts the gendered terrain of academic authority but still questions the efficacy of white teachers; here it is not the brutal white slave master but, rather, the sympathetic white woman, Miss Bodwin, who "taught [Denver] stuff" (266). Although we do not know the nature of this white woman's teaching, it is clearly more benign than schoolteacher's. Still, when Paul D. hears that Miss Bodwin is "experimenting" on Denver in hopes that she might attend Oberlin College, Paul D remains silent and yet thinks, "'Watch out. Watch out. Nothing in the world more dangerous than a white schoolteacher'" (266). Such an observation reinforces the insidious racializing impulses that still inflect the work of the most seemingly "liberal" white critics and teachers. Recent scholarship bears out the dangers inherent in this racialized academic dynamic. For example, Abel questions the fitness of white feminist scholars, insisting that their "readings of black women's texts disclose white critical fantasies" that focus almost exclusively on African American women's biological and textual bodies in their critical practices as a way of "rematerializing and rejuvenating" an "attenuated white feminism" (477, 479). And Lisa Gonsalves has shown how well meaning white instructors sensitive to the racial dynamics in their classrooms can suffer from a "hyper-awareness . . . [of] how to 'be' with a Black male student" in particular. She contends that, while such white instructors may be "aware of the some of the educational issues faced" by African American students, they may be "unable to use this knowledge to be a better teacher" for those students (443). Such warnings are not meant to scare off white teachers and scholars from working with African American texts or students, but they are meant to alert us to the ways that problematic racial difference insinuates itself into white scholars' academic endeavors despite their best efforts.

I begin this collection by highlighting the horrifying nature of some fictional white teacher-scholars not to imply that white teacher-scholars today are all horrifying—the truth is far from it, of course. I do think we need to start, however, by acknowledging the omnipresent historical context in which we all operate. As Hoyt Fuller so elegantly puts it, "the glass through which black life is viewed by white Americans is, inescapably . . . befogged by the hot breath of history" (5–6). History is here a sentient form that imposes itself on the present. If, à la the fantasies of Octavia Butler and Phyllis Alesia Perry, we grant to African Americans implicit authority about the experiences of slavery and racist oppression, then mustn't we implicitly grant to whites similar authority? The horrors of being the slave master or mistress are, of course, of a quite different sort than those of being enslaved. Yet don't some white folks, then, have an undeniable connection to that past? I suggest that we really can't have one historical connection without the other. Of course, acknowledging the contemporary potency of our slave past does not make contemporary African Americans into literal slaves, just as it does not make contemporary whites into slave masters and mistresses. Yet, as bell hooks claims, the racialized white body historically has represented "the terrible, the terrifying, the terrorizing" in many black communities (*Black Looks* 170). It is precisely these ghostly bodies that overlay contemporary academic settings and signify upon living white bodies.

Indeed, if we follow Butler's and Perry's lead, we would imagine the ways that enslavers' bodies *inhabit* living white bodies. There would, however, be no bleeding whip marks or manacle wounds to mark that passage—predictably, the history of enslavement would be barely perceptible to our present senses if routed through white bodies. Yet, when Perry's protagonist describes European kidnappers who steal her great-great-grandmother from Africa as "ghost[s] with hair like fire and no color eyes" and students look to me, do those ghosts materialize before their eyes? Are white scholars who stand before their students and colleagues interpreting African American texts just different versions of white stars such as Elvis Presley, the Rolling Stones, Britney Spears, and Eminem, "contrived and promoted" as Greg Tate argues, "to do away with bodily reminders of the Black origins of American" pleasures—"pop" or not (4)? Already labeled as "ghostly" in some African American traditions and made doubly so by the history that haunts our scholarly communities, perhaps it is the white form that embodies history, the absent and yet omnipresent body whose hot breath befogs our view of contemporary life. It is these bodies that we need to acknowledge more explicitly.

Although many of the contributors to this collection might take issue with the particular historical context in which I have situated our work here, I do believe that most would agree that tackling this subject is a delicate task—and not one, despite my initial turn to history, aimed at provoking "guilt" from white folks for the crimes of their literal or symbolic ancestors. Rather, it is a task with a variety of means and ends—first, of becoming comfortable with the past, with being able to wear the mantle of historical violence without letting it envelop white scholars in unproductive and ultimately self-serving shame or denial. It means being willing to run the risk of *seeming* uninformed, unenlightened, or, that most dreaded of all labels, "racist," as white scholars inevitably work out their own racial consciousnesses in academic publications and in their classrooms. It means that white scholars need to continue to learn and to solidify their own academic authority while remaining receptive to the critical work and counsel of their African American colleagues. And, finally, it means always looking toward the future—resisting history's claims on us when they lead to paralysis and testing the categorical imperatives that could keep us mired in unproductive ruts.

The essays contained in the following pages take up these tasks—sometimes resolutely and sometimes with trepidation. They have been organized into four parts: (1) Liberalism, Authority, and Authenticity; (2) Training and Working in the Field; (3) Beyond Black and White; and (4) Case Studies.

The essays in part 1, "Liberalism, Authority, and Authenticity," explore the logics by which white scholars justify / make sense of their place in the community of African Americanists broadly and in the African American literature classroom more particularly. The essays focus on the palpable power of the instructor's raced body in the classroom and its relationship to the students and to the texts at hand. This section grounds the book not only in personal experience but also in recent, more theoretical discussions about the many ways that white scholars can(not) enter the African American classroom.

The first two essays in the collection situate the doings of white scholars in a white liberal tradition that holds the promise of change through individual action at the expense of more radical examinations of systemic and historical inequities. Russ Castronovo begins by exposing the implications of a "white liberal politics." Setting aside the good work done by white liberals, he focuses on the way the ideology of liberalism subsumes deep-seated discontent through the personalization of hierarchies and the internalization of injustice as white guilt. In the end Castronovo proffers what he calls a "negative pedagogy" for white scholars of African American texts, for, as he points out, "the critique of liberal critics is, itself, prone to liberalism." John Ernest extends this critique, focusing on the white supremacist culture that already races the classroom before anyone enters. Rather than looking at how "race is presented as something in the literature, or as a quality or identifier of the author, or as one among many social topics," he suggests we should look to race as "a social order that writers work to represent, or to which writers respond." In particular, Ernest describes some of the ways that African American texts are misinterpreted when they are placed within the established (read: white) literary tradition. In closing, he suggests that the challenge for white scholars is "learning to read not just the text at hand but also the white hand on the text—as well as the complex cultural history that shaped the hand of authority and that has defined the authority of the text."

Leslie W. Lewis shifts the terrain of this conversation, moving us from the ideology of liberalism to the crucial etymological and historical differences between authority and authenticity. Taking us on a journey through African American performance history that includes examinations of the minstrel show and hip-hop culture, Lewis dramatizes the destructive nature of discourses of "authentic blackness" for the African American community—and, subsequently, for white scholars. In the end Lewis argues that authenticity is not only problematic but also perversely essentialist and that more fruitful questions to pose of white scholars are through the tropes of authority. Based on her experiences as a professional blues musician and as a professor at Tuskegee University, a historically black institution, Barbara A. Baker also argues for the utility of authority. Indeed, Baker follows the lead of some of Tuskegee's finest alumni, Ralph Ellison and Albert Murray, in asserting the "mulatto" nature of African American arts and the power that can result when white and black readers or listeners become "aesthetically one."

"Training and Working in the Field" considers some of the ways that white scholars are shaped by and shape their teachers, curricula, peers, and perceptions of the job market. This part of the book, perhaps more than any other, suggests how much the field of African American literature has changed during the past three decades, and so, too, has the position of the white scholar. Here I have included senior and respected scholars as well as graduate students confronting for the first time the racial politics of this field. Because these essays explicitly consider issues of perceived access to resources and power, they are, perhaps, among the most controversial in the book.

William L. Andrews begins part 2 by tracing his professional coming into being as an African Americanist at the same time that African American literature was coming into being as a recognized specialization. Perhaps surprisingly, given his illustrious publications in the field, Andrews explains that he was not considered an African Americanist by his employers until relatively late in his career. He thus reminds us that doing good work can be an end in and of itself. Venetria K. Patton also describes her professional coming into being as a young African American scholar who found her way, finally, to African American literature. In particular, she describes in positive terms the white teachers and mentors who guided her early career. Patton testifies that white scholars who demonstrate "cultural literacy" can do African American literary criticism. Yet she honestly grapples with the realities of an insistently raced and racist academic world and her desire, then, to grab hold of a literature she sees as her own.

The remaining two essays in part 2 examine how white scholars are being trained as African Americanists today. Graduate student April Conley Kilinski and newly minted Ph.D. Amanda M. Lawrence share their recent experiences being mentored in African American literature and entering the African American literary classroom. They question rhetoric that suggests, sometimes unproblematically, that anyone can do African American literature if they "know their stuff." They argue, instead, that access to training and classes is not a problem for contemporary graduate students; access to candid mentoring and the development of a more fine-tuned racial self-consciousness can be. Finally, Barbara McCaskill explores her complicated relationship to the field as an African American scholar who is training a generation of largely white students. In particular, she contrasts her view of the profession as "vocation or calling"—an obligation she feels to the work because of her visceral and familial connection to the literature—to many of her white students' "careerism."

Part 3, "Beyond Black and White," attempts to problematize the black/white divide that structures the book. The scholars who contribute to this section do not feel that the white scholar / African American text format is sufficient to represent their experiences in the field—even if they are apparently black or white. Matters of nationality and sexual identity are foregrounded. Some question the presumed hierarchical power structure that privileges whiteness and the authority it supposedly connotes no matter the racial context. In acknowledging the structural power of the black/white divide, the contributors both attest to its power and resist its totalizing effects.

Sabine Meyer and Nita N. Kumar question critical traditions that have, each argues, relied on simplified identity politics and limited the role of the white scholar—and the possibilities of African American scholarship more generally. Meyer grapples with the "faulty analogies" that have been forged between queer and African American identities (and studies) through their supposedly shared distance from a normative center. She eschews queer scholarship that has made use of a white "attraction to and fascination with the racialized other" and offers, instead, a "queer commentary" as a useful means for interrogating racial categories in the classroom. Kumar rehearses how the exclusive black/white divide has been reinforced through twentieth-century African American scholarship and asks how the postcolonial other relates to the racial other. In particular, Kumar claims that "it is this dialectics between the subjectivity of the postcolonial reader and the subjectivity of the ethnic text that can be generative of new meanings" that break us out of the potentially stultifying black/white embrace that she sees as dictating African American literary study.

The following two essays examine how non-American scholars are able to enter American conversations and classrooms entertaining African American literature. Alessandro Portelli talks about teaching African American literature in an apparently "white" non-American country and of confronting the white scholar / African American text dynamic in the United States as a white non-American. He recounts his distinguished career as an African Americanist in the United States and Italy, tracing how his relationship to the literature has been contextually bound—by the initial absence of people of color in Italy and by his own sometimes ambiguously raced body in the United States. The recent emergence of what Portelli calls "African Italians" has yet again shifted that dynamic as he continues his work in his home country. And Ngwarsungu Chiwengo examines the interesting alliances and alienations of a Congolese scholar relating to African American literature in the United States. She posits that "twilight" faculty such as her signify on African American literature in complex ways. Trained in white colonial academic praxis and thus schooled in the same racist stereotypes as white readers, she explores whether or not African scholars—what she calls the "stepbrothers and sisters" of African Americans—read and teach African American literature better than whites.

Part 4, "Case Studies," looks at individual instances of how and why white scholars approach African American texts. What draws them to this work? An unabashed love affair with the beauty of African American literature? White liberal guilt? Personal history? Subconscious cooptation? A sense that the horrors of slavery and reconstruction are best able to express the invisible ills that afflict others? Some combination of all of them? How do anger, fear, and resentment—as well as aesthetic attraction, intellectual engagement, and goodwill—shape the white scholar / African American text dynamic? The authors in this section explore the works of the writers to whom they and other white scholars are attracted and consider why and how these writers might have responded to their own work.

Robert S. Levine sets the stage for this final section, beginning by asserting his essay is "a confession—because there *is* something personal about such a long-standing critical interest in a writer, and there are secrets." He goes on to reveal his long-term attraction to the work of Martin Delany, a nineteenth-century writer who often demonized whites as a group and asserted black superiority. Levine reflects on how he integrated Harriet Beeches Stowe, the well-meaning white liberal, into his studies of Delany in order to negotiate his own relationship to Delany's work. Finally, once he became director of Graduate Admissions at his institution, Levine claims he heard Delany differently, particularly noticing his warnings about how education is kept "beyond the reach of blacks." Dale M. Bauer examines her relationship to the turn-of-the-twentieth-century novels of Emma Dunham Kelley-Hawkins, which she consistently assigns in classes, despite fears that students may dislike the novels. What she has discovered is that they ignore the racial uplift rhetoric that might prompt discontent, instead embracing the "dream of a raceless world" offered in the novels, one imbued with "universal" Christian values. Bauer eventually connects her students' desires to her own deeply held assumptions about the classroom as the potential site of "moral victory over the forces of evil, racism among them"—assumptions that she subsequently finds specious given the violent history of student resistance to the white professor represented in the women's literature she teaches.

The essays conclude with two examinations of white scholars' treatments of African American writers. James D. Sullivan, a Gwendolyn Brooks scholar, addresses Brooks's late-life efforts to ward off white readers from her texts—particularly the "professional Negro-understanders." Sullivan chooses not to heed Brooks's warning nor to see those warnings simply as a sign of the times in which she wrote. Rather, he argues that they have made him more keenly attuned to his "frame of reference," and he subsequently examines the racism apparent in early critical appraisals of Brooks's work. And Kimberly Rae Connor situates this conversation in the "ambient ethnic diversity that is [her] son's unconscious entitlement, the multiculturalism that is his norm." She details how her attraction to Monica Sone's *Nisei Daughter*, which she includes in her multicultural literature classes, is conditioned by her foundational understanding of and training in African American literature. In the end she asks us to imagine a future world that will require interpretive acts reflective of a multiethnic reality that take us beyond the apparently black-and-white divide.

But, before turning to these new essays, I refer readers to the reprint of Nellie Y. McKay's *PMLA* column, which leads off this collection. McKay's work inspired many of the contributors, and her long-standing commitment to the issues we address here serves as a reminder of the ongoing, self-conscious efforts required of all African Americanists. In particular, McKay's seminal work provides a focal point for the important discussions that our profession needs more explicitly to engage in to explore the role of the white scholar in African American literary studies responsibly.

## NOTES

1. I need to acknowledge that I am comparing the results gathered by two different organizations under different circumstances. The annual Survey of Earned Doctorates (SED) is a census of all Ph.D. recipients in the United States in a given year administered by the National Opinion Research Center. In 1997 the Modern Language Association, the national professional organization for students and scholars in literature and languages, completed a twenty-year study of the Ph.D. placements of students in the modern languages. Thus, the different means and ends of these two studies could produce results that don't articulate perfectly. Moreover, recent changes in the way information about race and ethnicity is gathered by the SED might also slightly skew recent results. The new format introduced to the survey in 2001 "asked respondents to mark all racial categories that apply to them, rather than a single category as had been requested since 1973 when race and ethnicity questions were first added to the SED questionnaire" (Hoffer et al. 14). This new policy potentially could increase the number of Ph.D. recipients marking any number of racial and ethnic categories.
2. In particular, Karen Elias and Judith C. Jones, Reddy, Rebecca Meacham, Fred Ashe, Kevin Everod Quashie, Virginia Whatley Smith, Gĩtahi Gĩtĩtĩ, Daniel P. Liston and Sirat Al Salim, Gary L. Lemons, A. Yemisi Jimoh and Charlene Johnson, write specifically on the racial dynamics in classrooms focused on African American texts (See TuSmith and Reddy).
3. Anne E. Goldman has also outlined how in *Beloved* "both the body and the word become commodified; texts upon which the white man makes his mark." She situates this "politics of production within what appears an equally curious literary establishment" (314). Goldman argues that in stealing an enslaved woman's words, her literary production, as well as her children, her reproduction, a character such as

schoolteacher "will enhance his reputation as litterateur and replenish his pockets[;] his enactment of abuse is performed in order to deny his dependence on the woman whose objectification enables him to produce his own identity" (324). Goldman begins her article with a self-referential moment acknowledging how she, as a white scholar, is implicated in this dirty literary business and thus implicitly bolsters my reading of the pedagogy not just of but also about the white teacher that Morrison delineates.

# Naming the Problem That Led to the Question "Who Shall Teach African American Literature?"

## or, Are We Ready to Disband the Wheatley Court?

NELLIE Y. McKAY

We whose names are underwritten, do assure the World, that the POEMS in the following Page, were (as we verily believe,) written by PHILLIS, a young Negro Girl, who was but a few Years since, brought an uncultivated Barbarian from Africa. [. . .] She has been examined by some of the best Judges, and is thought qualified to write them.

–Attestation in Phillis Wheatley's *Poems on Various Subjects, Religious and Moral*

The poems written by this young negro bear no endemial marks of solar fire or spirit. They are merely imitative; and, indeed, most of those people have a turn for imitation, though they have little or none for invention.

–Anonymous reviewer of Wheatley's poems in 1764

It WAS NOT NATURAL. And she was the first. [. . .] Phillis Miracle Wheatley: The first Black human being to be published in America. [. . .] But the miracle of Black poetry in America, the *difficult* miracle of Black poetry in America, is that we have been rejected [. . .] frequently dismissed [. . .] because, like Phillis Wheatley, we have persisted for freedom. [. . .] And it was not natural. And she was the first. [. . .] This is the difficult miracle of Black poetry in America: that we persist, published or not, and loved or unloved: we persist.

–June Jordan, "The Difficult Miracle of Black Poetry in America; or, Something like a Sonnet for Phillis Wheatley"

More than two hundred years have gone by since the spring of 1773, when Phillis Wheatley, subject of the epigraphs of this essay, an African slave girl and the first person of her racial origin to publish a book in North America, collected her best poems and submitted them to public scrutiny. In search of authentication, she appeared with them before eighteen white men of high social and political esteem, "the best Judges" for such a case in colonial Boston. Wheatley's owners and supporters arranged this special audience to promote her as a writer. According to popular wisdom of the time, Africans were intellectually incapable of producing literature. None of the Anglo-Americans beyond her immediate circle could imagine her reading and writing well enough to create poetry. But when the examination was over and the men were satisfied among themselves that Wheatley was the author of the poems, they put into writing an "attestation" that declared the works hers and, by extension, eligible for publication under her name. In a stunning repudiation of the white supremacy espoused by such Enlightenment luminaries as Immanuel Kant and David Hume, the Senegalese slave girl proved the skeptics wrong. Unfortunately, not even the words of Boston's most honorable men could overcome white opposition; no printer in America was willing to undertake this publishing venture. Consequently, Wheatley's book first appeared in England later that year, and on British soil she accepted the only public honor she would ever receive for her writing in her lifetime. The American edition of *Poems on Various Subjects, Religious and Moral* was published in Philadelphia in 1786, four years after her death.

The problems that Wheatley faced before the "court" of eighteen "judges" remained almost unchanged for the next two hundred years. Outright rejection of black literary production persisted through generations of talented African American writers who were dismissed, denied, and denigrated by literary authorities. Not until the 1960s, in the wake of the black civil rights movement, did black writers begin to gain the public recognition they deserved. It did not come easily either, originating in the disruptive, sometimes violent demands of raucous black students who wanted black studies added to the curricula of white colleges and universities across the country.

Today, first credit for the advances made by black literature in the academy belongs largely to two groups of black women and men. The first was a generation of less than a handful of mature black men of letters, veterans of the struggle to keep African American art and culture alive, who were recruited away from historical black colleges by well-known white universities in the mid- to late 1960s, the most turbulent period of the student disruptions. Among them were such stalwarts as Blyden Jackson (University of North Carolina, Chapel Hill), Darwin Turner (University of Iowa), Saunders Redding (Cornell University), and Charles Davis (Yale University). Though small in number, this group of men, by temperament and the advantages of the quiet respect for their work that they had earned over many long years of negotiating the academic shoals outside the white academy, were well suited to bring black literature into these institutions through their teaching and scholarship and to begin the work of training a new generation of black and white scholars in this field. The second group to whom early credit goes is the black studies generation of critics and writers, a generation of white research university–trained young black literary scholars who entered the professoriat at white institutions between the middle and the end of the 1970s. For many of them, their most sustained prior training in black literature was the work they did in writing their dissertations. But their chosen mission was to turn black studies into the dynamic field that it is today, and by working with one another and sharing information, they developed expertise in the field. Joining them in this quest was a new generation of African American writers who stood among the most gifted authors the country had ever seen: Toni Morrison, John Wideman, Alice Walker, and many others. In the 1970s there were more published black writers than in the previous five decades. The students demanded courses anchored in the African American experience across disciplines; the literary scholars and writers read, studied, and championed the cause of black literature in the classroom and in their writings.

Teaching and research in black literature were new to the white academy. Much that had to be done was learned on the job. For the younger black scholars, the field was exhilarating in its newness and in its unprecedented promises of rewards in the untrampled research pathways that lay open before them. On the one hand, there was the breathtaking excitement of excavating lost or forgotten works of the past. On the other, there was the fierce battle to ensure that contemporary writers were fully recognized on their merits.

Unfortunately, though not unexpectedly, many white faculty members resisted the changes that the new field made inevitable within long-established traditional English departments. From the mid- 1970s through the mid- 1980s, adversaries dismissed African American literature as a fad, ridiculed its differences from traditional American literary productions, warned interested white graduate students away from the courses, and discouraged and sometimes even refused to supervise Ph.D. dissertations that focused on black writers. Such hostility hurt the new black faculty members. Widely dispersed across the country, many young black scholars were intellectually isolated in their departments, with no mentors or even supportive white colleagues. The situation was less difficult for those in black studies programs, who, even when they were the lone literary scholars in those groups, could enjoy the camaraderie of colleagues in black history or sociology or other disciplines in the new field. Happier exceptions were those who joined the small groups of mature black literary scholars at leading white institutions.

To fill the need for mentors and supportive colleagues, black intellectual networks developed spontaneously among faculty members across institutional divides. Eager to make professional connections, excited to establish themselves in this important field, and hungry to satisfy the demands of the new work, they attended academic gatherings that offered them opportunities to meet each other and work out ways to keep in close contact, exchange ideas, discuss their work, and develop deep, meaningful, and lasting friendships, often over long distances. They lingered long and sat up late at these gatherings, stitching together the brave new world of black literature. Not all the stories ended well, and casualties were unavoidable. Everyone was sad when some colleagues failed to achieve tenure in their institutions.

Skeptics of black literature did not go away even after it began to prove its worth. In time, the formalist dismissals of the 1960s antagonists gave way to poststructuralist condescension. That change did not alter the situation for black scholars, who continued to find themselves defendants in the same court of opinion that had judged Phillis Wheatley two centuries earlier and found her wanting. Still, the work went on—teaching, research, and writing—and African American literature did not evaporate as predicted. Instead, as the 1970s wore on, a new area within it surfaced and before long made drastic changes to the face of the field. Early in the decade, in reaction to male domination of the black studies movement and to the male-centeredness of black literary studies, angry black women faculty members, with the help of the rising women's studies movement, aggressively set out to break into worlds from which their voices and experiences had been excluded. Women critics and writers searched out, engaged in long conversations about, and began to give courses in women writers. They shared discoveries; dispensed new information on writers and books; excavated, photocopied, and dispersed out-of-print texts, in a kind of black feminist samizdat, to make the works widely accessible for classroom use; and created a new domain of research and writing about the books and their authors.

Perhaps the spark was lit by such works as Toni Cade [Bambara's] *The Black Woman* and Toni Morrison's *The Bluest Eye*, both published in 1970 and today proudly held up as among the early founding texts of contemporary black feminism. In the middle of the decade Alice Walker's "In Search of Our Mother's Gardens" (1974) and "In Search of Zora Neale Hurston" (1975) and Mary Helen Washington's *Black-Eyed Susans* (1975) soared like battle hymns of this new republic in letters. What followed were Barbara Smith's "Toward a Black Feminist Criticism" (1977) and Deborah McDowell's "New Directions in Black Feminist Criticism" (1980), her response to Smith. Barbara Christian's *Black Women Novelists: The Development of a Tradition* (1980) was pathbreaking. By decade's end, these and other such publications defined the terms of the black feminist critical and theoretical debates, conversations, and dialogues of the time. Until close to the end of the decade, black male critics and writers paid scant attention to developments in black women's literatures, little suspecting that in the first consciously black feminist teaching and research efforts were the foundations of what would become the thriving area of scholarship in which they would participate. By then, black feminist writers and critics had made clear that black literature was going to be different and black women were at its center. Their work brought new and exciting ideas to black studies and women's studies and to English departments, the latter still trying to cope with the shifting ground that black literature and white women's literature represented to them. But no one could ignore the black women's academic movement any longer, and the rest is history.

Although this revolutionary period of ferment inside the African American literary community took place in full view of the whole intellectual community, white scholars and university administrators lagged far behind in their awareness of it—a lapse that has caused grave misunderstandings and persistent problems for white institutions. This essay examines three critical problems that help to keep the Wheatley court in session and hold African American literature hostage: the insufficiency of the black Ph.D. pipeline, the efforts to discourage white graduate students from exploring black literature, and untrained white scholars' undertaking of scholarship in black literature. Perhaps the most frustrating is the thirty-year interdisciplinary shortage of African American faculty members, a shortfall that negatively affects almost every white college and university across the country. Students protest, administrators mumble, and liberals wring their hands, yet in 1998 the crisis is nearly as severe as it was in 1965. Back then, black student pressure oftentimes forced even the most prestigious institutions of higher education to offer appointments hastily and unwisely to unqualified black candidates. Nowadays, the same institutions grapple over the tiny pool of star scholars, and many positions go unfulfilled. As we can see today too, the scarcity of African American Ph.D.'s in our discipline is one manifestation of the white academy's earlier reluctance to recognize the significance of developments in black literature.

According to MLA [Modern Language Association] figures, there are roughly 2,600 English programs in the country. About 140 of these offer the Ph.D. in English and American literature.[1] Each year beginning a decade ago, sometimes under pressure from administrators scrambling to diversify faculties, a significant number of these programs in white colleges and universities advertise for a recently credentialed specialist in African or African American literature. Many of the searches target an African American scholar. But the number of such scholars is small. Smaller still, naturally, is the pool of the most promising among them, most of whom are snapped up immediately by prestigious institutions that can offer them the highest salaries, the lightest teaching loads, the most research time, and geographic locations with advantages beyond academe.

How small is the pool? In the 1992–1993 school year, there were eighteen African American recipients of Ph.D.'s in English and American language and literature; in 1993–1994 there were twenty-six; and in 1994–1995 there were another eighteen.[2] Although the figures do not specify specialties, it is reasonable to speculate that most of these doctorates are in African American literature but that at least a small number are in other areas. One does not need to have great mathematical skills to recognize the magnitude of the imbalance between the number of minority Ph.D.'s entering the pipeline and the demand on the other end. For the majority of the employing institutions, sadly, no African American candidate materializes. Many reject well-qualified white applicants for these positions in hopes that a black candidate will appear next time. If not this year, runs the unspoken anxiety, then maybe next year. Institutions are caught in the fear that if they fill a position with a white candidate, there will be no place on their horizon for a black candidate. Too often one sees the same position advertised and re-advertised from one year to the next, while the most qualified nonblack candidates are turned away, important work is left undone, and the crisis is allowed to continue unabated. Even if some "black magic" could insert several hundred new African American Ph.D.'s into the job market, it would not solve the problem overnight.

First, there is no such magic at hand. Second, the training of Ph.D.'s, even in this era of scarce resources for graduate education, inevitably requires a longer time than we would like. Beyond that condition lies a host of familiar and formidable challenges: among them, limited resources, minority recruitment obstacles, and market uncertainties. The complications are many and the solutions difficult. The best time to have addressed these "pipeline" problems, moreover, would have been thirty years ago. But that could only have happened had the Wheatley court been disbanded and black studies, broadly defined, been taken seriously by Ph.D.-granting institutions. Closer attention to developments in African American literature and history, to name the most obvious disciplines, would have made today's black Ph.D. pipeline crisis considerably less severe. Given that approximately 140 departments of English and American literature grant doctorates, it is difficult to justify the size of the black Ph.D. graduating classes in the 1990s. But as Homer said, once harm has been done, even a fool understands it. Had intervention occurred thirty years ago, many more black faculty members would be in place today, and we would have discovered that where the faculty is reasonably diverse, the question of who has the right by ethnicity to teach what is irrelevant. Furthermore, white faculty members would have no cause to direct interested white graduate students away from African American literature. It is one of the world's preeminent literatures—why should it not be as fascinating as any other?

The reason offered for directing white graduate students away from African American literature returns us to the problem of making particular groups of people the targets for particular positions and relegating candidates' qualifications to a secondary role in the hiring process. We discourage these students from their preferred choices on the grounds that "the market" offers no jobs for them in that area because of who they are. But who is the market? As faculty members who make appointments to vacant positions in our departments, we are the market. In short, when we reject the nonblack candidate for a position in African American or another minority literature on the basis of the candidate's ethnicity, we create a problem, which we then attribute to a faceless entity we conveniently call "the market." What passes unnoticed in this linguistic dance is the real cost to students, black and otherwise, and to the future of our discipline. The alternative to having a black professor of African American literature should not be not having a professor of African American literature. The sad truth is that most institutions of higher education have no one, black or white, able to attract the next generation of scholars to this important part of the life of the mind. Such is the result of our failure to address the problem in a timely manner.

Another serious problem in the willful continuing marginalization of the field by the larger profession is the recent flood of new scholarship in African American literature by white scholars who, without training in the area, assume authority to teach, write about, and serve on panels that review black literature. At the same time, African American scholars seeking appointments in more traditional fields for which they were trained confront an automatic assumption that they are better able to teach, say, Morrison than Milton. Such blatant disrespect and contorted logic, such reluctances to learn about African American literature, its background and long history of serious scholarship, and to understand what Toni Morrison calls its structures, moorings, and anchors ("Interview" 151), cause major distress for black scholars and discredit the integrity of our profession. Disregard for the work of black pioneers in the field is reprehensible. Having black academic friends does not qualify white professors trained in Milton or Shakespeare or the Victorians or William Faulkner, for that matter, to teach, write on, or proclaim their authority in matters relating to African American literature. To presume otherwise is to appropriate and commodify the "other" and to imply ignorantly that African American literature is as wanting in intellectual depth as reviewers found Phillis Wheatley's poems more than two hundred years ago. To those with such a presumption, this is not real literature. It requires neither competence nor training.

Such misguided thinking cannot be taken lightly and should never be permitted to pass unremarked. It poses dangerous threats to the health and welfare of teaching and scholarship in African American literature. Print travels fast and far, and it authenticates ideas. In our profession, most ideas are disseminated through the written word. Faulty and careless notions passed on to unknowing students and teachers are as self-propagating as sound ones and will do irreparable damage to what is still a field struggling toward its maturity. It is not unwarranted pique or territorial jealousy when black scholars condemn incompetents' claims to authority in African American literature. But the task of speaking out against such misdeeds should not fall solely on the shoulders of black scholars. As new areas of literary studies become part of the family of our whole literature, the entire profession needs to be on guard and to assume the responsibility of raising its voice against all attempts to misappropriate intellectual authority over any area of our discipline.

Thus, the problems of the pipeline through which African American Ph.D. graduates in literary studies pass are connected with the limited access that white graduate students have to nontraditional literatures and with the behavior of white faculty members who have no regard for the integrity of African American literature. I contend that, for all appearances to the contrary (e.g., the popular and academic successes of black women writers, the new scholarship in this literature by white colleagues, the anxiety of publishers to get hold of almost anything written in the field), the Wheatley court remains in session. These are not problems for which there are easy solutions, but until we are prepared to pay them more than lip service, which comes cheaply, we will be forced to live in this self-destructing house of our own making.

There is a place to begin another conversation. Contrary to much of the angry rhetoric associated with ideologies of essentialism that some black scholars engage in, there is nothing mystical about African American literature that makes it the sole property of those of African descent. Toni Morrison reminds us that "it can be learned" ("Interview" 153). To learn it is to "know" it, and only those willing to learn will know. When African Americans say that black people "know" white people, the statement is neither presumptuous nor overreaching. For centuries blacks as a group have had to know whites; their lives depended on that knowledge. A reading of Charles W. Chestnutt's late-nineteenth-century stories provides a good education in the hows, whats, and whys that forced blacks to learn about whites. On the other hand, for those same centuries white people as a group have not felt the need to know black people. Instead, whites projected onto blacks a myriad of stereotypes that reinforced racial hierarchy. That treatment of the other is no longer acceptable in academic life or in our society as a whole. Black literary critics (like black scholars in other disciplines) have never been willing to play the grinning darky or colonized object for those who would make sport of their art, history, and culture. But beyond the emotions and actions of African Americans, if our profession is to overcome situations such as the empty black Ph.D. pipeline, the closure of African American academic positions to white scholars, and the hostility of black scholars toward white scholars who inappropriately make claims of authority on black literature, then white academicians must first learn how to treat minority cultures with due respect. This is not an issue of vocabulary or a denial of the value of theory in criticism on black literature but, rather, a denunciation of critics who know not whereof they speak and write. We must disband the Wheatley court so that African American literature can become a full member of the company of world literatures, open to all who wish to participate in its bounty. But, first, white scholars who want to engage black literature must learn it. Training and learning are at the center of the remedy for this problem.

In spite of the gloomy picture I have just painted, we need not reinvent the entire wheel either. There are models in place on which we can build. First, there is a great deal of excellent work already done in the field by non–African Americans, past and present, so it can be done. My generation (the black studies generation) of African American specialists were fortunate to have several excellent anthologies, comprehensive and specialized, that introduced us to much of the material then known to only a few people. These works supplied us with invaluable background information and directed us to important sources of additional readings. Without them our work would have been a great deal harder. Among the best of the comprehensive texts was *Black Writers of America: A Comprehensive Anthology* (1972), edited by Richard Barksdale and Keneth Kinnamon, black and white colleagues whose collaboration greatly enriched the field for more than two decades. *Black Writers of America* has only been superseded in importance by the new anthologies in the 1990s. The strength of the Barksdale-Kinnamon effort was that it demonstrated a solid foundation in knowledge of earlier work in the area, including that splendid collection *The Negro Caravan: Writings by American Negroes* (1941), edited by African American scholars Sterling A. Brown, Arthur P. Davis, and Ulysses Lee. But in addition to being familiar with the materials, Barksdale and Kinnamon committed themselves to producing a work as scholarly as any anthology at the time. *Soon, One Morning: New Writing by American Negroes, 1940–1962* (1963), edited by Herbert Hill, a specialized anthology by a non–African American, also belongs among important contributions to black literary studies since the 1960s. An ambassador without portfolio in the court of this literature, Hill was absorbed in black literature and music decades before the entry of black studies into the academy. In our own time the field would be much poorer without the contributions of non–African American scholars such as William L. Andrews, Robert Hemenway, James V. Hatch, and Jean Fagan Yellin, to name only a handful of the most visible. But these are colleagues who invested time, energy, and commitment to the work, in efforts equal to those required of any other area of literary studies. Collaborations between black and white scholars—such as the editing of *The Norton Anthology of African American Literature* (1996) by Henry Louis Gates Jr., Nellie Y. McKay, and nine period editors with the help of dozens of multicultural-multiethnic faculty advisors; the compiling of *The Oxford Companion to African American Literature* (1997) by Andrews, Frances Smith Foster, and Trudier Harris; and the splendid stewardship of Joe Weixlmann as editor of *African American Review*—are also ways in which all groups share a continuing learning experience that enriches our collective teaching and research.

Repairing past damage will be difficult, but following along the previous path will make life worse for all of us. More than two centuries after Wheatley proved her authorship of the poems she wished to publish and contemporary reviewers declared them "merely imitative" and without "invention," at the dawn of a new millennium we seem not to have traveled very far toward resolving the problem. We owe it to ourselves to make the hard but necessary changes, but most of all we owe it to the generations that will follow us. When and if we are ever willing to disband the Wheatley court once and for all, a black pipeline of eager young scholars will flow as it should, and the walls of African American scholarly resentment toward white academic interlopers and of the fears of those guarding white, black, and all other intellectual territories inside our common property will come tumbling down around us. Then we will all be free to claim our full American literary heritage. And if we do not abolish that court, African American literature will stand because as the poet June Jordan eloquently states, "the difficult miracle of Black poetry in America [is] that we persist, published or not, and loved or unloved: we persist" (261). But is this really the best that we have to offer the future? Consider the great loss that would be to everyone.

## NOTES

I wish to thank all my friends, of all colors and ethnicities, across the country with whom I have shared learning experiences and conversed for many years on ideas of teaching and writing about black American literature. These relationships are the bulwark of my professional accomplishments. I also especially thank my colleagues and friends in the Afro-American studies and English departments and the women's studies programs at the University of Wisconsin–Madison, whose day-to-day generosity always gives me support to do my work. My very special thanks to Susan Friedman, who will not let me forget the many intersections of all our lives; to Craig Werner for his willing readiness to help whenever I need him; to Tim Tyson, who took precious time from completing his own manuscript to make editorial comments that gave coherence to the early drafts of this essay; and to my graduate students, in all their diversity, past and present: the generations who give meaning to our struggle.

1. The MLA database of postsecondary language programs in the United States contains 2,598 institutions with at least one English program.
2. Thurgood and Clarke, app. table A-2; Simmons and Thurgood, app. table A-2; Henderson, Clarke, and Reynolds, app. table A-2. These numbers are for United States citizens and non–United States citizens with permanent visas.

# PART ONE

# Liberalism, Authority, and Authenticity

# Theme for African American Literature B

RUSS CASTRONOVO

The title of this essay takes its cue from Langston Hughes's "Theme for English B," in which the gulf between a white instructor and a black college student is temporarily narrowed by the knowledge they exchange and create together.[1] Narrated by the only black student in a class at Columbia University, the poem seemingly validates liberal institutions, presenting an optimistic take on the power of education to span the distrust, misunderstandings, and inequities that constitute the racial divide. At first, however, an intense racial awareness paralyzes the speaker who is faced with the assignment to "Go home and write / a page tonight." How can he or she write a personal essay for an audience that may have no clue about the pathways that bring a twenty-two-year-old African American from North Carolina to the Ivy League? How will a white instructor understand, not to mention evaluate, this page that "will not be white"? The misgivings that animate these questions suggest the poem as a primal scene that precedes the white critic who struggles with black texts. For, prior to the moments of fumbling, self-examination, and authority that are the stock and trade of white literary critical approaches to black literature, there exists an even more fundamental conflict experienced by the black writer who would author a black text that can be consumed, interpreted, historicized, even "discovered," by white critics and teachers.

Hughes's speaker solves this problem by making his or her page not wholly a black text but, rather, a hybrid articulation. The student asks, "So will my page be colored that I write?" and yet does not offer a satisfying answer other than to say that the page "will not be white." Refusing to be overcome by silence and inertia, the student will take home this white page and cover it with black marks. He or she rejects whiteness, whether it is understood variously as the sign of stymied expression or an identity vested with tremendous amounts of institutional authority. But neither does a countervailing sense of "color" reign. Just as quickly the student asserts:

> But it will be
> a part of you, instructor.
> You are white—
> Yet a part of me, as I am a part of you.
> That's American
>
> As I learn from you,
> I guess you learn from me.

Sweet to our national ears are these lines, which *almost* bring the poem to a close with this image of saccharine unity and equal exchange as the speaker, after some reluctance, intuits writing, creation, and consumption as a dialectical arena that unsettles assumptions about fixed, separate identities. The *you* and *me* quite literally exchange positions. In fact, each recognizes the other as a subject in this scene that reveals knowledge as a collaborative project. (Ears tuned to frequencies other than the national, however, might construe these lines differently, hearing in the repetition of *a part* the separatism of *apart*). Such is the scene of liberal education, a flash of interracial understanding triumphing over differences in institutional location and centuries of historical inequality. But the poem only *almost* comes to this reassuring conclusion. The speaker adds an important afterthought by way of an *although* that qualifies this momentary elation, reminding the reader that the white instructor, no matter the appreciation and respect that black cultural expression will earn, remains different, which, in this case means "older," "white," and "somewhat more free." The gulf yawns as wide as ever.

Deep within this gulf lies a troubling question: can whites teach, research, and write about black texts without making these texts conform to a liberal agenda that validates consensus over radical critique, accord over disjunction, and quaint lessons about mutual understanding over a more insurgent pedagogy dedicated to examining enduring inequalities? We can answer yes if we stay securely within the framework of that liberal agenda, abiding by assumptions about the ability of people to interact as free and autonomous individuals without the impingement of larger social, economic, or institutional structures. Hughes gives voice to this optimism in the black student's certainty that he or she learns from the white instructor. Such confidence is immediately undercut, however, in the skepticism—"I guess you learn from me"—over whether the instructor, bearing an individuality that never stands free and clear of whiteness and authority, reciprocates. If we attend to the centrifugal force of *although* and move outside this framework to consider a broader swath of literary history, we see that the answer to this question has long been no.

Such oscillations between yes, no, and although sum up the literary traffic that connects white liberals and black antislavery writers and narrators. On the one hand, whites assuredly learned invaluable moral, political, and ethical lessons from the likes of Frederick Douglass, Martin Delany, Harriet Jacobs, and Sojourner Truth. Building on his studies of black responses to *Uncle Tom's Cabin*, Robert S. Levine in his contribution to this volume illustrates how Stowe was instructed by Delany's criticisms of her novel to rethink her portrayals of black resistance in her next antislavery saga, *Dred*. Even unsympathetic and decidedly illiberal whites stood to learn something despite their own predispositions. At an 1858 antislavery meeting in Indiana, Sojourner Truth delivered a shaming lesson to the men who demanded that she expose her breasts in order to prove she was not a male hireling stumping for the newly formed Republican Party. Disrobe she did, asking her interlocutors if they wished to suckle at her breasts as had the white children of the men she had served. On the other hand, whites learned often only what they wanted to learn, which meant that black stories could be received in ways that provided neither a sense of ethical commitment nor moral urgency. Black stories ran the risk of telling whites little more than they already knew, their narratives conveniently reframed in ways that would confirm the "truths" about Southern immorality, the virtue of New England conviction, or the magnanimity of white philanthropists. A white Methodist minister, Hiram Mattison, thus used the story of an octoroon woman, Louisa Picquet, to verify his worst fears about concubinage. Fugitive slaves Milton and Lewis Clarke's apostrophe to the Bunker Hill Monument supported Boston Brahmins' denunciations of slavery as a betrayal of Revolutionary ideals (43). And Lydia Maria Child glommed onto Harriet Jacobs's *Incidents in the Life of a Slave Girl* as evidence of sisterhood's ability to transcend racial divisions. In each case the moral outrage, earnest belief in racial cooperation, and paternalism that are the hallmarks of liberalism ring forth loudly from these texts, so loudly, in fact, that literary articulations of blackness are made to service the self-image of whiteness as open-minded, generous, and principled.

Most black writing in the antebellum period remained dependent upon the goodwill and charity of well-meaning white activists. One way of summing up this situation is to say that, historically speaking, the theme for African American literature has been assigned by white instructors. Write about slavery. Tell us about your dehumanization so as to enable our indignation. Give us the details of interracial rape so that we can be shocked. Express your suffering in a way that proves how we all suffer. Another way to contextualize the situation is to invoke the case of Phillis Wheatley, as Nellie McKay does, gesturing to the 1773 examination of "an African slave girl and the first person of racial origin to publish a book in North America" by a panel of eighteen white men ("Naming" 18). From its origins African American literature needed the imprimatur of white authentication and authority in ways that "remained almost unchanged for the next two hundred years" (18). While no longer embodied in the persons of Boston's intellectual elite, the "Wheatley court," McKay implies, has continued in one form or another in the syllabi, hiring practices, disciplinary assumptions, and notions of canonization operative within academia. But it is not only that this tribunal of judgment has remained in session across the institutions of higher education in the United States. More to this essay's point, an ascendant liberalism allows many in the position of power—the enlightened men of colonial Boston who entertained the possibility that a woman abducted from Senegal could compose verse, abolitionist editors who facilitated publication of slave narratives, and the college instructor who asks for a personal essay from the only black student in English B—to feel good about that power.

While hierarchy cannot be denied,[2] liberalism does its best to concentrate instead on the moments of agreement and accord that this power enables. Quite reasonably, the objection could be raised that accusations about the self-satisfaction of liberals are beside the point. Abolitionists combined their influence and zeal to wage a legislative and rhetorical war against slavery. Who cares if a few white antislavery men and women found it easier to sleep at night after a day's struggle on behalf of the oppressed? And because of the instructor's tolerant outlook a black student is moved to express himself or herself and educate those who would educate him or her. Finally, the liberal commitment to individualism stands as the foundation of an interracial dialogue that brings knowledge and new understanding to the participants. Do not such positive results provide their own justification?

The quickness with which philanthropy, open-mindedness, and other signs of liberal sympathy can be dismissed is cause for concern. In this regard Hughes's speaker seems relatively unconcerned with what goes on inside white interiority, as he both dismisses and doubts whatever it is that the instructor thinks or feels ("I *guess* you learn from me"). What, after all, is to be gained from obsessing over the potential specter of liberal self-satisfaction, especially when this cynical fantasy overshadows and discounts the verifiable good accomplished by well-intentioned white activists, readers, students, and scholars in any century? Perhaps the critics of liberalism should remember that these do-gooders were fighting against the slave power, institutional injustice, and segregation. Such persons, we might also remember, are called do-gooders for reasons that are not entirely cynical. White self-satisfaction seems a small price to pay given the stakes of the battle. Does the radical critique of liberalism risk mistaking allies for enemies?

Both the defense and indictment of liberalism, especially when connected to thorny questions of race, have their merits. Each position, however, fails to engage the other, since liberals and their more radical detractors tend to focus on different levels along the sociopolitical terrain and thus speak past one another. Whereas liberals see progressive change occurring along a level playing field in which autonomous subjects attain recognition and reciprocity, radicals instead emphasize the larger structural conditions that encompass those individuals. Economic disparities, social bias, and unacknowledged political entitlements, for instance, make the idea of a level playing field just that—a nice idea that can only be sustained as an illusion because any sense of either historical contingency or realpolitik would reveal that playing fields are never level. Only our unexamined attachments to liberal perspective, after all, allow what is in actuality a terrain pockmarked by constitutive inequities and striated by differences to be misrecognized as a smooth, unbroken sociopolitical arena. A liberal outlook conveniently forgets that not everyone enters the conversation on equal terms; as Hughes's' "Theme for English B" puts it, some come to the level playing field "older—and white—and somewhat more free."

And in terms of this essay's "Theme for African American Literature B," when liberal commitments individualize the historical arena of social hierarchies, white critics can take up black texts as though they were generic readers examining generic texts. Just as classic liberal theory presumes an abstract generic self, one unmarked by embodied considerations such as race or sexuality, so too the liberal academy imagines that African American writing can be accessed, interpreted, and taught when individual readers put aside enough social prescriptions and cultural baggage to read purely as individuals.[3] This scene of evasion as interpretation requires a double move. First, the individual critic expresses sympathy or empathy. To be sure, these identifications are more than mere show; such goodwill is necessary to removing the distrust that mars any possibility of a level playing field. The genuine desire to recognize and understand another as an expressive subject can undoubtedly be a powerful political moment. But, as Andrew Lakritz argues, "what sympathy or empathy must always cover or neglect is the very relationship between elite and subaltern" that is much more complex than a personal interaction and, instead, involves broader social and political arrangements of power and privilege (9). Such feelings become instrumental at the second step at which the white critic understands the black text precisely because he or she can relate to it in the same manner that one liberal self relates to another because each has the same generic outline. This interpretative position has occasioned trenchant criticism. As Ann duCille writes, "The white scholar understands 'the African American experience' not in its own *right*, not on its own terms, but because he can make it like his own. With his voice, he can translate another's silence into speech. He speaks through and for the Other" (42–43; italics added).[4]

Yet for all its force and relevance, duCille's assertion describes the "African American experience," which must include literature, as autonomous and independent as though it had the status of a liberal subject. Black texts are the bearers of rights that are violated by white critics who approach the field as "an anybody-can-play pick-up game," paying no attention to the forerunners who pioneered this area of study (duCille 31). Incisive and bold, duCille's essay represents a classic piece of black feminist criticism, but the problem with its argumentation at this juncture is that it tends to individualize objects of knowledge and artifacts of culture to the point where interpretation becomes a matter of personal investment. Without a doubt, duCille touches many a sore point when she charges that white critics come to black texts motivated either by feelings of guilt or a romantic primitivism that fetishizes black culture. Yet, however accurate, this intervention traps both critic and text within a psychodrama ("I really don't want to be 'the man' when I read and assign Charles Chesnutt, but what's a white Negro like me supposed to do?") that confirms the boundaries of liberal subjectivity. Guilt, sympathy, self-satisfaction: all these feelings translate African American literature to scenes of inner struggle, doing damage to the political and public animus that fuels the most profoundly affective texts from *Incidents* to *The Souls of Black Folk*. In addition to reducing the complexities of reading to a confrontation of self and text, this confusion of the critic's feeling with the affect of the text creates doubts in one's ability to speak about the text in the first place. As Linda Martin Alcoff writes, "The claim that I can speak only for myself assumes the autonomous conception of the self in classical *liberal* theory" (108).[5] Once the white critic cops to the charge that he or she can speak only for the self, the text's ability to engage broader moments of social crisis or political difference is drastically scaled back.

Do not mistake me: it is entirely appropriate to rebuke white critics who have amassed cultural capital from reading black texts, especially when these professional profits are reaped without expressing an indebtedness to earlier black scholars who established the discipline.[6] Nevertheless, the alternative situation of nonengagement with black texts is just as troubling. If white critics do not "worry" about black texts, are they then justified in thinking only about themselves? White critics certainly want to avoid falling into what Alcoff calls a "discursive imperialism" that legitimates a "narcissistic yuppie lifestyle in which a privileged person takes no responsibility whatsoever for her society" (107). Politics are scaled back to the limited horizon of the self: the casualty here is the possible development of a critical perspective that attends to the larger economic, social, and cultural structures that keep various forms of injustice in place. While the rebuke of white critics effectively delegitimates the nauseating "feel good" emotions of various do-gooders, it represents a critical position still deeply mired in a liberal ideology that personalizes hierarchies and internalizes injustice as guilt.

In short, the critique of liberal critics is itself prone to liberalism because it often fails to interrogate the personal stakes and privatized outcomes that include hand-wringing, confession, accusation, and other anguished professions of autonomy. It does not matter whether such protestations are genuine or self-serving. Instead, the more radical point is that each of these reactions sacrifices a public, political vision for the anxieties of subjectivity. Unlike liberalism, which tends to highlight small-scale dialogues between individuals, radical knowledge proceeds by focusing on the conflicts that position individuals not only against other individuals but *within* an array of social forces and historical relations marked by hierarchy, subjection, and subject making. By emphasizing the broader structural conditions outside the individual and, indeed, by examining the structural conditions of race and economy that define critical selves, a radical perspective always situates reading as an institutional practice, keeping in mind that institutions (e.g., the professorate, higher education, and book publishing) are determined by forces more complex and intricate than any single self. Thus, in Hughes's "Theme for English B" the final reciprocity between black student and white instructor is not a concluding image of interracial understanding because it is never final. More factors, especially social factors involving age, race, and relative freedom, must be brought into play. And for this essay's "Theme for African American Literature B"? A radical critique insists on a political perspective whose final destination can never be the liberal subject. Such a commitment does not signal a disregard for individuals but, instead, acknowledges that human beings as democratic actors can never be fulfilled by their own autonomy or the singularity of personal relationships.[7]

The shift from liberal pedagogy to radical criticism effectively resets the parameters of interpretation beyond the stakes of personal investment. "My" guilt or "your" sympathy are irrelevant when even the interrogation of these positions continues to give pride of place to the liberal subjects that have and, no doubt, often enjoy such feelings. Indeed, as Hughes's poem suggests, the white instructor is very much beside the point, which is to say that within a radical pedagogy for African American literature the critic does not matter so much as his or her whiteness. Once political formations, cultural memory, and other such considerations properly become the focus of interpretation, the white critic as individual no longer merits so much attention; instead, what comes into focus are the larger factors that give authority and privilege to the whiteness that the critic bears. Refusing the distractions of a private racial drama, a radical perspective calls for an examination of the histories that allow white critics to lay claim to remorse or responsibility in the first place.

But in an academic world in which liberalism is regnant and often unacknowledged, the risk remains that the trenchant radicalism of black texts will take a backseat to individual perspective, rarefied scenes of interracial understanding, white self-examination, and the other ideological passengers riding at the front of the critical endeavor. When African American literature thus serves as the vehicle that transports critics to such singularized insights, the result is that other destinations on the map of racial justice are never pursued. It is in this context that P. Gabrielle Foreman expresses skepticism over "the current racial vogue [which] works as synecdoche, allowing liberal culture to express an interest in 'race' without addressing the injustices and pain experienced by communities of color" (532).[8] For all its accuracy, however, this statement misses the mark by presupposing the existence of some sort of ideal speech community in which injustice can be addressed. Within the critical field that is suggested by a "Theme for African American Literature B," an *although* always looms. Foreman and the white critics she scrutinizes would have little difficulty in coming to an accord about the need to read and interpret in ways that do not disavow any of the complicated histories within the national family—although does the vision of redress itself depend upon an evasion of abiding social factors? It is not that injustice can be addressed; rather, the lesson is that injustice cannot be addressed. It is not that pain can be assuaged; rather, the point is that pain can never be healed.

While such a negative pedagogy does not make us feel good, it does enable critical readings of African American literature that will always remember the sociopolitical imbalances and historical injuries that frame and motivate so much of this body of writing. Such a pedagogy is forever sentenced to dissatisfaction. The lesson is that there is no solace in researching or teaching African American literature: while liberal strategies that prioritize individual responses or even interracial understanding among autonomous subjects can turn a blind eye to institutional patterns and more encompassing hierarchical structures, a radical perspective necessarily considers contingent social and historical factors that make individual scenes of racial understanding acceptable to the liberal nation-state. When racism and injustice are healed by individual awareness, broader social action seems unnecessary. Scenes of blacks and whites transcending centuries of distrust and inequity have a special place in the cultural imaginaries of American literature, film, and education, as though the accumulated effects of slavery, lynching, segregation, and discrimination are counteracted by singularized epiphanies of interracial understanding and awareness. When such visions as Huck and Jim lounging on the raft, Mel Gibson and Danny Glover living up a high-speed pursuit, or a white critic sincerely reading a black writer are taken as the sole sign of racial progress, integration becomes a spectacle in which the "materiality of cultural relations"—with all their asymmetries—"are superseded by the dreamscape of 'America's' production" (Wiegman, *American* 132). Left intact and unquestioned are the effects of the market and the state, two institutions that American liberalism holds dear, rarely daring to investigate their role in fostering inequities within the very systems of individual fair play that they supposedly establish.

Despite its ability to expose liberalism's blind spots, a radical perspective should not be heralded as either a success or a solution. As it attends to larger contextual factors that frame individual scenes of reading, for instance, radicalism only reveals the extent to which the critical endeavor must always fail as a sociopolitical project. Failure, however, need not be a bad thing. Can white critics or, for that matter, black critics construct an appropriate theme for African American Literature B? That is, can the institutions that house academic professional practices adequately respond to the insistent agitation for equal treatment and human recognition that are an abiding concern of so many, if not all, black texts from the nineteenth century? The no that this essay provides in answer to these questions is not in the end countered by an affirmative pedagogy, an approach that would make everyone, especially do-gooders, feel good again. There is no yes that envisions a speech situation in which the politics of black texts are not transmuted, traduced, or translated to arenas of liberal consensus. Instead of seeking to overcome this no, we must deal with it by embracing a pedagogy of negative dialectics for African American literature. Justice certainly lies within African American texts, but we can never obtain it; like Moses who can only see the Promised Land from afar, our political desires remain unsatisfied. Justice exists, but, as with salvation, we will never achieve it.

This messianic approach to African American literature is suggested in a different context by Theodor Adorno who declares that literary works necessarily "point to a practice from which they abstain: the creation of a just life" (194). Steeped in negativity, this approach raises the (im)possibility of glimpsing the radical import of African American writing before it is inevitably absorbed by liberalism. At one level a radical perspective is no different from a liberal reading because each identifies the appeal for justice as central to black texts. But at another level these two modes part company with radicalism's painful awareness that justice will never be completed by interpretation. While liberalism tends to misread the individual's participation in the critical project as a broader remedy, a radically contextual approach acknowledges the continued deferral of meaningful social redress. This negative pedagogy contends that justice can never be secured, least of all through its own critical project. Instead, the lesson of such disheartenment is that the striving for justice will never be complete.

The problem lies not only with the precepts of American liberalism that underlie contemporary critical practices. Even radical readings of African American literature can confront justice only in a manner that is negative and indirect. Again, Adorno's insights can guide our understandings of a pedagogy that points to what it cannot do—but it is a gesture we must follow with great caution lest it seem to encourage fruitless comparisons between genocides. As Adorno ponders the fate of aesthetics in the wake of the Nazi Holocaust, he argues that any effort to represent concentration camps and systematized murders artistically "does an injustice to the victims." Such aesthetic failure stymies any attempts to produce art with unambiguous political commitments, but this failure is also the condition of an ethical practice. Adorno thus qualifies his initial statement about aesthetic representation as injustice by tacking on an *although*: "yet no art which tried to evade [the victims] could confront the claims of justice" (189). The same might be said of an ethical African American literary criticism. Readings of black texts can never fulfill the political yearnings in works such as *The Marrow of Tradition* and *The Bluest Eye*—although any belief that a critical project did successfully accomplish this task would mistake the complexity and depth of these desires.[9] And, as I've been arguing, liberal readings are prone to just this sort of error, misrepresenting individual triumphs as broader social interventions. Unless criticism assumes a radical perspective that confronts its tendency to individualize interpretation and its eternal estrangement from justice, readers will never attain a glimpse of what ethical interpretations might look like. We need not have any rosy faith that criticism of African American literature will one day result in such interpretations, but it would be nice to know that they exist as possibility, even if it is a possibility whose political potential lies in its forever being deferred.

## NOTES

1. The complete text of the poem is as follows:

The instructor said,

*Go home and write*
*a page tonight.*
*And let that page come out of you—*
*Then, it will be true.*

I wonder if it's that simple?
I am twenty-two, colored, born in Winston-Salem.
I went to school there, then Durham, then here
to this college on the hill above Harlem.
I am the only colored student in my class.
The steps from the hill lead down into Harlem,
through a park, then I cross St. Nicholas,
Eighth Avenue, Seventh, and I come to the Y,
the Harlem Branch Y, where I take the elevator
up to my room, sit down, and write this page:

It's not easy to know what is true for you or me
at twenty-two, my age. But I guess I'm what
I feel and see and hear, Harlem, I hear you:
hear you, hear me—we two—you, me, talk on this page.
(I hear New York, too.) Me—who?
Well, I like to eat, sleep, drink, and be in love.
I like to work, read, learn, and understand life.
I like a pipe for a Christmas present,
or records—Bessie, bop, or Bach.
I guess being colored doesn't make me *not* like
the same things other folks like who are other races.
So will my page be colored that I write?
Being me, it will not be white.
But it will be
a part of you, instructor.

You are white—
yet a part of me, as I am a part of you.
That's American.
Sometimes perhaps you don't want to be a part of me.
Nor do I often want to be a part of you.
But we are, that's true!
As I learn from you,
I guess you learn from me—
although you're older—and white—
and somewhat more free.

This is my page for English B.
(*Collected Poems of Langston Hughes* 409–10)

2. For a recent study of the hierarchy and condescension that could often persist within nineteenth-century brands of liberal reform and charity, see Ryan, *Grammar of Good Intentions.*
3. On the particularistic—but often disavowed—components of the abstract individual, see Warner, "Mass Public."
4. This problem is not only one of speech and speaking for. As Carla Kaplan suggests, there is also the need to listen. But how can we learn to be good listeners and an ideal audience? Kaplan explores this desire to listen by way of Zora Neale Hurston.
5. Also see Leslie Bow who carries this point still further by examining the cultural and institutional problems that attend acts of self articulation (48).
6. McKay ("Naming") reminds us of the first generation of black critics such as Blyden Jackson, Darwin Turner, Saunders Redding, and Charles Davis who brought attention to African American writers and trained younger scholars.
7. My understanding of this radical orientation is, in fact, developed from Frederick Douglass's *My Bondage and My Freedom.* See my book *Necro Citizenship* 2–61.
8. Foreman's critique raises a tricky point because she includes me in her list of scholars whose efforts contribute to liberal bad faith. Little room thus exists for me to address her critique without falling prey to the personal and doing a disservice to the social questions she raises. Instead, for a judicious working through of these questions, see Levine, "Commentary."
9. Morrison's afterword to her novel speaks to this realization as she cites the failure of *The Bluest Eye,* which may touch readers emotionally but not move them ethically or socially (211).

# Race Walks in the Room

## White Teachers in Black Studies

JOHN ERNEST

Can white teachers teach African American literature? This question, asked either directly or indirectly, often provokes a frustrated or even indignant reply from white teachers. One hears complaints about identity politics, comments about teachers who specialize in the medieval period (even though they are not themselves medieval), ideal visions of interracial cooperation (an imagined beloved community of scholarship), or condescending dissertations on the fundamental principles of scholarship and professional authority. Often white teachers assume that their authority can or should be based only on their "mastery" of the material—by which they most often mean a relatively detailed knowledge of the subject, a good store of information. By this logic race becomes the charge against which the white teacher must defend herself or himself, the unfair attempt to undermine the authority of a white teacher who, after all, knows the subject. But, in stating the question bluntly, I do not mean to undermine the efforts of those many teachers who devote themselves to a careful understanding of their subject, though I do wish to raise questions about what constitutes the subject of study and what is involved in the presentation of the subject to students in university classrooms. Nor do I want to limit these considerations to those who specialize in African American literature, for I think meditations on the teaching of African American literature should account for a community of engagement that extends beyond specialists in the field, encompassing those who recognize that they should represent a diverse body of literature in their courses and so are in search of an appropriate text by an African American writer—with appropriateness often measured by a body of concerns specific to the course, concerns often uninformed or unencumbered by a deep knowledge of African American literary history, let alone a working understanding of the field of Africana studies. Perhaps, then, we should shift the question and ask whether white teachers can or do teach African American literary history (even those teachers who focus on the occasional selected text by African American writers), whether white teachers can or do engage themselves in conversations about black aesthetics, or whether white teachers can or do teach within the social and ideological contexts that form the subject of black studies.

And these questions take us into the classroom—not just to the forum in which we present the subject but to the students gathered there, the teacher employed there, and the interactive dynamics involved in teaching. This essay's title refers to a situation frequently referenced in conversations about race at the University of New Hampshire (UNH): a class with only one black student, led by a white teacher. Most teachers at UNH are accustomed to teaching either all-white classes or classes in which there are no black students though other social groups are represented—and when they get one black student they are usually self-conscious, often cautious, and sometimes defensive. In conversations about the familiar "one-black-student situation," they are likely to talk in terms of both problems and possibilities. For the possibilities they look for ways to engage the black student in class discussions—and our black students frequently complain about being placed in the position of being race representatives, whose task it is to teach the other students about race. If teachers encounter "problems" relating to the one black student (as the teachers present it, these problems can range from the student's lack of engagement in class discussions and material to open discomfort about or resistance to the teacher's authority), they will sometimes talk with the student in a private conference, looking for "sensitive" and "fair" resolutions.

Of course, race does not enter the room only when a student of color comes in; race is always already there, for the classroom is very much both the product of and forum for the ideological imperatives of a white supremacist culture. The black student simply, and merely by her or his presence, exposes the presence of race in the room. She or he disrupts the controlled racial dynamics necessary to maintaining the illusion of whiteness as a nonracial or racially neutral ideological condition. There is, in effect, never just one black student in the classroom, for black students are transformed into race representatives when they walk into the white theater of education. And, consciously or not, in their approach to their subject or in their orchestration of class and small-group discussions, teachers often respond to this exposure of whiteness by working to re-contain race—largely by isolating the student, either through praise or benevolent discipline, a performance either of one's credentials as a racially informed teacher or of one's strict adherence to "standards" regardless of race. Whiteness, that is, works to maintain control over its environment through a (white) liberal (re)staging of racial conflict and resolution.

A predominantly white university offers, so far as I can tell, little more than a reasonably controlled and controllable theater for maintaining and manipulating established cultural scripts. Certainly, the familiar notion of race—the race of a cultural claimant, race as attitudinal, race as a set of social affiliations—operates in this social setting, and much can be learned from encounters with this experience of race. But the race of the individual is also used to veil (intentionally or otherwise) the reality of race as a cultural construction—race as economic, legal, political, educational, historical, and social order, that which controls one's understanding of the past and one's theater for the imagined future. Within the social laboratory of the university, as in the world beyond the campus, the study of race requires an awareness of something like Heisenberg's uncertainty principle. If you study the individual, your understanding of the system will be skewed; if you study the system, your understanding of the individual will be skewed. Friendships are made, and white students believe that the "problem" of race is overstated; subjects are presented with care, and white teachers are astounded when their black students insist on seeing them as part of the problem. As both culturally determined individuals and institutional representatives, we should not be surprised when black students claim that they can see familiar traces of the dysfunctional academic memory embodied in the white teacher standing at the front of the room. As Charles W. Mills has noted, "Nonwhites . . . find that race is, paradoxically, both everywhere and nowhere, structuring their lives but not formally recognized in political/moral theory" (76).

What is white about the white teacher, in short, is not simply the color of her or his skin but, rather, the historical and ideological situation that has made "white" bodies such able predictors of experience, understanding, and access to privilege and cultural authority—a whiteness, in other words, that cannot be transcended simply by the reach of the teacher's consciousness (however greatly bolstered by knowledge or professional expertise). Behind the comforting screens of narratives of racial progress, beyond reminders of the international settings within which the nationalist determinants of race have functioned, beyond the developing emphases on the complex mix of individual genealogical narratives, the cultural landscape of white supremacy stretches out like a Mandelbrot set—endless replications of an always adaptable matrix of ideological imperatives, economic networks, and public practices. To attend to the historical process by which race has been constructed is, after all, to recognize that, instead of race being *somewhere*—in individuals, who await the purifying touch of antiracist advocacy—race is, in fact, *everywhere*: in the way we live, the way wealth and access to power are passed on from one generation to the next, the way that schools are funded, and the ways in which education is defined, inscribed in textbooks and standardized tests, administered, and presented to students. To talk of white teachers, then, is not to talk about *who they are*—"white people"—but, rather, to address *who, where, when*, and perhaps even *why they've been* people living in a culture in which the ideological matrix of whiteness has had and continues to exert considerable force over individual experience and identity formation.

What happens, then, when a white teacher walks into the room to teach courses on African American history or culture? Certainly, race walks into the room, this time visibly the race of the teacher, for the subject matter rather usefully highlights the teacher's whiteness. Still, race remains bound and determined by its association with blackness—the blackness that the teacher both does and does not represent in leading the class, the blackness that the teacher orchestrates through the course of the semester, determining when and how "race" (i.e., as an explicit and acknowledged presence, in a delimited and contained form) will enter the public space of class discussion and the epistemological realm of course evaluation material (essays, exams, and the like). Since they work with African American materials, the dangers for white teachers of African American literature can be even greater than for other teachers, for they have it within their power to shape the text of African American literary and cultural history to the tacit imperatives of a white supremacist culture. White images of black identity, Toni Morrison has observed, are actually representations of white identity projected onto black America, there to be manipulated and controlled according to the needs of white America. Those needs include the need to transgress and protect the boundaries of white identity and also the need to keep an awareness of whiteness *out* of white experience—that is, to make white Americans feel that race is something that applies only to others. Through the "representation and appropriation" of the Africanist narrative, Morrison argues, white Americans have long worked to transform African American experience into a domesticated tale, one capable of serving multiple functions. The white narrative of African American life "provides opportunities to contemplate limitation, suffering, rebellion, and to speculate on fate and destiny"; it is "used for discourse on ethics, social and universal codes of behavior, and assertions about and definitions of civilization and reason"; and it is "used in the construction of a history and a context for whites by positing historylessness and context-lessness for blacks" (*Playing* 53). Vehicles of the (immediate and professional) institution's ideological imperatives, teachers serve as directors of the semester's restaging of literary history, guiding both textual and human actors into a developing drama of African American literary history (or of the place of African American literary production in the "larger story" of American literary history). Throughout this performance teachers will often have occasion to reflect on the accuracy of Morrison's observations, though such occasions often slip by unnoticed. More often than not, we've seen this show before, and the restaging amounts to a new production of a settled plot.

In thinking about raced texts, racial classroom performances, and racial understandings, I am applying Saidiya V. Hartman's concept of "performing blackness," in which "blackness is defined . . . in terms of social relationality rather than identity." "Blackness," Hartman argues, "incorporates subjects normatively defined as black, the relations among blacks, whites, and others, and the practices that produce racial difference." Blackness, in Hartman's persuasive formulation, "marks a social relationship of dominance and abjection and potentially one of redress and emancipation; it is a contested figure at the very center of social struggle." In her term *performing blackness*, then, Hartman means to convey "both the cross-purposes and the circulation of various modes of performance and performativity that concern the production of racial meaning and subjectivity, the nexus of race, subjection, and spectacle, the forms of racial and race(d) pleasure, enactments of white dominance and power, and the reiteration and/or rearticulation of the conditions of enslavement" (56–57). To speak of black texts, accordingly, is to speak of textual sites of social struggle in which the multifarious relations involved in that struggle are highlighted and dramatically restaged.

In the classroom this performance is not only restaged yet again but is placed within an ideological theater that controls the terms of the social drama—making it necessary to think not only about white teachers but also about white classrooms. Keeping in mind Stephen Henderson's emphasis on the performativity fundamental to the (re)production of black literature (and to black expressive culture generally) and of the varying modes and degrees of *saturation* in black culture fundamental to such (re)productions, such improvisational reiterations of the original text, we should ask ourselves what kind of performance of African American literature is staged in academic theaters directed by white teachers. Most white teachers simply lack the deep cultural background and experience essential to the collective classroom staging of black aesthetics, and they bring with them, understandably enough, sensibilities shaped by their own saturation in a United States culture that positions whiteness in complex but influential ways. Too often, this saturation shapes the presentation of the literature and the orchestration of the classroom dynamics. As Robert E. Washington has argued, "most scholars writing about black literary works simply assume those works have been socially consequential but fail to explain how they operate—sociologically speaking—in cultural space" (10), and I would emphasize here the importance of these operations in the overdetermined cultural space of the classroom. Indeed, often these texts are not allowed to operate at all beyond the usual modes of inspiration and ethical affirmation or as case studies in the problematic history of race.

In those classrooms, just as white teachers often isolate or contain the black students in their courses, so they can also isolate or contain African American literature, keeping it at a distance from the broader concerns of black studies. It is either contextualized within established notions of the literary tradition and approaches to literature or is placed in "conversation" with various literary traditions in the service of an idealized multiculturalism. One is often reminded of the justice of Mills's observation that "the recent advent of discussions of 'multiculturalism' is welcome, but what needs to be appreciated is that there are issues of political *power*, not just mutual misconceptions resulting from the clash of cultures" (125). Race is presented as something in the literature or as a quality or identifier of the author or as one among many social topics, rather than a social order that writers work to represent or to which writers respond or within the particular contingencies of which writers develop an approach to the art of what can be said against the force of the unspeakable. Race, that is, enters the literary tradition when African American literature walks into the syllabus. Literature by white writers remains racially neutral (accomplished, in part, by identifying certain works or moments in texts as racist, so as to distinguish these racial moments from the "nonracial" mainstream of the tradition), and teachers work to isolate or contain African American literature—again, either through praise or discipline. There is, after all, much to support Washington's argument that, in the twentieth century, "the liberal-left white intelligentsia both fostered and culturally subjugated the dominant black literary schools" (330). As a result, African American literature usually is kept so busy *representing* race in the curriculum that it is not given the opportunity to represent the race that extends beyond blackness and to retheorize the cultural order that constitutes race.

Following the trajectory that Washington illuminates in his study of the white manipulation of African American literary self-representation, one might suggest that, just as the category of race relations can be used (consciously or not) as a means of avoiding the deep structures of the social order that "race" has both defined and justified historically, so engaging in racial theory as a study of "identity politics" can serve as a means of avoiding the cultural history that has produced African American literature. Such approaches come with their own logic, including the tempting possibility of rejecting the category of race so as to avoid an easy categorization of individuals, a rejection that arguably simply replicates the historical pattern by which the endlessly flexible white supremacist order has maintained its illusion of racial neutrality. This is not to say that I am unsympathetic to Paul Gilroy's view "that there is something worthwhile to be gained from a deliberate renunciation of 'race' as the basis for belonging to one another and acting in concert" (*Against Race* 12), though I am afraid that many white folks will be only too happy to get on this particular bandwagon. Nor do I want to miss what Gilroy suggests is "a chance to break away from the dangerous and destructive patterns that were established when the rational absurdity of 'race' was elevated into an essential concept and endowed with a unique power to both determine history and explain its selective unfolding" (14). I am, however, left with that history that has been determined, unfolded, and explained. How do we revise a history narrated according to the imperatives of "the rational absurdit[ies] of 'race'" if we do not attend to the realities of the manifestations and effects of a social order that race *is*? What do we do with the sites of memory we encounter daily—the movies, music, textbooks, indexes of books—that continually lead us back into the matrix of race, reminding us that, however much we might want to avoid dwelling in the past, we cannot avoid the multifarious ways in which the past dwells in and around us? Even if we can give up "race relations" or racial group identities as a way of categorizing and understanding social behavior and envisioning possible worlds of understanding, we should be careful about dismissing race as a category for understanding the cultural geography of the economic, political, and historical order.

To apply this to the study of literature: it is important, I think, to note that renouncing race will have no effect on how most people teach and write about white literature, but it will affect gravely the ways in which we read, respond to, and apply the lessons of African American literature—making much of that literature a response to a category of thought that no longer has currency, leading us to lose the ways in which that literature responds to a matrix of concerns, a historical/systemic order, that remains all too current. One is still more likely, after all, to encounter an essay, or a pedagogical approach, that "complicates" the category of race in the study of, say, Zora Neale Hurston's work than to encounter a complication of the racial dynamics in Ernest Hemingway's work. Indeed, one is still more likely to see, in anthologies and classrooms, "units" devoted to race that focus more on the Hurstons of the literary world than on the Hemingways. The project of renouncing race as a category of thought, in other words, is complicated by the fact that white culture has for quite some time been engaged in the practice of renouncing and repressing race as a category of thought for many of its writers—to the extent that it is still rare to encounter specialists in Hemingway or other writers who even consider race to be one of their most pressing research concerns, and certainly it is rarer still that such scholars will identify themselves as specialists in white national literatures. And, aside from those actively engaged in "race studies," many literary theorists will be satisfied to enter and exit the subject of race with a good (mis)reading of Gilroy and a few others. Many will be satisfied, indeed, if the rest of us renounce race and send the message up to the head office.

Away from that head office, however, the social experience of race does not cave in under the weight of a racialized global capitalist market for black style, and it doesn't organize itself under the various and exclusive tents of racial politics. White teachers need to confront the whiteness of worlds still untouched by racial theory, the whiteness of colleagues who are not required to think about whiteness, the whiteness that follows one home. In her characteristically compelling and challenging essay "The Highs and the Lows of Black Feminist Criticism" Barbara Christian reminds us of the intimate force of literature, at once both private and public, bound to the moment and carried from the past. "Because language is one (though not the only) way to express what one knows/feels," Christian writes, "even when one doesn't know one knows it, because storytelling *is* a dynamic form of remembering/recreating, we found that it was often in the relationship between literatures and the world that re-envisioning occurred" (48). Too often, I would suggest, the relationship between African American literature and the white teacher's world is under-studied and under-theorized and is rather underwhelming, overdetermined, and all too predictable in its manifestation in classrooms and conversations. For Christian, famously, African American theorizing is not something to be applied to the text but, rather, something presented in and through the text, in the performance of one's reading of African American expressive culture. That theorizing has much to say about the position of white readers and audiences as well. The literature speaks of communities beyond the text, communities that are then (re)positioned when race walks into the classroom, the white teacher with text in hand.

In thinking about her own position within the academy, Christian thinks about the various communities with which she is affiliated and in which she lives, and white teachers of African American literature would do well to follow her lead. "Because I am a black literary/feminist critic," Christian writes, "I live in a sharp distinction between the high world of lit crit books, journals, and conferences, the middle world of classrooms and graduate students, and the low world of bookstores, kitchens, communities, and creative writers" ("Highs and Lows" 50). The complex interplay between these worlds, and the still more complex interplay between these various communities as they have developed historically and as they are staged in the present, defines the particular challenges Christian faces as a scholar-teacher. Applying a similar dynamic of individual position to the subject of interracial understanding, theologian James H. Cone has argued that "what whites fail to recognize is the fact that all decisions made with regard to what is important or worthwhile are made in the context of participation in a community. It is in the community that values are chosen, because the community provides the structure in which our being as persons is realized. It is not possible to transcend the community; it frames our being because being is always *being in relation to others*" (97). White teachers of African American literature engaged in a dream of transcendence—whether it be considered a scholarly, theoretical, or social achievement—would do well to consider Cone's commentary on the multiple contingencies of individual identity as they identify their own highs, middles, and lows to explore "the relationship between literatures and the world" that constitutes the heart of the central question about teachers and subjects raised in this essay and in this collection of essays.

In his reflections on the defining conditions of black theology, Cone seems to anticipate the question. He asks, "Is it possible to change communities?" And he answers: "To change communities involves a change of *being*. It is a radical movement, a radical reorientation of one's existence in the world" (97). Cone's answer is deceptively simple if evaluated by the standards of white liberal history but more challenging if evaluated in the worlds and by the standards presented in African American literature as contextualized by black studies. No doubt, many white people are ready for a "radical reorientation" of sorts, but we tend to want to control the terms of that reorientation, with a particular investment in the visibility of our radical status. But Cone's keyword here is *community*, and the communities represented by African American literary history might well lead to research projects that focus less on the cutting edge ahead than on the solid but dull blade behind and to approaches to teaching that include labor-intensive work in institutional reform, a deep acquaintance with recruitment and retention offices on campus, and attendance at student events. One might be reminded that community outreach has long been considered an essential feature of black studies, and one might begin to attend to the often striking transition from the world of the campus to the neighborhoods that surround the campus. Changing communities, in other words, might begin with one's approach to one's professional life and responsibilities.

This "radical reorientation" might begin with the realization that African American literary history has yet to be fully recovered or constructed and that the U.S. educational system rarely prepares its constituencies for a complex understanding of the nation's past. My work is in the nineteenth-century, so my comments are directed primarily to a field of writing that is usually sampled selectively and contextualized loosely. Even today, some might teach or even write about the *Narrative of the Life of Frederick Douglass* without reading Douglass's other autobiographical writings, or they might present this text as a representative of the "slave narrative genre" without reading more than a handful of narratives. Sojourner Truth can still be trusted to ask regularly, "ar'n't I a woman?" Both the system of slavery and the antislavery movement might still be presented as monolithic enterprises—and students report encountering confident correctives that the Civil War had little to do with either slavery or race. Complex mixed-genre textual performances—for example, William Wells Brown's *Clotel; or, The President's Daughter: A Narrative of Slave Life in the United States* and Harriet E. Wilson's *Our Nig; or, Sketches from the Life of a Free Black, in a Two-Story White House, North*—are often identified unproblematically as novels and, consequently, viewed as rough though historically significant examples of early African American attempts at literary mastery, the beginnings of an evolutionary development that would eventually lead to Toni Morrison.

Reenvisioning this literary history might well begin by bringing more of it into view, and what is radical about this work might be little more than the insistence that we attend to an African American calendar of literary scholarship. By this I mean simply that white writers have received a great deal of attention over the years, leading to biographies, reference works, literary histories, revisionary literary histories, and detailed readings and rereadings of individual texts. But, while the efforts of Dorothy Porter, Henry Louis Gates Jr., Frances Smith Foster, William Andrews, and many others have made a great number of nineteenth-century African American texts available again, much work remains—including the work of attending to the writers and texts thus recovered, piecing together some sense of the complex cultural process that shaped the writers' various approaches, and rethinking what it might mean to talk of African American literary history. We need to follow the direction of texts that extend out in various directions, attend to the narrative imperatives of a fragmented community, and explore political and biblical subtexts that cannot be reduced to an easy footnote or a peremptory gloss. We need to enter into an understanding of racial constructions that is chaotic rather than Euclidean so as to attend to a world of race beyond the neat dimensions of the color line, the line so essential to white understandings of racial activism, the line that offers the seductive prospect of heroic transgressions—including the ultimate transgression of eliminating the line, as if it were the problem all along. We need to piece together what can be known of individual lives and avoid the generic constructs (with its exceptional figures) characteristic of voyeuristic white approaches to African American identity from the antislavery movement to the present. The community of the past makes its own demands—most fundamentally, the demand for recognition—and these demands come down to simple questions about how one should spend one's time, what scholarly priorities one should set for oneself, and how one should present the always-previsional story of African American literary history in the classroom.

Without this work we are likely to fall into a kind of professional default mode, a willingness to accept a received story of literary history and received conceptions of what constitutes literary art, if only to reorient received wisdom to create a new scholarly movement. In the classroom, particularly in courses that offer broad surveys of American literature, this can mean a reliance on the usual "inclusion" model involving strategic insertions of African American writers and related social movements into an already formulated master narrative. And the narrative can indeed master its subjects—for, while early African American literature is sometimes viewed as the primitive anticipations of the more recognizably *literary* achievements of later years, the achievements of contemporary writers are often located along different genealogical lines altogether. In Ishmael Reed's *Flight to Canada*, for example, Reed's representative

Raven Quickskill encounters William Wells Brown, expresses his admiration for Brown's work, and tells him that "Flight to Canada" (arguably, both Quickskill's poem and Reed's novel) imitates Brown's style—but Quickskill notes that this influence will be missed by most and that "the critics are going to give me some kind of white master" (121). And, indeed, on the back cover of the book Reed is praised by the *Saturday Review* for writing a novel in the tradition of Mark Twain, while Brown's work still struggles to find readers receptive to its complex representation of the fractal national landscape as defined and regulated by the system of slavery.[1] White teachers, drawing from their own education and cultural experience, are all too likely to resemble the reader represented on the back of Reed's book.

Can white teachers teach African American literature? I can't offer a simple answer to this question or a neat conclusion to this essay, not even for myself in my own teaching and scholarship. It seems to me that white teachers have a lot of work to do in thinking about their approach to this field. It is not enough to borrow authority from black scholars and writers; it is not enough to base one's authority on a relatively expansive body of knowledge; and it is not enough to base the authority of one's scholarship and teaching on what amounts to easy conversion narratives ("I once was white, but now I see"). Whiteness is a complex web of contingencies, and white teachers have a responsibility to understand and work with and against these contingencies. What I have in mind is something that Toni Morrison has addressed in her commentary on Herman Melville: "If . . . a white, nineteenth-century, American male took on not abolition, not the amelioration of racist institutions or their laws, but the very concept of whiteness as an inhuman idea, he would be very alone, very desperate, and very doomed" ("Unspeakable" 381). Although I don't want to suggest that white teachers of African American literature are necessarily "doomed," I do want to indicate the depth of the challenge white teachers face, a challenge rarely noted in the work of white scholars and rarely seen in "white" classrooms.

If our real question is not whether white teachers *can* teach but whether they *may*—that is, whether we have the right to do so—then one can only note that the question has been decided, for white teachers do teach African American literature. No doubt, too, most of us can find students or colleagues willing to give us some stamp of racial approval, something to hang on the walls of our self-conscious houses of thought. But, if our question actually has to do with the challenges specific to white teachers of African American literature, then we need to engage ourselves in the fullness of the subject before us and dedicate ourselves to the challenge of learning to read not just the text at hand but also the white hand on the text—as well as the complex cultural history that shaped the hand of authority and that has defined the authority of the text. We will need to consider the cultural theater in which we teach and the communities beyond that theater with which we ally ourselves. Following Cone, one might approach one's challenges by drawing from the methodologies of black liberation theology—a theology that emphasizes the importance of a community defined by its multiple contingencies, historical and social; a theology that places "orthopraxis" over orthodoxy as its means of self-evaluation; and a theology devoted to an ongoing interrogation of the institutional and political frameworks within which it operates. Perhaps one might hope for "a radical movement, a radical reorientation of one's existence in the world" (Cone 97). Certainly, one can identify some white scholars and activists who might be taken as standards against which one's own performance might be measured, though John Browns and Jonathan Kozols are all too rare. Still, the demands of African American literary history are great, the whiteness of the teacher cannot be transcended, and the semester's performance cannot be contained within the classroom walls. In the end, and along the way, we will be known by our acts.

## NOTE

1. The other back-cover blurbs complete the picture, though not quite in the way that Quickskill/Reed anticipated. The excerpt from the *New York Times Book Review* presents *Flight to Canada* as "a demonized *Uncle Tom's Cabin*," while the excerpt from the *Baltimore Sun* presents Reed as one who "wears the mantle of Baldwin and Ellison like a high-powered Flip Wilson in drag."

# Naming the Problem Embedded in the Problem That Led to the Question "Who Shall Teach African American Literature?"

## or, Are We Ready to Discard the Concept of Authenticity Altogether?

LESLIE W. LEWIS

Black Is . . . Black Ain't

–Marlon Riggs

Keepin it real, y'all.

–A phrase made popular by numerous hip-hop artists

It's uh known fact . . . you got tuh *go* there tuh *know* there.

–Zora Neale Hurston, *Their Eyes Were Watching God*

The concept of racial authenticity poses more problems than it solves, in part because authenticity itself does so. In philosophical contexts authenticity often signifies the ethical imperative to be true to oneself; in historical contexts it may refer to verisimilitude; and in the world of art and artifact it seems to mean that an object is what it claims to be with regard to mode of production. Within the construct of culture, and within related scholarship focused on race, numerous book and article titles and subtitles demonstrate that contemporary deliberations about authenticity are quite common—and useful.[1] But this essay is meant to be cautionary because there are conceptual limitations implicit in authenticity's definition, limitations that are most obvious in the context of racial authenticity. Consider this: in all cases questions of authenticity require answers from authority, a quite different conceptual creature and not even etymologically related. Nothing (and no one) gives *itself* a certificate of authenticity, after all, so that authenticity's dependence on authority means that, characteristically speaking, authenticity is extrinsically, rather than intrinsically, anchored. In other words, authenticity may seem to be about *being* real, but it is always, in truth, about being *perceived* as real, and, consequently, authenticity is a representational rather than an existential concept. Further, and this is perhaps most significant, since judgments that characterize something (or someone) as authentic, or not, are made on the basis of authority, not authenticity itself, these two categorical claims to knowledge, while sometimes linked, are neither congruent nor separate but equal. Authority defines authenticity, but the inverse does not hold, and we must consider here that, while we very regularly discuss black authenticity and other forms of racial authenticity, this does not extend to a discussion of white authenticity, a phrase that may even strike some as oxymoronic. Conceptually, we have a fraught state of affairs, indeed. This essay, then, will interrogate authenticity's role in arts and letters and in the academy but will do so by first examining black authenticity issues within African American performance contexts as well as the commodification of authenticity in these same contexts. I begin here because African American performance history makes very clear black authenticity's representational, rather than existential, roots, and, as such, this history reminds us that "blackness" is a contested identity within African American circles and also reminds us that playing authenticity means playing a game long defined by the dominant culture.

As I understand it, there is a question sometimes put to white scholars of African American literature (or studies) that involves the genuineness of our relation to the materials we read and contemplate, discuss and teach, analyze and interpret. I think it is a mistake for white scholars to feel singled out by this question, as if unfairly challenged in some way that is impossible to address; it is not as if black scholars are not sometimes challenged by some version of the same question. But, ultimately, questions of this sort are bad questions, unproductive questions, and moments in African American writing help explain why. W.E.B. DuBois does not ask if he can sit with Shakespeare, move arm in arm with Balzac, summon Aristotle and Aurelius; he simply notes that when he does so there are no winces; there is no scorn, nor condescension (*Souls of Black Folk* 76). James Baldwin recognizes that, although he has white friends whom he cares for and trusts, he can never convey their humanity to Elijah Muhammad and with this insight recognizes, "in the eeriest way possible . . . what white people must go through at a dinner table when they are trying to prove that Negroes are not subhuman" (*Fire Next Time* 70–74). Taken together, these examples, by analogy, remind us that there is no point in asking whether interracial love affairs between scholars and texts should exist; they already do. But justifying them to anyone who believes them inherently wrong is a no-win situation. As I hope to demonstrate in the second section of this essay, questioning the authenticity of relationships between scholar and text points toward the ways in which authenticity, as a perversely essentialist concept, is insufficient for scholarly purposes. This is not to say that the desire to relate epistemology and ontology, knowing and being, or even the exegetical and the metaphysical,[2] is itself misguided but only that these relations need to be drawn in ways that authenticity cannot fathom.

## Black Is . . .

As Nellie McKay notes in her article "Naming the Problem That Led to the Question 'Who Shall Teach African American Literature'; or, Are We Ready to Disband the Wheatley Court?" the issue of authenticity has plagued African American writers at least since the Wheatley court was asked to judge whether Wheatley was capable, or not, of writing poetry by her own hand. Yet, as the first two epigraphs McKay chose for her essay also indicate, eighteenth-century American society as represented by the Wheatley court had rigged the game. The question that the judges considered, as McKay presents it, was the question of authenticity, which is inherently a question of agency: did Phillis Wheatley write the poetry that she claims is hers? To the detriment of American literary and intellectual development, however, even while these judges attest that Wheatley's poems were indeed written by her, reviewers state that these authenticating claims do not matter. "Authentically what?" these critics could ask about Wheatley's writings. Racism (and sexism, no doubt) foreordained the answer: even if Phillis Wheatley wrote the words on the page, what she wrote, said the critics, was not poetry—that is, not *real* poetry. The Wheatley court may have answered the question of agency, but it never considered the deepest questions of authority: for example, there is no indication that Wheatley's judges, or any other leaders of this eighteenth-century colonial American society, could conceive of the idea that Wheatley herself might join *them* on the scholarly "bench" once she has passed her exams. Indeed, as Thomas Jefferson echoes in his *Notes on the State of Virginia* (1787), contemporary opinion determines that, while Wheatley's hand may have written her poems, because that hand was black those poems were by definition merely imitative, not creative; for Jefferson, in the context of his musing that "blacks" are somewhere between "whites" and "Oranootan[s]" in the great chain of being, "Phyllis Whatley" [*sic*] cannot be a poet, and "the compositions published under her name are below the dignity of criticism" (986). Whether Phillis Wheatley really wrote her poems or not, they did not count because she did not count, and no eighteenth-century American court would reconsider that judgment.

Critical response to Wheatley's poetry, then, makes clear that the question of racial authenticity in the context of eighteenth-century white supremacy is the question of whether or not nonwhite people are authentically human. We know through the scholarship focused on the history of white supremacist thought, on the development of early African American letters, and on the relation between the two that, as race becomes a categorical imperative, blackness becomes a commodity, first through the market economy of slavery. In mid-nineteenth-century society this commodification develops as cultural institutions are created that mediate white psychic responses to white culpability for the oppressive political regime known as the antebellum United States. Consider this 1860 echo of Jefferson's "Oranootan":

> "WHAT IS IT?"? Is it a lower order of MAN? Or is it a higher order of MONKEY! None can tell! Perhaps it is a combination of both. It is beyond dispute THE MOST MARVELOUS CREATURE LIVING. It was captured in a savage state in Central Africa, is probably about 20 years old, 4 feet high, intelligent, docile, active, sportive, and PLAYFUL AS A KITTEN. It has a skull, limbs and general anatomy of an ORAN OUTING and the COUNTENANCE of a HUMAN BEING. TO BE SEEN AT ALL HOURS AT BARNAM'S MUSEUM.[3]

This is the text that accompanies a Currier and Ives lithograph of P. T. Barnum's "What Is It?" exhibition, in this rendition a picture of the creature in its "wild" state. This exhibition opened in New York during the 1860 presidential campaign and was soon put to use by anti-Lincoln political propagandists. As with other exhibits in his "Gallery of Wonders," Barnum here sells the "authenticity" of this creature, whom viewers are invited to see and then define for themselves (man? or monkey?). Not surprisingly, as later scholarship has revealed, this "What Is It?" creature was played by African American actors ("Lost Museum Archive").

In the context of this exhibition and then postbellum nineteenth-century American culture more generally, Barnum's "What Is It?" question shifts the American public's attention from a focus on authentic humanity to a focus on the authentically black—a shift in all likelihood hastened by the fact that authentic blackness sells. In the "What Is It?" example it is the dominant society's fascination with questions about what blackness is that sells the exhibition to the general public, not that society's fascination with questions of fundamental humanity, and whatever authentic blackness is in this context, it is clearly constructed by the dominant society for consumption by the dominant society. My point with this "What Is It?" example, however, is not simply that authentic blackness is delineated by white society in order to fulfill that society's needs; my point is that the shift from questions of authentic humanity to questions of authentic blackness forever changes the racial game. Here is where we must consider racial authenticity issues as they play in postbellum American performance history: as the Civil War ends, the first "all-colored" blackface minstrel troupes are formed, which means that black men darken their faces with burnt cork and so impersonate white men impersonating black men—and all this under the sign of authenticity, selling themselves as "original Georgia" minstrels. As Marlon Riggs and others have documented, black performance history begins from within and by signifying on the racial stereotypes of blackface minstrelsy.[4] But, as Riggs later interrogates in the posthumously released *Black Is . . . Black Ain't*, questions of authenticity as they pervade African American communities are often detrimental to African American people.

If we carefully consider the career of any famous turn-of-the-twentieth-century African American minstrel or vaudeville performer—Billy Kersands, Sam Lucas, or Bert Williams, for example—we see that, while such a performer may have been popular with white audiences directly because of the purportedly authentic blackness that he represented, what made him popular with black audiences was more complexly related to issues of black authenticity. A significant passage from Tom Fletcher's *One Hundred Years of the Negro in Show Business* demonstrates, through observations and reminiscences by Fletcher's maternal grandfather, "born on the Gold Coast of West Africa [Ghana]," that minstrel show performances like the cakewalk have their origins in steal away gatherings on the plantation and retain elements of African culture and music (19). As Fletcher's later descriptions of specific performances also indicate, however, black performers are not so much set on retaining African elements in their shows as they are invested in creating new spectacles for their audiences, often by appropriating and then signifying on black stereotypes. In discussing his own involvement with the Georgia Minstrels, Fletcher reports that "everybody wanted to be original and creative in those days," so that end men Frosty Moore, Willis Clarke, Lew Jones, and Standford McKissick "would each take his mirror and his makeup, go to a different corner of their dressing room and put on makeup. All the end men used burnt cork on their faces and grease paint on their lips. When they had finished, each would put his hand over his mouth until time for the curtain to go up, then reveal the makeup on his mouth. The shape and size of the mouth on opening night was yours for the season and none of the other end men was allowed to use your mouth style all that season" (59). These contests, of course, allowed the end men to spoof what blackness "is," by focusing on the stereotype of big lips, and so to continue to sell creative interpretations of blackness to their white and black audiences.[5] The skit that comedian and dancer Billy Kersands made famous, "his stunt of dancing while holding two billiard balls in his mouth," which "proved sensational," worked similarly (61).

One final example from African American performance history will add appropriate complexity to our survey of representations of / significations on black authenticity at the turn of the twentieth century. Consider Sam Lucas, of

Callender's Original Georgia Minstrels, who published the song "Carve Dat Possum" in 1875. Lucas was perhaps the most successful black actor of his day and, as Fletcher says, "had been a star and a big feature of all the big colored shows, minstrels, musical comedies, dramas, melodramas and variety" (67). "Carve Dat Possum" was a song he made famous. The first verse of the song is:

> De possum meat am good to eat,
> Carve him to de heart;
> Yo'll always find him good and sweet,
> Carve him to de heart;
> My dog did bark, and I went to see,
> Carve him to de heart;
> And dar was a possum up dat tree,
> Carve him to de heart.

And the chorus goes:

> Carve dat possum, carve dat possum, children,
> Carve dat possum, carve him to de heart;
> Oh, carve dat possum, carve dat possum, children,
> Carve dat possum, carve him to de heart. (N.p.)

These lyrics, however, are sung to the tune of a song easily recognizable, at least by African American audiences, as the great spiritual "Go Down, Moses."[6] "Go Down, Moses," the song of deliverance whose lyrics focus on Old Testament images but obviously also refer to enslaved Africans in the Americas, has a distinctive melody that is "wonderfully strong," to use James Weldon Johnson's words (*Autobiography of an Ex-Coloured Man* 181). In Johnson's opinion, in fact, "Go Down, Moses" contains the strongest theme "in the whole musical literature of the world" (*Books of American Negro Spirituals* 13). In the context of late-nineteenth-century African American performance, then, when we consider Sam Lucas singing "Carve Dat Possum" with overtones from "Go Down, Moses," from the minstrel stage and for a racially mixed audience, we begin to get a sense of just how tangled the performance of racial authenticity is with signifying and commodity production and get a sense as well that this tangle is embedded in the very origins of race performance.

Keeping this origin story in mind, then, if we jump approximately one hundred years to examine issues of authenticity within hip-hop culture, in order to better understand the complexity of racial authenticity in contemporary American life, we are immediately confronted with the phrase "keepin' it real." Kembrew McLeod's research suggests that artists use this phrase as an invocation of authenticity whose precise "meaning changes depending on the context in which it is invoked" ("Authenticity within Hip-Hop" 139). DJ Muggs says that he did "about 200 interviews last year and in every one was that question

'What's keepin' it real to you?'" Hip-hop journalist Angela N. states, "You haven't lived until you've edited a 2-hour interview and heard 'keepin' it real' after every other sentence, tried to cut most of them out of the finished product, then have your boss ask you 'could you do *something* about all of these "keepin' it real's"?'"(qtd. in McLeod 139). These and other examples demonstrate that one main aspect of the claim "keepin' it real" is that an artist's music has not been overly commercialized, which seems to mean calculatedly produced for a crossover (i.e., primarily white) audience. Method Man, a Wu-Tang Clan member and multiplatinum solo artist, says: "Basically, I make music that represents me. Who I am. I'm not gonna calculate my music to entertain the masses. I gotta keep it real for me" (140). This claim specifically seems to mean that this artist is not *intending* to make records that sell to white suburban teenagers and get played on MTV, which emphasizes the racial aspect of the music's definition. As McLeod summarizes, popular artists risk inauthenticity, and, "by disassociating . . . from 'blackness,' a hip-hop artist opens himself or herself to charges of selling out" (141). Hip-hop, however, is contentious racial territory, and many artists and scholars offer quite sophisticated analyses of its relation to market authenticity. In "Nigs R Us, or How Blackfolk Became Fetish Objects" Greg Tate observes, in a discussion of Eminem, that "for some a white rapper will always be an oxymoron; others, like retired basketball star Charles Barkley, find great humor in the irony of living in a time when the best rapper (his words, not mine) is white and the best golfer is Black" (8–9). Tate edits *Everything but the Burden: What White People Are Taking from Black Culture*, a collection of essays that presents "the myriad ways African Americans grapple with feelings of political inferiority, creative superiority, and ironic distance in a market-driven world where we continue to find ourselves being sold as hunted outsiders and privileged insiders in the same breath" (14).

One of the essays in Tate's collection, "Pimp Notes on Autonomy" by Beth Coleman, brings us forcefully into this arena of market authenticity. Coleman, who is very clear on what we might characterize as one of the newest black aesthetics, opens her essay: "If one had to say it fast, the slave economy in America produced the American pimp. Pimping may be the second-oldest profession in the world, but it was in America first that the pimp became a black pop star. It is the particular undying racial swagger of the pimp as he has become famous in America that I pursue here" (68). Coleman concludes her essay with a series of statements about what she characterizes as "pimp theory." First, she says, "Pimp theory understands that one cannot refuse representation." Next, according to Coleman, "Pimp theory is a formal readdress of the mechanism of mastery even as it is a form of repetition compulsion. It relies on the double spin, playing the black fetish. It is a philosophy that states that *a priori* the consolidation of power happens—with or without your consent" (79). Finally, as Coleman explains, "Pimp theory is to be that thing so thoroughly for your audience (whores, patrons, colleagues) that one is able to rob the man and have him thank you for it. That is the magic trick, the moment of transformation, and that's why he's a Black Nationalist hero" (80). Coleman's "magic trick" is also a more generally invoked contemporary strategy for alternative success. When the desire for the accomplishment referred to in an earlier era as "getting over on the man" merges with panoptical object knowledge stemming from living under constant surveillance, and so knowing how to do exactly what the observing eye expects, the result is sleight-of-hand behavior that convinces the eye that something indeed happening is not. We might characterize this as a new version of the old strategy to "change the joke and slip the yoke,"[7] but the notable point is that pimping is not about freedom but money. Further, pimping relies on the appropriation of people as commodities, as its origins in the slave economy would suggest, and so pimp theory seems also to accept black (market) authenticity at the expense of the struggle for human authenticity.

What seems, at least sometimes, to be the complete merger of black authenticity with black market authenticity, particularly as we focus on contemporary popular culture, is also what R.A.T. Judy characterizes as "nigga authenticity," as when he states that "*nigga* defines *authenticity* as adaptation to the force of commodification" (229). In his important and influential essay "On the Question of Nigga Authenticity," from *boundary 2*, Judy characterizes hardcore rap as responding to the "inevitable loss of experience to commodified affect" in this "age of hypercommodification, in which experience has not become commodified, it *is* commodification, and *nigga* designates the scene, par excellence, of commodification" (228). In this context, Judy says, "authenticity is hype, a hypercommodified affect, whose circulation has made hip-hop global," and "nigga is not an essential identity, strategic or otherwise, but rather indicates the historicity of indeterminate identity" in the "global hypercommodification of cultural production, in which the relation of cultural object to group being no longer matters politically" (229). With his analysis of "nigga authenticity," however, Judy leads us away from the conceptualization of racial authenticity and back to questions of human authenticity. That is, as Judy states, "In other words, nigga poses an existential problem that concerns what it means (or how it is possible) to-be-human. . . . Hardcore's nigga returns us to the existentialist preoccupation with the difference between the subject of knowledge and the subject of experience" (230). Here, then, Judy ultimately claims much more for nigga authenticity than Coleman allows within pimp theory.

For Coleman "the serious limitation on pimp theory as a liberation ideology is that it must reproduce the structure from which it hails," her way of making a point similar to Audre Lorde's well-known statement that "the master's tools will never dismantle the master's house" ("Master's Tools" 112). For Judy, however, concepts fundamental to liberation theory are not givens. His claim is that hip-hop is “an emergent utterance” that questions the *a priori* subject identity that is the foundation of liberal knowing and that nigga authenticity, “a strictly existential matter,” is about exploring different types of human consciousness, which, through translation, become valid for all forms of human life. If we now return to the Wheatley court wherein we began this definitional excursion into questions of racial authenticity, we see the fundamental difference between the proof of human authenticity that Wheatley's court demanded compared with the nigga authenticity Judy describes. In the process of proving Wheatley's writings authentic, the Wheatley court equates human authenticity with white life as the Judges know it. Consequently, Wheatley must prove her humanity by proving herself to be recognizably like her Judges. The authenticity Judy pursues, however, is unmoored from whiteness and so suggests the possibility of something other than the same ol' structures of consciousness. His question of human authenticity, in other words, expands the range of possibilities for human existence, at least in a postmodern theoretical context. Through the production of the hypercommodified nigga of late-twentieth-century popular culture, according to Judy's argument, this figure that stands in the American imagination as the most racially authentic performative subject has now undone what P. T. Barnum's “What Is It?” exhibition created a century earlier. Commodified, racialized object becomes the hypercommodified, racialized subject that refocuses our attention on questions of human being rather than on questions of black being. Yet, in spite of the radical possibilities in Judy's argument, it does also seem that the concept of racial authenticity might be likened to the proverbial tar baby, in that the more we struggle with it the more we become stuck in it.

## . . . tuh *know* there

There are two premises that seem most significant as we consider representations of African American life and culture in the college classroom. The first is that black subject matter is off-limits to no one, including white students and white professors: it's not a “black thing” in the sense that cross-racial understanding is impossible—difficult, perhaps, but not impossible. Paul Gilroy makes this point in *The Black Atlantic*, in the concluding pages of his chapter “Black Music and the Politics of Authenticity.” About music, he says: “Looking back on the adolescent hours I spent trying to master the technical intricacies of Albert King and Jimi Hendrix, fathom the subtleties of James Jamerson, Larry Graham, or Chuck Rainey, and comprehend how the screams of Sly, James, and Aretha could punctuate and extend their metaphysical modes of address to the black subject, I realize that the most important lesson music still has to teach us is that its inner secrets and its ethnic rules can be taught and learned” (109). The second point is that any claim to blackness that excludes other claims to blackness is wrongheaded. This is the point that Kendall Thomas makes in "'Ain't Nothin' like the Real Thing,'" an essay that explores the "jargon of racial authenticity" as it relates to African American sexual politics and reminds us of the heteronormative logic that ascribes "'authentic' black identity on the repudiation of gay or lesbian identity" by quoting O.G. (Original Gangster) Ice Cube saying, "true niggers ain't gay" (61, 59). Thomas's conclusion, of which we must take note, is that "the obsessive preoccupation with proof of racial authenticity deflects attention and energy away from the need to come to grips with the real, material problems in whose resolution black Americans of both genders and all sexual identifications have an immediate and urgent interest" (67). Here, then, we are also reminded that whatever nigga authenticity brings us in the theoretical realm, it is still true that hardcore rap's virulent misogyny and homophobia has certainly hurt real black people.

Turn-of-the-twentieth- and turn-of-the-twenty-first-century African American blackface and hip-hop performance examples show us the attendant difficulties and complexities involved in efforts to define authentic blackness. Even fairly standard definitions of black cultural authenticity such as the black nationalist Larry Neal's formulation in "The Ethos of the Blues" that how we define a cultural tradition depends on the ethos, the "emotional archetype" or "characteristic personality" shared by the makers of the tradition and their intended audience or supporting community (42), seem insufficient in this era of "global hypercommodification of cultural production," as Judy names it (229). Who really is, in other words, the intended audience or supporting community for the hardcore rap that reaches into white suburbs and across national boundaries? What is the ethos, in Neal's terms, of the nineteenth-century blackface minstrel shows performed by African Americans to racially mixed audiences? Here, however, I want to suggest that issues of authenticity are not just confusing and complex but also potentially deadly and that particularly with regard to scholarship—and the classroom—we need work marked by authority rather than authenticity. In part this is an etymological point. As previously mentioned, the words *authority* and *authenticity* are not etymologically related.[8] *Authenticity* derives from the Greek, *authentes*, which is a contraction for *autoentes*, meaning perpetrator, or, from Liddell and Scott's Intermediate Greek-English Lexicon, someone who does something with his own hand, literally a murderer. *Murderer* is the best translation of the word in Sophocles' *Oedipus the King*, for example, in which Creon says early in the play: "The God commanded clearly: let some one / punish with force this dead man's murderers [*autoentas*]" (ll. 106–107.) Other examples of the word's usage in Greek texts are translated similarly. Proving authenticity, then, involves proving agency and, consequently, proving oneself genuine. *Authority*, by contrast, is from the Latin *auctoritat*, from *auctor*, or "author": one that originates or gives existence, from the Latin *auctus*, past participle of *augere*, to increase. In the realm of authority, then, we ask what we add to literature or scholarship, how we increase what we know, how we support opinion or demonstrate knowledge. This, I want to suggest, would have been and is the more fruitful question to ask of the eighteenth-century Phillis Wheatley, of the twentieth-century African American scholarly pioneers whom Nellie McKay discusses in "Naming the Problem," and of twenty-first-century white African Americanists. Replacing the question of authority with the question of authenticity has been and still is, I repeat, potentially deadly—and most consequentially to the study of African American letters itself.

Ann duCille takes up the academy's difficulty in distinguishing authority from authenticity in her essay "The Occult of True Black Womanhood: Critical Demeanor and Black Feminist Studies," and her concerns and examples help us to focus on many of the ways that various searches for authenticity, or attempts to authenticate scholarship, go wrong. As duCille states, "the question of who is authorized to teach African American discourse is riddled with ironies, paradoxes, and contradictions," so much so that black scholars whose fields are not African American literature or African American studies are often "expected to be ready, willing, and able to teach black studies courses" (32). Moreover, as duCille also observes, when white scholars are hired to teach African American literature or studies (whether qualified to do so or not), in institutional practice the same white African Americanists often are not expected to play the myriad roles we expect from black scholars, for example, to provide "a black reading" of a colleague's work or "black representation on a committee or black resources for . . . students." This is the "paradox of critical demeanor," as duCille names it, in which the "difference between authority and authenticity" is recognized but nevertheless conflated so that "Black scholars on predominantly or overwhelmingly white campuses are rarely authorized simply as scholars" but are also treated in such a way that "our racial difference is an authenticating stamp . . . that . . . casts us in the role of Caliban in the classroom and on the campus." The consequence for black women scholars on predominantly white campuses is "both a hypervisibility and a superisolation." Further, duCille reminds us, "when their canonical year rolls around, all too often these same black women faculty members who have been drawn on as exemplars and used up as icons will find themselves chewed up and spit out because they did not publish" (33). And, I would add, grimly, that we have lost to early deaths too many of the black women scholars who have published—and taught and served—perhaps at the expense of personal and vital needs.

DuCille is most pointed, however, in her critiques of scholars' personal statements about why they are engaged in the work at hand, including Jane Gallop in *Around 1981*, John Callahan in *In the African American Grain*, Missy Dehn Kubitschek in *Claiming the Heritage*, and Houston Baker in *Workings of the Spirit.* The statements duCille objects to are those that might be categorized as naming one's own subject position. There are, indeed, so many examples of such statements that they have become standard, and even anecdotal evidence suggests that more than a few scholars working with materials that represent life experience not congruent with their own perceived gender or racial identity category have been told by mentors that such prefatory statements are required. Still, as duCille recognizes, scholars in this position at times make very awkward confessional statements that really do nothing to buttress their own authority. I read such statements as misguided attempts to play by the rules that require authenticity as well as authority in matters of race yet am sympathetic to white writers who want to claim, in some way, an identity, or standpoint knowledge, that is not white or is not limited in the ways that white identity is seen to be limited. After all, as James Baldwin has said, white is a metaphor for power ("a way of describing Chase Manhattan Bank"), and, while white may be a state of mind, there is a way in which white is, as Baldwin puts it, a "moral choice" ("Black English" 57, 59). If this is true, it should be at least possible for white people to choose to be otherwise. And in this regard there is a developing literature composed of significant biographical explorations by men and women whose lived experiences are not quite white and another growing body of literature that focuses on white antiracist activism.[9] Nevertheless, as Becky Thompson reports, one wise activist's approach to her work is not to talk but to do—good advice, in my opinion, for any white scholar of African American materials searching for authenticity (*Promise* xviii).

DuCille articulates some of the complexity of naming the problem of authenticity in her critique of Houston Baker's *Workings of the Spirit: The Poetics of Afro-American Women's Writing*, in which she describes her impatience with Baker's turn to African American women writers. According to duCille's reading of Baker, he "tells us in his conclusion that the shared horror of a friend's rape led him to seek solace in the 'expressive resistances of Afro-American women's talking books'" (45). DuCille paraphrases and quotes Baker again, reporting: "The writings of black women authors like Hurston, Morrison, and Shange helped teach him and his friend to move beyond being victim to being survivor. 'The texts of Afro-American women writers,' Baker says, 'became mine and my friend's harrowing but sustaining path to a new, common, and, we thought, empowering discourse and commitment. To "victim," in my friend's semantics, was added the title and entitlement "survivor." Are we not all only that? Victim/Survivors?'" (duCille 45; Baker 208–209). This statement by Baker is not read sympathetically by duCille, however, who summarizes her negative response: "Although Baker is certainly entitled to tell his story, using his friend's rape to claim entitlement to the texts of black women writers—to authorize his entry into a field he has virtually ignored—makes for a story that I, for one, resent being asked to read as part of his critical discourse. For me, this maneuver compromises the integrity of his intellectual project; it makes the feminist concept that the personal is political a kind of joke. . . . Baker's conclusion makes me distrust not his cultural competence, perhaps, but his gender sensibility—his ability to handle with care the sacred text of me and mine" (45–46). Baker's attempt to use his "friend's" rape to authenticate his own connection to texts written by black women, in other words, undermines, for duCille, his critical authority.

I have here quoted duCille's difficulties with Baker's text at such length because the public record shows that this example brings with it tremendous complexity. In *Workings of the Spirit* Baker intimates, but does not say, that the "friend" who has been raped is his wife, Charlotte Pierce-Baker.[10] She, however, has written her story, and other black women's, in *Surviving the Silence: Black Women's Stories of Rape*, and so we do know, in retrospect, that Baker is making reference to his own family's trauma. We might wonder: should this identification change duCille's reading of Baker's conclusion to *Workings of the Spirit*? Who is to say, and why and how, that black women's writing should not be read for the way that it demonstrates the strength of survival? Is that not what some texts teach to some readers who need such knowledge? Does referencing texts that tell of endurance by black women necessarily mean referencing Mammy stereotypes, as duCille indicates? (45). Isn't Alice Walker's "In Search of Our Mothers' Gardens" read differently? Part of the project of duCille's essay from which I have quoted so extensively is to "problematize the admitted possessiveness of our disciplinary concerns," is, again in duCille's words, to explore "the sense of personal stake that permeates the scholarship by black women about black women." I concur with duCille that for black women scholars it may be time "to interrogate in new and increasingly clinical ways our proprietary relationship to the field many of us continue to think of as *our own*" (34). It is in the spirit of "complementary theorizing," as Sharon Holland through Ann duCille names it, that I offer these thoughts on racial authenticity and its limitations (qtd. in duCille 51).

In the end Baker's *Workings of the Spirit* should be analyzed based on what it does as literary criticism, not on whether its origins are legitimate. Certainly, there is a story that Baker has begun to tell that movingly articulates what it means to be the black husband of a black wife who was raped by two young black men who broke into their house while they and their nine-year-old son were home.[11] In light of this story, is Baker's own relation to the both/and construct of victim/survivor one of outsider or insider (or perhaps both)? In other words, do we really dare ask whether the path that brought Baker to read and write about black women's texts should be considered "genuine" or not? This, I am suggesting, is where authenticity is a conceptual failure. By suggesting that lines are clear, that some are of the group and some are not, that some have a legitimate claim to connecting to the life experiences a literary text presents and some do not—all strictly by virtue of who readers are in terms of recognizable race or gender identity categories—this is, we now recognize, a dangerous shortcut through the very complex relation between being and knowing, experience and learning. Charles Johnson has his character Captain Falcon declare: "Dualism is a bloody structure of the mind. Subject and object, perceiver and perceived, self and other—these ancient twins are built into mind like the stempiece of a merchantman. We cannot *think* without them. . . . They are signs of a transcendental Fault, a deep crack in consciousness itself. Mind was *made* for murder" (*Middle Passage* 98). We who are Johnson's readers, however, know more than Captain Falcon. I propose that we take our cue from the writers we study and become, at least at times, dead serious responsible readers who reexamine issues of agency and representation and knowledge. Let us uncouple mind and murder, and let us begin by abandoning the logic that one must "be" one (or be very much like one) to "know" one, since "oneness" so posited makes murderous dualism inevitable.

If, as scholars of African American literature, we are to abandon quests for authenticity and begin again, I have three suggestions for alternative starting points. The first is contained within the moment when Janie in *Their Eyes Were Watching God* learns that she "has an inside and an outside now and suddenly she knew how not to mix them" (72). Self-division, as Barbara Johnson articulates, means that authenticity's sign is self-difference, not self-identity, and reexamined this means a definition of subjectivity unlike any authenticity can really name ("Metaphor, Metonymy and Voice"). A second alternative starting point would focus on the process of achieving our own authority, James Baldwin's language for people who are "unshakable" in their knowledge, who have indeed suffered but have survived "the fire of human cruelty that rages" and so know what no school or church can teach (*Fire Next Time* 99). These would be people who possess a certain kind of self-certainty, not the "I am what I am" certainty of authenticity but the "I know what I know" certainty of authority. Finally, I suggest that we take seriously and begin to articulate carefully how it comes to be that some people "get it," even while others do not, a problem whose solution was partially posed long ago by Frederick Douglass in *Narrative of the Life of Frederick Douglass* (1845), when he characterized listening to the sorrow songs expressed by slaves on their way to the Great House Farm as the best possible path toward understanding slavery. "If any one wishes to be impressed with the soul-killing effects of slavery," Douglass says, "let him go to Colonel Lloyd's plantation, and, on allowance-day, place himself in the deep pine woods, and there let him, in silence analyze the sounds that shall pass through the chambers of his soul" (57–58). Such people in such situations, says

Douglass, will be moved, "impressed," if they are indeed human. Let us better understand this mode of hearing that leads to the understanding that Douglass begins to characterize so well. If we do so, then perhaps the field of African American studies, literary and otherwise, will mature in such a way that we will know what it means "tuh *go* there," even with a text, and know this so well that we, as African Americanists, contribute an epistemology of "*go* there" to the larger academic community and to American society as well.

## NOTES

My thanks to Kim Middleton Meyer for conversation and suggestions for reading that allowed me to explore cultural commodification within a comparative ethnic literatures frame of reference; to Portia Maultsby for years ago sharing her knowledge of black performance history and theory; and to Marjorie Pryse for conversation and clarifying comments on earlier drafts of this essay.

1. See, for example, Newman, *Inauthentic Culture and Its Philosophical Critics*; Siemerling and Schwenk, eds., *Cultural Difference and the Literary Text*; Hartman, *Scars of the Spirit*; Levin, *Africanism and Authenticity in African-American Women's Novels*; Favor, *Authentic Blackness*; Griffiths, "Myth of Authenticity"; and Mufwene, "Investigating Gullah"; in addition to the texts cited subsequently in this essay.
2. The juxtaposition of *metaphysical* and *exegetical* comes from the epigraphs to chapter 8 of Henry Louis Gates Jr.'s *Figures in Black*:

   Nigger, your breed ain't metaphysical.
   Robert Penn Warren, "Pondy Woods," 1928

   Cracker, your breed ain't exegetical.
   Sterling Brown, interview, 1973

3. This text is taken from the Currier and Ives lithograph as it is reprinted in Hughes and Meltzer, *Black Magic* 62.
4. Riggs's film *Ethnic Notions* is particularly powerful in this regard.
5. According to Fletcher, when very popular performers such as Billy Kersands with the Richard and Pringle Georgia Minstrels performed in towns with large black populations, "theaters in the south, which had only a small space in the gallery for colored customers . . . often would split accommodations in half" so that colored customers occupied "a full half of the theater from the ground floor or orchestra section right up to the gallery, with whites filling the other side" (*100 Years of the Negro in Show Business* 62).
6. One matches "Go Down, Moses" to the words of "Carve Dat Possum" as follows: in the first verse the first line of "Go Down, Moses," "When Israel was in Egypt's land," becomes in "Carve Dat Possum," "De possum meat am good to eat," and the subsequent and repeated "Let my people go" becomes "Carve him to de heart." In the chorus "Go down, Moses, way down in Egypt's land" becomes "Carve dat possum, Carve dat possum, children," and additional lines and verses continue in this way.
7. Ralph Ellison's phrase, from the essay by the same title.
8. Gregory Hartman's foreword to *Scars of the Spirit* seems to indicate that he believes, incorrectly, that the etymology of *authenticity* is related to the Latin *auctoritas*, or *authority* (vii).

9. See Williams, *Life on the Color Line*; Reddy, *Crossing the Color Line*; Jones, *How I Became Hettie Jones.* See also Thompson, *Promise and a Way of Life*; Russo, *Taking Back Our Lives*; Rothenberg, ed., *White Privilege.*
10. In his conclusion to *Workings of the Spirit* Baker's first reference is to "a best friend" who was raped, and in his afterword he says: "My greatest gratitude goes, as always, to my wife, Charlotte Pierce-Baker, and to my son Mark. If any two people deserve the ancient spiritual's inscription about trouble seen, it is they" (212).
11. This story is told by the pseudonymous David, the author's husband. See Pierce-Baker, *Surviving the Silence* 252–263.

# Turning Impossibility into Possibility

## Teaching Ellison, Murray, and the Blues at Tuskegee

BARBARA A. BAKER

> When the white man steps behind the mask of the trickster his freedom is circumscribed by the fear that he is not simply miming a personification of his disorder and chaos but that he will become in fact that which he intends only to symbolize; that he will be trapped somewhere in the mystery of hell (for there is a mystery in the whiteness of blackness, the innocence of evil and the evil of innocence, though being initiates, Negroes express the joke of it in the blues) and thus lose that freedom which, in the fluid, "traditionless," "classless" and rapidly changing society, he would recognize as the white man's alone.
>
> —Ralph Ellison, "Change the Joke and Slip the Yoke"

The students at Tuskegee University, where I have taught African American aesthetics in a variety of literature courses for the past seven years, are overly polite. In the first weeks of class they do not articulate the resistance registered on their faces when the gospel according to Ralph Ellison and Albert Murray pours from my mouth. If pressed, their reaction to a white woman teaching the African American vernacular tradition to black students at a renowned historically black college comes in single words: "ridiculous," "absurd," they say. No matter how carefully executed my teaching strategy, I often encounter the kind of resistance that flourishes in an environment where students have come purposefully seeking a black milieu, believing they might enjoy, for once, the comfort and power that comes from being a member of the majority. The typical Tuskegee student has gone to a great deal of expense and trouble, often knowingly sacrificing the accoutrements, accommodations, and benefits of better-funded state schools, in order to experience what I will call "not-otherness," not being a representative of a minority. Recognizing many of my students' pronounced desire for this not-otherness, as well as acknowledging my own need for not-otherness in the classroom, has been key to most of the success I have achieved as a white scholar of black texts at a historically black institution. If I succeed, I see my students' expressions change from resistance to acceptance, and I hear my students using words like *respect* and *passion* when discussing their experiences studying African American aesthetics. While it is unlikely that most white scholars of black texts will find themselves in precisely my situation, my hope is that the insights I have gained through this unique experience are applicable to situations of otherness in general and to white scholars of black literature in particular.

To begin, the fact that I find myself in this seemingly unlikely circumstance is no accident. Although I grew up in New York State culturally removed from the Southern surroundings that bred the African American vernacular—folktales, spirituals, blues, and jazz—I accepted without knowing Ralph Ellison's challenge to all who would claim American culture as their own; that is, we must all also recognize black experience as part of our own. In "The Art of Fiction" Ellison says that the African American experience is one that all Americans must identify with and recognize "as an important segment of the larger experience . . . not lying at the bottom of it, but intertwined, diffused in its very texture" (172). I accepted this easily as a musician who discovered my voice singing "Swing Low, Sweet Chariot," went on to become a professional rhythm and blues player, and then a scholar of African American literature and culture. My students, however, have made it abundantly clear to me that there is a big difference between a white person embracing African American culture and a white person pretending to know African American experience. Teaching black students has forced me to reconsider the negotiation between blackness and whiteness that informs the cultural productions that have been important to me all along, from my days as a musician to my experience teaching African American literature at a predominantly white institution and my teaching of black aesthetics at Tuskegee.

A teacher (much like a musician) usually needs to experience some level of oneness with her class (or audience), and this sense of being on the same page enhances the learning (or listening) experience for both the teacher and the student. When my academic audience changed from majority white to majority black (I am usually the only white person in my class at Tuskegee), I found a marked difference in the way that I addressed issues of cultural negotiation between blackness and whiteness as manifested in American literature and music.

When speaking to a majority white class about issues of African American aesthetics, I remember feeling as if I were talking about someone else, the "not-me," as Toni Morrison refers to it in *Playing in the Dark: Whiteness and the Literary Imagination* (38). I could talk about how Elvis appropriated the blues, for instance, and take comfort from that fact that my students and I were neither the perpetrator nor the victim of such an appropriation. We were innocent bystanders, eyewitnesses at best. Being a member of the majority in a classroom situation created a sense of ease that helped me remove myself from implication and allowed me to look at these American cultural occurrences as a point of discussion, an artifact of ongoing history. And, even if my need for oneness with my mostly white students necessitated collusion with the appropriator, my students and I could share in the blame and comfort ourselves in regret. Black students in the class, always few in number, usually seemed overwhelmed by the wave of invulnerability created by the majority. Most of us were oblivious to our own vulnerability to oppression. We were excused from really knowing the experiences of which we were speaking.

At Tuskegee, however, I cannot speak as if I am talking about somebody else. The immediacy and delicacy of my face-to-face encounters with my students eliminates the possibility of sidestepping my complicity in oppression. In accepting my complicity, I also must accept my vulnerability. As Ellison might put it, I must be willing to lose the freedom that is so often recognized as belonging exclusively to white people and become that which I had previously intended only to evoke for the purposes of discussion. I am no longer swept into the tide of the majority where I cannot really experience otherness. In surrendering the invincibility provided by my status as a member of the majority, my students and I can get on the same page, the place where all people are susceptible to the oppression that accompanies otherness as well as endowed with the privilege that comes with not-otherness. At Tuskegee my students and I talk about the realities of this kind of oppression as an experience that is intertwined in the very texture of American life and that all people, black and white, can experience it and, therefore, know it.

Of course, this is not the same thing as experiencing and knowing blackness, and I do not intend it to be. Instead, I intend to make real for my students the possibility of identification with both sides of the negotiation table, the presumed winner and the presumed loser, to realize that both parties share in the experience, that both are susceptible to the privilege of not-otherness and the lack of privilege that otherness often creates. My point is illustrated best by American art that is most influenced by African American aesthetic strategies, and, therefore, I have a natural inclination toward this way of thinking, since I am a musician who identifies with African American musical forms. Yet it is not necessary for a white scholar of black texts to be a musician or to teach at a historically black college in order to relinquish the automatic assumption of privilege and freedom that comes from majority status. It is necessary, however, I think, to identify beyond the group of which one is a member and understand that freedom and privilege are extremely fluid conditions. In my classes I illustrate this by openly addressing the crimes of appropriation, for example, in a way that explores the possibility of identification with both parties involved with the act, pointing up the privilege that comes with creating something so desirable that someone else wishes to claim it as his own. Doing so helps to direct the class toward the hard-won acknowledgment that my students and I are aesthetically one, our artistic choices reflecting the irrevocable diffusion of blackness within whiteness and whiteness within blackness of American art.

It is not coincidental that the latter assumption was formulated and articulated by two Tuskegee intellectuals, Ellison and Murray. The Tuskegee Institute of the mid-1930s that educated Ellison and Murray did not intend to produce cultural critics, let alone novelists, but the atmosphere, then as now, was one of charged artistic energy seeking release and recognition. Tuskegee was and is a place where American art becomes living art rather than artifact because the students often come with intentions of defining themselves against their perceptions of the dominant culture's consensus about their possibilities or lack thereof.

Although Ellison and Murray came to Tuskegee under different political circumstances than students today, they learned there that the most desirable position for a would-be artist was the position of not-otherness; both intentionally rejected the trappings that accompany minority status. Instead, they sought status among the finest artists in the world, irrespective of the Southern political climate that reinforced their perceived differences from the majority. When Albert Murray returned to Tuskegee in 1999 to deliver the Ralph Ellison Memorial Lecture, he reiterated this point. He prefaced his reading from *Trading Twelves: The Selected Letters of Ralph Ellison and Albert Murray* by bluntly telling the students: "Ralph and I didn't write books to be read during African American History Month. We want to be read every month by everyone." This had been their shared goal from the beginning of their educations, and they knew that, in order to achieve it, they would have to engage in an aesthetic identification with as many of the greatest artists of the world as possible.

At Tuskegee they found in the Hollis Burke Frissel Library a literary world that informed their expansive vision of artistic possibility, which helped them to formulate an aesthetic framework that fitted African American contribution into a global and modern perspective. They were able to achieve the recognition they desired through an understanding of American art that reflects Ellison's claim that blackness is diffused and intertwined in the very texture of American life, and they came to this point of view by absorbing the craft and technique of the finest literature in the world, which was available to them on our campus. Ellison says, "So in Macon County, Alabama, I read Marx, Freud, T. S. Eliot, Pound, Gertrude Stein, and Hemingway. Books which seldom, if ever, mentioned Negroes were to *release* me from whatever 'segregated' ideas I might have had of my human *possibilities*" ("World" 116; italics added). To their literary inheritance they added knowledge of African American fine art as it is embodied in the African American vernacular tradition, especially through the blues and the folk tricksters Brer Rabbit and Brer Bear. Ellison makes it clear, however, that he does not use folklore in his work because he is black "but because writers like Eliot and Joyce made [him] conscious of the literary value of [his] folk inheritance. [His] cultural background, like that of most Americans, is dual" ("Change" 58). Ellison claims no privilege or lack of privilege because he is an African American artist; rather, he emphasizes the discipline necessary in aesthetically identifying beyond oneself.

Like Louis Armstrong, the most universally recognized American trickster of all, the Tuskegee/American/world-class aestheticians Ellison and Murray gathered all that could be known about their craft and forged a theory that shows that blackness is fundamental to the most uniquely American contributions to the art of the world. Various manifestations of the African American vernacular tradition, especially blues and jazz (and I would add hip-hop music), are universally recognized markers of American culture. When students are reminded that black Americans contributed the most profoundly recognizable American artistic productions to the world, they rightfully share in and claim the respect that Murray and Ellison demand.

Pronouncing this out loud in the classroom remains as necessary today as it was when Ellison and Murray initiated the discussion in the mid-twentieth century because, as Henry Louis Gates Jr. asserts, Murray's and Ellison's joint enterprise inverted the notion held for generations, and I believe in many circles still today, "that the word 'American' tacitly connote[s] 'white.'" According to Gates, this inversion is "the most breathtaking act of cultural chutzpah this land had witnessed since Columbus blithely claimed it all for Isabella" ("King of Cats" 76). As Murray and Ellison illustrate in their cultural critiques and in their fiction, in terms of our aesthetics, our much beloved music, and our collective disposition toward confrontation in the face of adversity, America is perhaps more correctly an African America, or, as Murray calls it, an "Afro-U.S." (*Stomping* 65).

Students seem astonished to hear me say this, but, with music as a metaphor for our Afro-U.S., little by little they not only see the point, but they also deeply appreciate the significance of the fact that the point is made by a teacher in whiteface who is not simply miming a personification of blackness but embracing the blackness as well as the whiteness of the American cultural and literary productions I love and therefore teach as part of my own aesthetic heritage.

I make it a point in the classroom to reiterate the claim that I have heard Albert Murray make on many occasions; that is, American culture is incontestably mulatto. He first made this claim in *The Omni-Americans: New Perspectives on Black Experience and American Culture*, his groundbreaking study of the fallacies inherent in the American political landscape published in 1970. In a 1996 interview with Tony Scherman, Murray clarifies the term *omni-*

*American*, saying that "it reflects my basic assumption that the United States is a mulatto culture. . . . The omni-Americans are the Americans. My conception makes Americans identify with *all* their ancestors" (128). In the classroom identifying with *all* of our ancestors can be as painful as a family reunion, and I would be kidding myself if I did not admit that suggesting to my students that we share ancestry and heritage makes for some tense moments. Those awkward moments present an opportunity to initiate discussion about just exactly what is so terrifying about our shared ancestry. Do my students fear that I, the symbolic representation of the enslaver, am attempting to steal from them what is theirs and theirs alone? Do I fear relinquishing my privilege if I acknowledge that it is constructed from a lie? Or, as one student put it, "the dominant race doesn't want to admit that we are like them and feel what they do because then they would have to give up their superiority." Once we address these questions, we sigh relief and then realize that we have gone where many other literature classes simply cannot go, especially if teacher and students are not on the same page.

Ellison says that there is a great "joke at the center of the American identity," and that is that white people "can be so absurdly self-deluded over the true interrelatedness of blackness and whiteness": "What's more, each [black and white] secretly believes that he alone knows what is valid in the American experience, and that the other knows but will not admit it, and each suspects the other of being at bottom a phony" ("Change" 54–55). In truth, blackness and whiteness are initiates of each other; they begin and end each other: "Negroes express the joke of it in the blues" (53).

For his part Murray says that "the blues is white America's heritage too" (Scherman 127), and this is one reason that some white people can qualify to teach courses in African American studies. He writes that what is needed is more white scholars "who will take the time to study and try to understand what *American Negroes* are all about, who can identify with their glories and therefore truly empathize with their defeats" (*From the Briarpatch* 95). He suggests that whiteness does not preclude the necessary identification that must precede true empathy. I would add that white Americans who possess a predisposition toward the blues are more apt to identify with the glories and defeats of their black ancestors because, when we engage in American music, our shared ancestry becomes undeniable, not to mention extremely desirable.

It would be an enormous error in judgment to assume, however, that whiteness in any way better prepares or qualifies someone (whether a musician or not) for the privilege of teaching African American aesthetics. Such an assumption would merely be another misdirected, masked appropriation of black art. Conversely, although I am in complete agreement with current hiring practices at predominantly white universities that seek to diversify faculties in an effort to provide a more well-rounded education for the masses, it is a destructive insult to our African American heritage to limit the teaching of African American aesthetics to black teachers or to black students. The teaching of African American aesthetics, culture, literature, and history should be elevated to its rightful position at the forefront of American studies, taught, learned, and shared by all members of the American intellectual community. Yet I would caution white scholars of African American studies who choose to join me on this slippery slope that, by the very nature of their choice, they must address the whiteness of blackness, and vice versa, with passion and respect that recognizes that they can never know black experience. It is most useful for me to articulate to my students that, as mulatto as my culture is and as much as I identify and empathize with black experience, I know that I can never be "Negro American," because, as Ellison explains,

> being a Negro American has to do with the memory of slavery and the hope of emancipation and the betrayal by allies and the revenge and contempt inflicted by our former masters after the Reconstruction, and the myths, both Northern and Southern, which are propagated in justification of that betrayal. . . . It has to do with a special perspective on the national ideals and the national conduct, and with a tragicomic attitude toward the universe. ("The World" 131)

As scholars of African American literature trying to get to the reality of the American cultural configuration, our best hope lies in identifying with the glory and empathizing with the defeat to which most Americans are subject. We can learn something about the way American art expresses the fluidity of our culture by looking to American blues music, which succinctly and profoundly expresses the adaptability necessary to confront ever-changing circumstance.

Engaging in the blues in the fashion that Ellison and Murray suggest, however, is not a simple exercise in imitating down-home, three-chord stomps. Blues is not as simple as it appears on the surface; very much like the literary achievements Ellison and Murray admire and produce, it is a matter of discipline and craft. It is also a matter of aesthetic identification beyond the culture that produced it. Let me return to the example of Louis Armstrong.

In *The Blue Devils of Nada: A Contemporary Approach to American Aesthetic Statement* Albert Murray devotes a chapter to explaining Armstrong's significance to his aesthetic theory. While Armstrong appears as a jester or a trickster, in fact, his musical disposition is reflective of the way black aesthetic maneuvers speak to and for the American character in general: "he took jazz from the level of popular entertainment and into the realm of a fine art that requires a level of consummate professional musicianship unexcelled anywhere in the world" (63). And he did this much the same way that Ellison and Murray accomplished their aesthetic achievements, by studying and practicing his craft, consuming all that went before him, aesthetically identifying beyond his own community, reiterating the great riffs of the finest musicians, and stylizing them into American aesthetic statements. Louis Armstrong was "destined to make music that is . . . representative of American affirmation and promise in the face of adversity" and became "a globetrotting goodwill ambassador for the irrepressible idealism of his native land because it was such an irresistible expression of what so many people elsewhere think of as being the American outlook on human possibility" (Murray, *Blue Devils* 54, 71). Armstrong is a good example of American blues music speaking to our mulatto identity because he is a national emblem recognized as uniquely American, embraced by most Americans, black and white, and a disciplined craftsman who stylized European and American music in a completely African American way. To me he also embodies the ideal strategy for a white scholar of African American literature—that is, the strategy of the "good trickster."

In "Change the Joke and Slip the Yoke" Ellison says that the masking trickster has long played a role in the irony of the American struggle for self-identity, and the core of the struggle comes from an unwillingness to recognize the blackness of whiteness of our authentic identity: "out of the counterfeiting of the black American's identity there arises a profound doubt in the white man's mind as to the authenticity of his own image" (53). The "evil" trickster does not recognize that his own image is made out of the blackness he masks as he uses the mask to usurp the identity of the other. The "good" trickster, however, uses the mask to imagine himself differently in the name of discipline; it is a matter of understanding the other as well as oneself, playing the role that imagines the composite whole, and expanding on what is known in creative movement toward the future. Any teacher of African American aesthetics, literature, or culture must play the role of the good trickster, learning and teaching the craft and discipline of the great American writers, understanding our shared culture and the interconnectedness of blackness and whiteness, absorbing and expanding on what is known in the name of hope and possibility. For the good trickster "masking is a play upon possibility and ours is a society in which possibilities are many" (Ellison, "Change" 54). In the classroom I have found that students are rarely moved by the teacher-as-innocent-bystander who does not really identify with the text. It is impossible to teach well that which one does not accept as her own, just as it is unlikely that a musician can sing or play well a song with which she does not in some way personally connect. One of the best compliments a musician can receive is: "You play it like you own it."

Perhaps the need for this volume comes from the fact that we as Americans still have a difficult time imagining that so-called white people accept so-called blackness as part of their own identities. Similarly, when I discussed the topic of this book with my students, they were surprised that there would be any need for it because they had not considered the fact that white people have taken so much scholarly interest in African American art. Part of their education in my classes involves unveiling the reality of African American heritage as central to American culture. Students often arrive on campus completely unaware of the profound impact of black culture—and, more specifically, the contributions of intellectuals related to Tuskegee—on America. Learning these things inspires an intellectually motivated self-respect.

I have learned that I can make the same point by encouraging students to make their own aesthetic choices and then studying the craft and ancestry of the choices they make. Often I begin the semester by assigning students the task of finding a song within their own CD collection that speaks to them. I ask them to type up the lyrics and bring in a copy of the recording. They typically choose classics such as Stevie Wonder's "Pastime Paradise," James Brown's "Say It Loud (I'm Black and I'm Proud)," or Al Green's "Love and Happiness." Or they choose sophisticated newcomers such as Talib Kweli, Big Boi and Andre 3000 of OutKast, or Missy Elliot. Often they choose the works of Tupac Shakur, an American classic who has taken on the mythic proportions of an Elvis. And, lately, many students have chosen the works of Eminem, a choice we find particularly amusing because his self-chosen name (M&M) allows us to laugh at the joke at the center of the American identity.

Once we have the music before us, we study it as literature, examining the aesthetic virtue of it. When students recognize that their own aesthetic choices play back through the African American vernacular tradition—from hip-hop to rap such as Grandmaster Flash & the Furious Five's "The Message" through the straight-ahead rhythm and blues of Brown and Green to Elmore James's "Sunnyland" and on back through Armstrong's "(What Did I Do to Be So) Black and Blue?" to "Swing Low, Sweet Chariot"—then we are ready, together, to read Ellison's *Invisible Man*, beginning, of course, with "The Prologue," in which the invisible man dreams his way through the continuum of the vernacular tradition, from the black sermon to the slave narrative and back to Louis Armstrong. Their resistance to my white appearance begins to melt away with the accomplishment of this exercise because of my respect for their aesthetic choices and because of my knowledge (gained through study and discipline as well as passion) of art that they had, until then, presumed to be theirs, their heritage, and theirs alone. It becomes apparent to my students that this music is my heritage, too, and, therefore, our cultural inheritance is the same. I become to them, one could say, "not-so-other" because I express and embrace my humanity in the same terms that they do. And the study of literature, no less so for African American literature than any other kind, is the study of human experience. Ellison writes:

> the Negro American writer is also an heir of the human experience which is literature, and this might well be more important to him than his living folk tradition. For me, at least, in the discontinuous, swiftly changing and

> diverse American culture, the stability of the Negro American folk tradition became precious as a result of an act of literary discovery. Taken as a whole, its spirituals along with its blues, jazz and folk tales, has . . . much to tell us of the faith, humor, and adaptability to reality necessary to live in a world which has taken on much of the insecurity and blues-like absurdity known to those who brought it into being. ("Change" 58–59)

So, as a class, we set out on our adventure through Ellison's prologue to *Invisible Man* with full knowledge that the continuum of expression known as the African American vernacular tradition, forged by African Americans from the first days of contact with Europeans in the United States to the present, provides the most useful metaphors for human experience to one of the most sophisticated American writers of the twentieth century. Along the way we discover that, if the invisible man is to speak for us and to us, we have to share in the glory and defeat of becoming visible to one another.

PART TWO

# Training and Working in the Field

# Before Positionality

WILLIAM L. ANDREWS

When Lisa Long first asked me to contribute something to this book, I wrote back the following email: "I'm a little ambivalent about this. I have to admit I have no theoretical position on this issue, nor have I ever spent much time thinking about whether I'm justified in doing the work that I do. I've been working on African American literature for over thirty years. It's too late for me to theorize about what my position on it should be."

Lisa's suggestion that some reflections on my three decades of work in this field might be worthwhile led me to compose the following reflections, the title of which, "Before Positionality," is somewhat ironic, since we are always already positionally situated in relation to any text, whether we want to recognize it or not. In 1972, however, when I published my first article on African American literature, I didn't give a second thought to the question of my positionality with regard to Charles Chesnutt, whose fiction I wrote about in that article, nor did the journal that published the article, the *CLA Journal*, ask me anything about who I was. I don't recall having read at that time anything that interrogated the role or responsibility of white critics in the study of black literature in the United States. In this sense I think of myself as having started working in this field before at least the academic discourse about positionality was invented.

In one of her essays in *A World of Difference* Barbara Johnson asks, under what conditions "explicitly speaking from *where one is* turns out to allow for an expansion rather than a contraction of the range of pedagogical experiences available" (44)? In the same spirit of curiosity, rather than confidence, I offer these few remarks, unsure of how much relevance my experience in the American academy over the last thirty years has to the kinds of issues that *White Scholars / African American Texts* engages. Although I hope my work and my example in African American literary studies helps anyone, regardless of color, who wants to pursue similar kinds of work in this field, I don't know that the ways I pursued my work thirty, twenty, or even ten years ago have particular relevance to the ways white people might undertake to teach or write about African American literature today. Yet, if there's one question I've been asked more than any other in my career, by black as well as white people, it's "how did you, a white man, get so deeply involved in this field?"

The short answer to this question is that there is no short answer. But it might be worth stating at least this much: I never had a road-to-Damascus experience that caused me at some point in my career to *decide* to become an African Americanist. Black literature drew me in like a gravitational force, but the process took years before I realized that, willy-nilly, I had become an African American literature specialist. One reason why it took so long for me to think of myself as an African American literature specialist is that it's taken almost as long for the literature I've been most interested in—black writing before 1920—to be considered literature at all, in other words, as a legitimate *field* of literary study in which a scholar might claim to specialize. Specialization implies, of course, that what one works on is sufficiently coherent and valuable in and of itself, that it merits particular focus and attention along with the intellectual and academic dignity that accrues from such attention. For a long time in my career the work I did on pre–Harlem Renaissance black writing didn't qualify for the honorific of a specialization either from Americanists, who tended to care about only a handful of canonical black writers, or from African Americanists, whose canon of black writers, though much more catholic than that of their white colleagues, was largely confined to the twentieth century. I realize the limited applicability of such generalizations relative to African American literary scholarship over the last forty years. Nevertheless, not until well into the 1990s have such generalizations about either field begun to lose their salience.

Given that the field I've devoted myself to wasn't regarded for a long time as a field available to go into is at least one good reason why I didn't think of myself as an African American literature specialist until pretty late in my career. I finished my Ph.D. degree in 1973 with a specialization in American literature before World War I. My dissertation was on Chesnutt, but, when Texas Tech hired me to start in the fall of 1973, they hired me as an Americanist. That was what I considered myself, although, if asked, I liked to call myself an Americanist with a special interest in black American writing. During my four years at Texas Tech I taught mostly freshman composition and sophomore literature surveys, with an occasional upper-level course in American literature. Our department's specialist in African American literature invited me once to lecture to her class, but I never asked to teach black literature, and no one at Tech proposed that I teach it. At that stage in my career I thought I was doing well to get to teach an American literature survey every other semester.

The senior faculty in my department knew from my early publications that I had a research interest in African American literature. One comment that I recall from an annual review of my scholarship read, "Needs to branch out from Chesnutt." By 1975 I had a chance to do just that when I was invited by some highly placed people in the Mark Twain Edition to become a coeditor of a volume in that prestigious scholarly project. In the 1970s participation in one of the multivolume textual editions devoted to what we used to call "major American authors" was the sort of thing that could lead to tenure and promotion. The chair of my department was himself a textual editor. I mulled over the invitation from the Mark Twain editors awhile but decided that I'd rather write a book about Chesnutt than edit one by Mark Twain. It didn't seem to me at the time that my decision was especially portentous, but, as I look back on it, that was one turning point in my career.

In 1977 I was hired to teach American literature at the University of Wisconsin–Madison. I didn't worry that my senior colleagues in American literature, almost all of whom were textual editors by trade, would not take my work on Chesnutt seriously. They had hired me to teach American literature before 1914. Chesnutt was an American writer whose important work was finished by 1914. So, I taught what I was expected to teach, got my book on Chesnutt published, and rose through the ranks. During my eleven years at Wisconsin I never taught an African American literature course. I taught plenty of black writers in my American literature courses, but there was no need and no request for me to offer courses in African American literature. The University of Wisconsin had an Afro-American Studies Department that offered black literature courses taught by my friends Nellie McKay and Craig Werner. Nellie, Craig, and I were quite conscious of the territoriality and turf consciousness of departments at Wisconsin then. Rather than seem to be shirking my duties to English or encroaching on Afro-American Studies, I chose simply to do what I had been hired to do. I hope that my teaching of American literature put black writers more prominently on the literary map than had been business as usual in the Madison English Department.

It was not till I got to the University of Kansas (KU) in 1988 that I felt I had finally been hired, at least in part, to teach African American literature. The chair I held at KU was the Hall Professorship in American Literature, but by that time my scholarly work in African American literature left little doubt about where my intellectual interests lay. Without neglecting opportunities to teach white American literature at KU, I also enjoyed for the first time offering classes exclusively on black writing.

I recount this aspect of my career simply because it might be inferred from my thirty years of published work on African American literature that I've been a teaching African Americanist for a lot longer than has been the case. I realize that the deferral of my teaching African American literature courses might seem to some a source of frustration or disappointment. For me, however, I think I had gotten rather used to researching texts and writers that I didn't often get to teach, at least not under the curricular rubrics and in the intellectual frameworks that I might have preferred. In light of the imposing authority of what we were learning to call the "canon" of American literature and in view of the fact, of which I was peculiarly well aware, that most early African American writing still could muster little claim on that canon, I thought it best to focus my research on building a case through scholarship for the existence and importance of pre-twentieth-century African American writing *as* literature.

To those who would like to work in African American literature but who seldom get an opportunity to teach it, I hope my experience might provide some encouragement. One lesson that whites who want to work in this field might draw from my experience is, to echo Booker T. Washington, "Cast down your buckets where you are" (99). If you have been trained in African American literature but the job opportunity you have obliges you to teach more broadly in American literature, why should such an assignment prevent you from researching African American literature or finding opportunities to teach black writing, albeit in the context of larger, multiethnic traditions? "Cast down your buckets where you are" is also my advice to those trained in American literature who still would like to pursue research on African American writing in a particular vein. Whatever you know best about American literature can enrich your research in African American literature. "Cast down your buckets where you are" also applies to those whites who find themselves attracted to African American research even though they weren't hired to teach or research black writing. If "where you are" in your mind and heart inclines you to this literature, you should give yourself the chance to find out where this literature might take you.

I'm not talking about a crystal stair here. There were few, if any, institutional incentives for me to study eighteenth- and nineteenth-century black American writing early in my career. My publications won praise from only a few colleagues. My salary raises were minuscule. I remember more than one senior professor at Wisconsin who seemed genuinely perplexed when they learned that I was researching the history of black American autobiography in the eighteenth and nineteenth centuries. "Did blacks *write* autobiographies back then?" "Is any of it good literature?" "Who was Frederick Douglass?" were some of the questions I received from well-meaning senior colleagues. To them my research seemed more appropriate to someone in the History Department than to an associate professor of English. But, even though I didn't get a chance at Wisconsin to teach most of the writers I wrote about in my book, *To Tell a Free Story*, I never once regretted engaging in that work. Investigating the slave narrative tradition gave me insights into classic white American texts that I could never have had any other way, which added new dimensions to my teaching. As a scholar, I gained a stronger sense of purpose and commitment to intellectual inquiry than I'd ever felt before. I also began to meet people who shared my sense of discovery and who have become friends, colleagues, coeditors, and collaborators in a common effort to reconstruct African American literary history and disseminate a wide range of African American texts.

After *To Tell a Free Story* came out in 1986 I planned to write a sequel carrying the history of African American autobiography up to 1930. But, because I've been involved in so much editing over the last fifteen years, I have yet to finish another critical book. Instead, I've given a great deal of my energies to editing various anthologies, reference books, collections, and classroom texts devoted to African American literature. None of this work represents the kind of scholarship that went into the writing of *To Tell a Free Story*. Yet it seemed to me then, and now, that a great need exists for skillfully edited texts and reference works devoted to African American literature, a need that white as well as black scholars can help to meet as long as they prepare themselves and take advantage of the opportunities available to them. Whites who feel uncertain about their role in African American literature might consider the advantages of collaborative work with black colleagues who share similar interests. Well over three hundred scholars contributed to *The Oxford Companion to African American Literature*, the most ambitious work of interracial collaboration in African American literary scholarship ever attempted, to my knowledge. When Frances Foster, Trudier Harris, and I discussed whom to assign the articles in the *Companion*, we didn't talk about a potential contributor's color or positionality—we just talked about whether she or he would do the job right and get it in on time. I know of no reason why African Americanists, black and white, can't find common purpose in similar kinds of collaborative work, particularly in editorial work. How many reliable or complete editions of major African American writers exist today? Phillis Wheatley, Douglass, DuBois, Richard Wright, Zora Neale Hurston, and Langston Hughes come to mind, but many other important figures remain.

Let me close by returning to the question of color as it has affected the way I've seen myself or others have seen me in African American literature. First, I've never written a preface or an introduction to anything I've done in which I identified myself racially or suggested that my identity was somehow significant to what I was doing. I think my reticence, indeed my silence, on this matter was influenced by my study of Chesnutt early in my own career. In a late essay in which he reminisced about his literary career, Chesnutt acknowledged that his own racial heritage "was never mentioned by the publishers in announcing or advertising" his first book, *The Conjure Woman* (1899). Chesnutt continued: "From my own viewpoint it was a personal matter. It never occurred to me to claim any merit because of it, and I have always resented the denial of anything on account of it" (193). Chesnutt's apparent refusal to identify himself racially when his first book came out can be interpreted in many ways, not all of them complimentary perhaps. But it seems to me that what Chesnutt wanted, by launching his literary career without reference to race or color, was to be read and judged on the basis of what he wrote, not what he looked like. Of course, this dichotomy is reductive, but for me it remains instructive.

When I wrote my first book, *The Literary Career of Charles W. Chesnutt*, which came out more than twenty years ago, I don't think it ever crossed my mind to mention anything about myself. There was no photo of me on the dust jacket of my book, and the only comment that the LSU Press printed about me was that I had gotten my doctorate from the University of North Carolina–Chapel Hill and was teaching at the University of Wisconsin–Madison. If any reviewer of my book brought up my color, I don't recall it. I do recall that early in the 1990s I was in a conversation at a conference with a senior African Americanist whose work I had long respected, who told me he'd read my book on Chesnutt many years earlier. After finishing it, he said he still hadn't been able to decide whether I was white or black. I took that as a compliment. Was I trying to write, or do I think it's possible to write, an "unraced" or "color-blind" criticism? No. I just don't see how featuring my color or race as a pretext or context for the study of someone else's text, regardless of their color or race, provides me a useful point of intervention as a critic.

I don't recall ever being asked by a scholar or teacher in African American literature to justify or explain my work on the basis of positionality or race. Once undergraduates see my name on the cover of their textbook, they don't question my authority to teach them African American literature. Maybe if I'd started teaching African American literature before I'd published very much in the field, I'd have more to say about how I've wrestled with the question of authority and how to establish it in the classroom or in one's criticism. All I can say is that my thirty years of work in this field have been guided by the conviction that, if as a critic I had something valid and worthwhile to say or if as an editor I made it possible for someone else to say something valid and worthwhile, my own identity as an individual would not matter, not in the long run, not to anyone whose judgment would ultimately matter to me. I think discussions of positionality do matter, but in the end, as long as grits is groceries, what I want to know most is not who did the cooking but what's in the pot.

# White Scholars in African American Literary Circles

## Appropriation or Cultural Literacy?

VENETRIA K. PATTON

Race has become a literary hot topic, particularly in reference to whiteness and blackness. Toni Morrison's *Playing in the Dark: Whiteness and the Literary Imagination* (1992), which developed from her William E. Massey Sr. Lectures in 1990, calls attention to the need to address the black presence within American literature while also studying literary whiteness. This call seemed to lead to a proliferation of studies regarding the formation of race in literature. Within the last fifteen years literary criticism has produced such texts as Dana Nelson's *The Word in Black and White: Reading "Race" in American Literature 1638–1867* (1992), Eric Sundquist's *To Wake the Nations: Race in the Making of American Literature* (1993), J. Martin Favor's *Authentic Blackness: The Folk in the New Negro Renaissance* (1999), Patricia McKee's *Producing American Races: Henry James, William Faulkner, Toni Morrison* (1999), and Kimberly W. Benston's *Performing Blackness: Enactments of African-American Modernism* (2000). In texts such as these, scholars have noted the arbitrariness of race and have argued that race is a social construct rather than something real and identifiable. In his introduction to *Voices in Black and White: Writings on Race in America from Harper's Magazine*, Henry Louis Gates Jr. points to Kwame Anthony Appiah's observation "that there are no white people—only people passing for white. Just as there are no black people, only people passing for black. For even the seemingly most brute aspects of our social identities are culturally constructed; 'race' is always refracted and inflected by a mutable fretwork of assumptions and beliefs local to our time and place" (Gates viii). Despite these intellectual explanations about the mutability of race and movements to de-essentialize race as a category of identity, American society and its literature has and continues to purport the existence of raced beings. It is this same contradiction that muddies conversations regarding the presence and role of white scholars within African American literature.

We are in an interesting period in which clamors for multiculturalism and greater diversity are pitted against taunts of reverse racism and political correctness. Yet, despite the attack on affirmative action in educational institutions, there continues to be a strong interest in African American literature as a field of inquiry. In *Black Looks: Race and Representation* (1992) bell hooks observes "that there is pleasure to be found in the acknowledgment and enjoyment of racial difference. The commodification of Otherness has been so successful because it is offered as a new delight, more intense, more satisfying than normal ways of doing and feeling. . . . ethnicity becomes spice, seasoning that can liven up the dull dish that is mainstream white culture" (21). Through the metaphor of "eating the other," hooks points to the dangerous "commodification of difference," which "promotes paradigms of consumption wherein whatever difference the Other inhabits is eradicated, *via* exchange, by a consumer cannibalism that not only displaces the Other but denies the significance of that Other's history through a process of decontextualization" (*Black Looks* 31). This seems to be the fear behind charges of cultural appropriation—is interest in ethnicity a sincere attempt to address difference or merely an idle diversion? African American literature is currently a hot commodity, but the reason for the popularity is unclear. Is it seen as "an anybody-can-play pick-up game performed on a wide-open, untrammeled field" or as a legitimate "discipline with a history and a body of rigorous scholarship and distinguished scholars underpinning it" (duCille 31)?

In her essay "The Occult of True Black Womanhood: Critical Demeanor and Black Feminist Studies" Ann duCille explores "what it means for black women academics to stand in the midst of the 'dramatically charged field'—the traffic jam—that black feminist studies has become." She asks, "Are we in danger of being trampled by the 'rainbow coalition' of critics—'black, white, male, female, artists and academics, historicists and deconstructionists'—that our own once isolated and isolating intellectual labors have attracted to the magnetic field of black feminist studies?" (23). DuCille suggests that the interest in black women has reached "occult status" while "increasingly marginaliz[ing] both the black women critics and scholars who excavated the fields in question and their black feminist 'daughters' who would further develop those fields" (25). Although duCille admits to feeling "ambivalence, antipathy, and, at times, animosity" about "the new-found enthusiasm" for black women's literature, she also confronts her "own dis-ease with the antagonism to which [she has] admitted and by which [she is herself] somewhat baffled" (26). She does not want to claim the work of black women writers "as the private property of black women readers," yet she continues to struggle with "enduring questions about co-optation and exploitation" (30–31). Rather than grapple with "this persistent (but perhaps inherently unresolvable) debate over who can read black female texts" in terms of race, culture, or gender as strictly or even primarily racial or cultural or gendered," duCille advocates the interrogation of more important questions "about professionalism and disciplinarity; about cultural literacy and intellectual competence" (31). This take on the dilemma seems a much more fruitful approach, which recognizes African American literature as a legitimate field of inquiry and not merely an exemplar of black life.

How, then, do we address the issue of white scholars teaching and researching in the field of African American literature—should this be seen as appropriation or cultural literacy? How one answers this question is inextricably linked to recent rethinking about the nature of race as a social construct and the continued lived experience of raced beings. Thus, what follows is an attempt to meld an intellectual response with my own personal experience as an African American woman trained primarily by white scholars to work in the field of African American literature. I will share some of my experiences from graduate school and the early days of my career while linking them to my reading of the experiences of some of the white scholars most crucial to my intellectual development. I hope to provide a nuanced reflection on my experiences and continued ambivalence regarding the persistent essentialism practiced within the academy. While I never fully settle my own internal debate regarding the role of white scholars in African American literary circles, I do believe that my discussion of cultural literacy is a useful, if not fully adequate, approach to the complexities of this issue.

Before getting to the heart of this piece—my thoughts about being trained in African American literature by white scholars—I need to step back and discuss my introduction to African American literature. It was not until graduate school that I enrolled in my first African American literature class and expected to have my first African American professor. I had never had a black teacher in K–12 or in college, but my expectation of an African American professor died a quick death when a blonde professor entered the room. I was disappointed, while a classmate was angry. I suppose, since I had never had a black instructor, it was easier for me to settle in and take comfort in the fact that this instructor had been trained by a leading African American scholar. I doubt it was merely by chance that this tidbit of information was shared so soon. I suspect my professor also felt some discomfort as a white woman teaching black literature. She was also relatively new and probably still in need of methods to claim some form of authority in the classroom. This gesture toward secondhand blackness was enough for me, but I know others were more resistant.

I would not be surprised if my professor's experience was not unlike my own experience teaching an American novel course. My first year on the tenure track began with African American survey courses the first semester, followed by a combined undergraduate and graduate American novel course the next semester. I had taught before at my graduate school, a prominent liberal arts college, and at a junior college. I also had the good fortune of obtaining my secondary education certificate while pursuing my bachelor's degree, so I had had course work about pedagogy and had actually been taught how to teach. This preparation probably made me less nervous than other brand-new professors, but I really struggled that second semester. The African American survey class I taught the first semester was a new course for me, and I hit the typical stumbling blocks associated with new courses and new books, but I didn't have my authority challenged as I did that second semester in the American novel class. My students the first semester expected me to be knowledgeable in part because of my brown skin—I am African American, so I must know about African American literature. It is seldom that I can acknowledge brown skin privilege, but I do think this is often at work when I teach African American literature. Yet I have also encountered the white student who knew more than me by virtue of her African American friends and *Jet* magazine. I suppose that there are two things at work here—students come to class with certain expectations about their professors, and African American professors, like other nonwhite professors, are typically subjected to additional scrutiny. Thus, when I teach a course about African American literature, I am perceived as being knowledgeable, not necessarily because of my training but, rather, by virtue of my experience as an African American. African American professors are often expected, however, to prove themselves to their students, who often suspect that we got our jobs based on affirmative action, not merit. Thus, we frequently encounter students who believe that they know more than we do, despite our years of education and experience. So, if I do have moments of brown skin privilege, they are few and fleeting.

In the case of the American novel class I do not think I had any such moments, even when discussing texts by African American authors. In fact, I suspect some students wondered why these novels were even included in the syllabus. Students seemed to question my notion of the American novel, which I must admit was probably more colorful than most but not terribly radical—I had writers such as Hannah Foster, Catharine Maria Sedgwick, Nathaniel Hawthorne, Henry James, Herman Melville, Harriet Beecher Stowe, Frances E. W. Harper, Mark Twain, William Wells Brown, Kate Chopin, William Dean Howells, and Theodore Dreiser. I had not abandoned the canon; I did insist, however, that we address issues of race, gender, and nation building. The foregrounding of these issues called attention to the racism and sexism embedded in our country's history and culture, and, while I thought this fostered fruitful discussions, many of my students could not come to terms with the discomfort associated with confronting some of the less pleasant aspects of our country's past.

I imagine that the resistance and challenges I faced in asking students to confront such hot button topics was not too different from what my African American literature professor experienced in teaching the other's literature. Our class was overwhelmingly white, with a few black students. I am not sure if our presence helped or hindered class dynamics, but ultimately this was a good class in which I learned a lot. Our professor insisted that we have informed discussions about the literature, rather than emotional responses. She presented the material as a valid category of knowledge to be studied and learned, not just experienced. The black students were not singled out as experts because of our lived experience. This is not to say our experience was discounted but, rather, that it was no more valid than the experiences other readers brought to the texts. It was in this class that I came to appreciate African American books as more than a reflection of black life but as high-quality literature.

My professor approached this literature with an appreciation for difference. Thus, as I took my first African American literature class, I did not feel as if I was getting a white reading of the literature, but, instead, I was presented with a multiplicity of approaches to and interpretations of the texts. Yes, my hopes were disappointed when I encountered yet another white teacher, but this disappointment was quickly replaced with excitement and inquisitiveness as I discovered not only her passion for the literature but also her respect for and understanding of the material. What really made the class work for me was that the books were discussed not in a vacuum but within the sociohistoric contexts of their production. This cultural context is essential to the ways in which African American authors present their visions of our world.

Thus far, I have focused my examples on my experiences with one particular white professor because she teaches African American literature courses and not just African American literature within American literature courses. The bulk of my training and mentorship, however, came from my dissertation advisor, who was not an African Americanist but did teach African American literature as a regular part of his American literature courses—and, yes, he is a white man. Rather than discuss his teaching methodology, I prefer to address his role as mentor, as this was crucial to my introduction to the discipline. Some might think that I would be handicapped by not having someone to introduce me to a network of African American scholars, but this was not the case. My advisor introduced me to several well-known African American scholars—women and men—and I have frequently spoken to scholars who have heard about me through my advisor. The fact that my advisor is part of this network of African Americanists suggests that he does not merely dabble in the area but, in fact, keeps up with the scholarship and the leading thinkers in the field. This type of networking can be very beneficial for a wide range of reasons: it keeps one's research up-to-date; it may help during the job search; it may lead to a fellowship; it can help in finding potential external reviewers; and so on.

One might wonder what an older white man can teach a young African American woman about African American literature, but my answer is—plenty. My advisor opened my eyes to the inner workings of academia regarding, among other things, hiring decisions, tenure and promotion, and publication. Yet I would not say that he treated me just like his white students but, instead, was very frank about how racial politics might effect my negotiation of academia. For example, we had lengthy discussions about the job market and my decision to go out early while still writing the first chapters of my thesis. He thought this would be good practice, and, as the Modern Language Association conference was nearby, it would not be terribly expensive. He warned me, however, that several schools shy away from "ABD" candidates and that this was often particularly true for people of color because of the potential political fallout if the degree was not completed in a timely fashion. We talked about all aspects of the job search, interviews, and contract negotiations, including essential issues such as the job talk to the minutia of clothing choices—yes a suit, preferably with a skirt. I don't believe we talked about hair—this conversation was reserved for my mother and close friends—but it was a crucial point: how might my hair be read as a statement about my racial identity and politics?

As I write this, I must remind myself that this is not meant to be a tribute to my advisor, but it is hard to resist the inclination because he is indeed an excellent mentor. My very positive experience is reflected by similar comments from his other students, but this is not always the case in student-mentor relationships, especially when race is an issue. Over the years I have come across a number of graduate students and junior faculty who have not had such an ideal working relationship with their advisor and committee members. Thus, I think it is particularly important that white scholars working in African American literature consider not only how to produce high-quality research but also how to work well with their African American students.

Many African American students will share my experience of wanting to study African American literature but having to rely on white African American literature specialists or American literature specialists with some interest in African American literature. With the exception of one African American woman, white scholars shaped my graduate training. I'm not sure if this is more or less ironic than the fact that, despite having had primarily American literature course work, I was always seen as an African Americanist by hiring departments, and interviews for positions described as American literature with an interest in African American literature were few and far between. I like to think that this was because I used my dissertation and conference presentations as a way to package myself as an African Americanist despite not having as much course work devoted to African American literature as I would have liked, but I suspect skin color also played a role in the way my expertise was perceived.

Despite the recent spate of criticism directed toward essentialism, essentialism is alive and well in department hiring practices. This desire to hire a specialist in ethnic literature or postcolonial literature and theory is often coupled with the desire to hire a visual representation of the other as well. This practice further complicates my response (and probably many similarly situated academics) to the presence of white scholars within the field of African American literature. While, intellectually, I view African American literature as a legitimate field of study available to all scholars, emotionally, I continue to feel a sense of ownership for a field intricately connected to my own culture and history. This possessiveness is also heightened by the fear that African Americans will be further squeezed out of academia if we do not have our own terrain. After all, how many African Americans are hired to teach Shakespeare, Victorian literature, or even American literature? Many of the few African Americans who do dare to leave the confines of African American literary specialties are still expected to teach African American literature because of some supposed experiential knowledge. Yet those with training and expertise in an area other than African American literature continue to be received with suspicion.

My personal experiences bear out the saliency of duCille's commentary regarding her conflicting thoughts regarding ownership of intellectual property and concerns about exploitation. This, in turn, brings me back to duCille's point about professionalism, cultural literacy, and intellectual competence. These are key ingredients for a successful scholar and teacher; I would argue, however, that those teaching African American literature are particularly in need of cultural literacy. The term *cultural literacy* was coined in 1987 by E. D. Hirsch Jr., who argued that people without adequate knowledge about American culture were disadvantaged in their reading comprehension. Although many scholars were attracted to his thesis, others took him to task for his construction of a very narrow list of cultural facts that every American should know because it did not adequately reflect the ethnic diversity of the United States.[1] Louise Giddings notes: "The argument which Hirsch presents seems reasonable and logical. Cultural knowledge leads to effective social communication, societal harmony, and literacy. It appears that cultural literacy would be a desirable and worthwhile goal for all members of society. However, the topic has sparked controversy" (110). Although Hirsch's book was one of the best-selling nonfiction books in the United States, he was attacked for inadequate representation of African Americans, Native Americans, and Latinos. Giddings, then, argues for "[a] broader, more diverse, and less traditional view of what it means to be a culturally literate person" (112). Rather than pursue an inclusive definition of *cultural literacy*, in this instance I would like to call for a specific cultural literacy with regard to the African American experience. One does not need to be

African American in order to read, teach, or study African American literature, but one does need to know about and understand African American history and culture in order to teach or research African American literature adequately. For example, neo–slave narratives, such as Shirley Anne Williams's *Dessa Rose* and Octavia Butler's *Kindred* will not be fully understood or appreciated without some understanding of the history of slavery as well as its lingering effects. Nor will students have a full understanding of African American literature without some discussion of the oral tradition and its connection to literature. Langston Hughes's blues poetry is not the same without some understanding of the blues and the role of music within African American culture. Thus, cultural contexts are essential to appreciate fully the way in which African American authors read and write the world.

For my thinking about cultural literacy I am borrowing from Henry A. Giroux's discussion of the connections between literacy, culture, and difference. Giroux asserts: "In the discourses of postmodernism, literacy in its varied versions can be taken up as both the politics of representation and the representation of politics. . . . Within a postmodernist framework, literacy restructures the boundaries and borders that have traditionally been used to constitute meaning, disciplinary structures, art, and life" (1–2). What I find particularly attractive about this definition of *literacy* is the recognition of the fluidity of meaning: "In this instance, literacy is not reduced to learning simply how to read, write, or listen. As part of a broader politics of difference, it also serves to focus attention on the importance of acknowledging that meaning is not fixed and that to be literate is to undertake a dialogue with the multiple languages, discourses, and texts of others who speak from different histories, locations, and experiences" (2). This broader definition of *literacy* is ideal for approaching African American literature because the texts often call for the recognition of different ways of reading the world. Difference, as a theme, is a recurrent presence in African American literature whether it's Toni Morrison comparing Pecola Breedlove's life to a Dick and Jane primer or Ralph Ellison's Invisible Man finally recognizing his invisibility. Difference within the black community is also confronted in such texts as Nella Larsen's *Quicksand* and Wallace Thurman's *The Darker the Berry: A Novel of Negro Life.*

Literacy must take into account "that people 'read' the world differently depending, for instance, on circumstances of class, gender, race, politics, and sexual orientation. They also read the world in accordance with spaces and social relationships constructed between themselves and others" (Giroux 3). A good teacher will understand that these different ways of reading the world will also generate a variety of interpretations of the literature and thus will be prepared to negotiate these differences during class discussion. A good scholar will also realize that different ways of reading the world will also lead to different ways of writing the world and will take this into account in conducting literary scholarship. Thus, a culturally literate teacher and scholar of African American literature would recognize the differences within African American literature and try not to homogenize the texts as merely American literature, nor would the literate teacher-scholar exoticize African American literature as completely other. A culturally literate teacher-scholar would have the tools to discuss the cultural, historical, and socioeconomic nuances embedded within African American literature.

As I attempt to bring this essay to a close, I'm still left somewhat unsatisfied with my attempt to delve into this very thorny terrain. Is it enough to take the intellectual approach and argue "that what is at issue is not simply the color or culture of the scholar but the kind, quality, and cultural competence of the scholarship" (duCille 40)? In many ways I feel as though I am in a lose-lose situation. DuCille asserts that "to claim privileged access to the lives and literature of African American women through what we hold to be the shared experiences of our black female bodies is to cooperate with our own commodification, to buy from and sell back to the dominant culture its constitution of our always already essentialized identity" (34). My insistence upon cultural literacy is an attempt to negotiate these equally problematic options, but then it opens another can of worms—who determines cultural literacy, and how do we know it when we see it?

Even as I write this, I cannot ignore my own response to scholarship written by nonblacks. There have been many times when I "knew" that the author was not African American based on the writing. What does it mean that I think about this? Is this indicative of bad scholarship? What does it mean if I am fooled or left unsure of the identity of the scholar? What does it mean that I have yet to mistake an African American scholar for a white one? Am I tapping into the presence or absence of cultural literacy? I suspect that my questions regarding the identity of the scholar are connected to my concern that so many critics feel entitled to speak about African American literature despite their training or experience. I should note that, when I refer to training, I am not limiting this to formal training, but I do expect scholars to acquaint themselves with the field before publishing in the area. When I read scholarship about African American literature and can identify the writer as white without the writer self-identifying, I do believe I am picking up on a lack of cultural literacy. Something that I have read suggests a lack of pertinent information about African American culture and history. I suspect that this is why I have taken culturally literate white writers for African Americans but have not misidentified an African American literary scholar as white.

I have struggled in writing this essay because it demands an encounter with the personal. I could not stay hidden behind the cloak of research and intellectual discussions. Time and again I asked myself: should I address this? do I dare mention this? what will others think? I am generally not so vacillating; I tend to be fairly direct about my opinions, but I find myself still rather irresolute regarding this topic. I cannot separate the intellectual response, which is in many ways based on an idealistic worldview, from the practical response that knows racism is alive and well in academia. DuCille notes that "despite the fact that many of our white colleagues and administrators may theorize African American and black feminist studies as open fields, as acquirable tastes ('You don't have to be one to teach one,' as someone put it), this intellectual position often is not lived up to in institutional practice" (32–33). This is the theory that many academics share, but there is still the craving for the "real thing." The black body is wanted to diversify departments, provide representation, and signal authenticity:

> when these same individuals want someone to provide a black reading of their work or black representation on a committee or black resources for their students or information about a particular black author or details about an event in black history, more times than not it is to black faculty that they turn, and not to the white Victorianists they have hired as African Americanists and have authorized to teach courses in black literature and history. (DuCille 33)

This really brings me back to where I started—the concept of race as an identity construction does not adequately address the practical lived experience of inhabiting bodies that are typically racially identifiable. In order to address this split notion of identity, perhaps I can don my rose-colored glasses of race construction while still peeking around the lens to avoid tripping!

## NOTE

1. See Hirsch, *Cultural Literacy;* Estes, Gutman, and Harrison, "Cultural Literacy"; Worsham "From Cultural Literacy"; Pentony, "Cultural Literacy"; and Giddings, "Beyond E. D. Hirsch."

# "Knowing Your Stuff," Knowing Yourself

APRIL CONLEY KILINSKI AND AMANDA M. LAWRENCE

APRIL: When I decided to specialize in African American literature as a master's student, I did so because this literature seemed to speak to me in ways that nothing I had read before did, and I naively believed that my visceral response was enough to validate my interest. The question I soon learned to ask myself, though, was WHY I felt so connected and drawn to African American literature. I was blindsided by how many times students in my, then, all white graduate program asked about my choice to specialize in this literature in ways that, to me, seemed accusatory. After all, this was not a question I heard asked of others who wanted to specialize in areas like Medieval or Renaissance literature. I was implicitly being accused of trying to co-opt something that didn't belong to me. When I spoke to my white mentor about my discomfort with having to justify my choice, he said that what people were really concerned about was whether or not I would be comfortable teaching to a majority of African American students.

AMANDA: One of the most surprising moments of my first semester teaching an African American literature course occurred well over a month into the class. Out of the blue one of my African American students asked: "Why are you here? Why do you do this? Don't misunderstand. It's not that you're not good at this—the class is great—but we just want to know why." She asserted that the question had been on everyone's minds from the beginning of the semester. Nervousness at teaching the course for the first time had led me to over-prepare for every eventuality . . . except this one. I rambled on about my love for the literature, my interest in constructions of race, my childhood in the South, the Harlem Renaissance class I took in college, and my master's work on Nella Larsen, but the students seemed disappointed, as if I were holding out on them. That day in class I remember wishing I had a more compelling story to explain my interest and for the first time feeling that my love of this literature itself might not be enough to establish me as an invested, valid teacher and reader of African American texts in my students' eyes.

As white students of African American literature, we have been told repeatedly by scholars in the field that the key to succeeding is to "know your stuff." Indeed, Nellie McKay and others contend that the way to prepare white scholars in the field of African American literature is to provide them with a thorough knowledge of African American literature and history. In this regard many graduate programs, including ours, seem to excel. Classes are taught on major black authors, the black aesthetic, race in American literature, black women writers, the Harlem Renaissance, and African American literary theory, and special topics courses are offered on thematic concerns and historical events. Graduate students in Ph.D. programs are also afforded the opportunity to take comprehensive examinations in this area. Outside of English departments, African and African American studies departments offer various courses in African American history and culture. The breadth and depth of these courses seem to suggest that access to knowledge is not the problem for scholars preparing to enter this field. If students take advantage of available course offerings, they will, in fact, know their stuff and will be able to embark upon their careers with confidence.

As our stories indicate, however, McKay's solution, offered in her *PMLA* guest column, fails to take into account the political realities of white bodies who seek to study and teach in the African American literature classroom. For white graduate students presently interested in African American literature, navigating the space between a theoretical understanding of race and the political reality of teaching about race can be challenging. That is, while our courses emphasize understanding race as a social construct, this kind of approach to understanding race often ignores the social and political realities of lived experiences. As Christie Farnham asserts in "The Discipline of History and the Demands of Identity Politics," "Although most scholars today argue that race is less a scientific concept than a social construct, the public seems to be largely unaware of this argument" (110). We have found that with the right to study and speak about African American texts comes an implicit expectation for personal and political justifications for interest in this literature. Consequently, since it is rare that a white person can embody a black subject position, white graduate students are often questioned about their decision to specialize in these texts. As we found, knowing your stuff is one thing, but negotiating others' desires to understand your relationship to it, as well as your own anxieties about having "sufficient" justification, is a different matter entirely.

In April's story a key assumption was at work in the questions asked by her white colleagues. In essence, assuming a "right" to speak about these texts without that justification was interpreted as tantamount to asserting the white privilege that Ann duCille rejects when she writes that African Americans "become objects of study where [they] are authorized to be the story but have no special claim to decoding that story. [They] can be, but someone else gets to tell [them] what [they] mean" (34). April did not assume any privileged access to these texts, but the questions she was asked made her wonder if her students would also share these concerns and if she would need to provide some kind of justification for them as well. Her mentor's comment, in hindsight, really seems to be saying that, in choosing this field, her primary obligation would be to the African American students who cross her path, since they are the ones who "matter."

In Amanda's experience it occurred to her after class that, given what many of the African American students had revealed about their intensely personal motivations for taking the class—to learn about their heritage in order to better understand themselves, for example—they might have been looking for something more personal from her. If most of them had come for a reason that ran deeper than fulfilling a requirement, they might naturally assume that their teacher had such a reason too. Also, the way in which the student asked the question perhaps implied that Amanda must have a personal motivation for teaching these texts. Maybe the expectation was that she would have an African American husband or maybe that she had grown up in a mixed-race family—that there was something about her background that would justify her investment in African American people and, as an extension, African American literature. Considering this experience now, we question whether the race of the student and the racial makeup of that class (largely African American) affected Amanda's need to explain herself and her interpretation of the students' "disappointed" response. We recognize that Amanda was anxious for her students' approval of her answer and, therefore, of her as a teacher. We question whether she would have been as unnerved if a white student in a largely white class had made the inquiry.

Reflecting on the implications of our encounters—the need for "sufficient" justification and an implicit hierarchy of students—we are left with a series of challenging questions about our roles as white scholars and teachers. Do we need to single out African American students in our classes in ways that we would not single out white students? What, if anything, do we need to say to justify our choices? Who needs to hear these justifications? Why was the self-referential moment seemingly so necessary for those who questioned our interest and so uncomfortable for us?

Ultimately, what these experiences and the questions they left us asking amount to is that our whiteness was being "raced" and that we were beginning the process of losing what Gail B. Griffin calls "white innocence." Griffin's contention that consciousness begins with a willingness to examine ourselves as racialized beings speaks to the process that we as white graduate students underwent when we began to study and then teach African American literature. As we trained for and entered the field, we encountered challenging questions from our colleagues and students that prompted an awareness of our position as "limited, known, identified" in relation to the literature as well as to the students we were teaching (7). In this essay we will examine how we came to this racial positionality and theorize about our own motives and anxieties in the classroom as graduate students teaching African American literature for the first time. We will argue that this awareness led us to think about our racial position in new ways and to enact a kind of self-referentiality that we see as both necessary and problematic.

In arguing that coming to a self-referential position was necessary in our development as teachers of African American literature, we are aware of the pitfalls that can be associated with what Michael Awkward calls the "self-referential impulse." Awkward challenges the practice of white critics who incorporate statements about their positionality into their writings. For Awkward the self-referential impulse "fails to make these scholars significantly more self-conscious in their involvement in a dialectics of race" and, further, can be a dangerous assertion of white power that limits their interpretive efforts and reinforces a white scholarly hegemony (600). Yet Awkward finds the work of white scholars who do not address their race as a factor in interpretation to be equally troubling. Thus, he seemingly leaves the white scholar in a double bind. For white critics to discount their race as a significant factor in reading is to ignore the power dynamics implied by their positionality. For white critics to embrace the self-referential impulse is to risk bringing those power dynamics to bear upon the text in negative ways.

DuCille sketches a similarly complex position. She criticizes Jane Gallop and Adrienne Rich, among others, for unintentionally demeaning the African American people they seek to honor in what she calls "*Driving-Miss-Daisy*, some-of-my-best-friends-are-black, I-once-was-a-racist confessionals" (45), which she claims also assert a kind of white privilege. DuCille contends that perhaps she should be more understanding of white writers' narratives of how they gained racial consciousness but also admits that this is difficult given that her racial consciousness was formed by enduring repeated acts of racism as a child and not from "reading Richard Wright's 'Big Boy Leaves Home' as an adult" (44–45).

As Awkward and duCille's work shows, the white scholar's role in African American critical discourse is far from uncontested. While it is frequently acknowledged that white critics of African American literature can produce informed, enlightened, and useful scholarship, how they address their own race in relation to that scholarship and what influence race might have over it are important questions still under debate. Because both of us are new scholars in the field and have limited publication experience, for the purposes of this essay we will examine these questions in the contexts of the training we received as graduate students and our first experiences teaching African American literature in freshmen and sophomore courses. We have found that, if self-referentiality is a problem in scholarship where the body is unseen, it is even more challenging when the white body is standing in front of a class, particularly if that body is a new teacher of African American literature facing students whose ideas about race are based on experience rather than theory.

AMANDA: The importance of what my racialized body represented in the classroom became clear to me when my African American literature class was discussing Amiri Baraka's 1964 play *Dutchman*, in which a seductive white woman manipulates a young black man on a subway. She taunts him until he explodes in rage and then uses his outburst as justification for killing him. During our discussion one of the black men in the class asked me how it felt to be a white woman teaching *Dutchman*. He commented that, as the teacher, I had black men like him "in my power," much as Lula had Clay in hers in the play.

I did not get the sense that the student was asking in order to insinuate anything negative about my motives or authority, but being compared to Lula was still incredibly uncomfortable for me. In asking his question, the student raced my whiteness and made me recognize that, as a teacher, I did not and could not occupy a neutral space. In drawing connections between the power dynamics in the play and those in the classroom, he was reminding us that we were the text of the class as much as the literature was and that the play was not so dated that a comfortable distancing was possible for any of us.

APRIL: One semester I taught Nadine Gordimer's "Town and Country Lovers" as part of a unit on race and gender issues in my Freshman Composition course. The story deals with an interracial relationship that is illegal during apartheid in South Africa. As part of our discussion, I told my students about some of my own experiences dealing with apartheid while growing up in South Africa that I felt would help them to better relate to issues raised in the text. I was caught off guard when an African American student asked if I had ever been accused of racism during my time as a teacher. I responded that I had not but that, if any of my students ever felt that I had a particular racial bias against them, it was most likely my white students. I further explained that this had much to do with my background growing up in Africa as often one of the only white people in a particular situation. I lamely finished by saying, "Although I look white on the outside, I don't really feel like it on the inside."

Afterward I realized that my response may have been a problem, so I went into the next class and began by clarifying my statement. I told my

> white students that they had nothing to worry about as far as my grading policies were concerned, since, when I said that my white students may see me as racially biased, I was referring to the way that I read and which political issues I usually sympathize with. I further clarified that, when I said I didn't "feel" white, I in no way meant to imply that I could possibly understand what it means to be a minority and that I am fully aware (no matter how much I hate it) of the privilege I am often accorded simply because I inhabit a white body. I assured my students that what I had really meant was that my racial consciousness was formed differently from what they might consider usual for white people in this country or in South Africa because of the different positions that I was often put into while growing up. The student who had asked the question very casually said:""I can't believe you have been worrying about that! I had no problem with your answer. I know because of your experiences that you are not racist, so I wondered if you had ever been falsely accused of it."

Our students' questions forced us into uncomfortable identifications with racist, white characters in the texts that we were teaching, identifications that, in turn, forced us to think about how our own racial consciousnesses conflict with what our racialized bodies represent. Amanda was identified with a malicious white female power over a black male. Because in teaching African American literature she often sought to show her students that she had an understanding of blackness and because she often found herself identifying with minority characters in texts, she did not want to acknowledge she might be wielding white power, particularly gendered white power, in the classroom. Her student's question drew her attention to the fact that, regardless of how race might be internally constructed for her, external constructions of race still defined her racialized position in the classroom. No matter how hard she tried to project herself as "black identified," her students would still see her as white, and it had been presumptuous of her to assume otherwise.

April's anxiety and need to clarify her statement to her students stemmed primarily from the fact that she did not want her two African American students to feel as if she were asserting a kind of affinity with their experience and racial position that she had no right to claim. The implication of her mentor's comments, that African American students are the ones who "matter," particularly influenced this discomfort, especially since she was a white person teaching a text about white racism. She wanted to distance herself as much as possible from the racism in the story. Our students' questions exemplify that to some extent we cannot achieve this distancing precisely because of our white bodies.

What is at work here is Charmaine Eddy's idea that "accepting the racial body as evidence of our cultural narratives erases the distinctions between the diverse cultural sites of ethnicity, nationality, culture, and race through the surety of corporeal chromatism" (82). When our students associated a particular cultural narrative with our white bodies, we were forced to see ourselves as "raced" white, which is a position we usually try to reject. Furthermore, when we became anxious about the acceptance of students whom we had visually identified as black, we made assumptions about their cultural narratives based on "corporeal chromatism," which informed our assumptions and behaviors. April's response about "feeling" white bears out the cultural significance in racial formation, as does her student's response about being in Africa making her exempt from racism. The fact, however, that she was concerned about her black student's response to her answer about racial consciousness and the fact that her black student knew that for some her body could be associated with racism bear out the extent to which the corporeal body becomes the site of reference in the classroom setting.

Our students' probing questions led us to examine our desire to identify with a black subject position in the classroom and the extent to which it is impossible for us to do so because of what our bodies represent to them. We also became aware that the anxieties that led us to want to black identify were based on assumptions we made about our black students' expectations based on what their bodies represented to us. Despite the problems with this series of assumptions, confronting them in the classroom setting opened up a space in which our classes could delve more deeply into the meaning of racial constructions. Amanda answered her student's question directly, revealing her own discomfort with the identification it foregrounded, and also asked the students to talk about their personal responses as they read *Dutchman*. In the end the class, including Amanda, was able to open up an important discussion of the continuing significance of the play and of the ways in which the historical legacy of relationships between black men and white women continues to inform our culture and our understanding of race. April realized that, even though her student's belief that being in South Africa made her different was correct to some extent, it did not fully account for the complexity of her position as a white teacher. By revisiting her response, she was able to acknowledge that she had wanted to remain comfortably in the black subject position that her students had granted her through their acceptance of her experience in Africa as "sufficient." Yet the white privilege that she had been accorded both in South Africa and in the United States precluded her from unproblematically adopting this position.

These realizations were painful for both of us, but we do not regret that we had to go through them. They produced positive results in our classes by creating the kind of safe spaces where students felt comfortable asking racially charged questions. They also represented necessary steps in our development as scholars and teachers of African American literature. We agree with Eddy that "only by crossing the racial boundaries and taking the risks implied in our intervention into the discourse of race will we begin to 'race' the 'non-raced,' and only by 'racing' the 'non-raced' can we interrogate through practice the critical, textual, and theoretical 'bodies' that form the foundation of our cultural discourse about race" (101).

Although we had begun this interrogation as students of African American literature, the classes in which we were students were predominantly white and were taught by white instructors. Therefore, we never had to race ourselves as scholars and teachers of African American texts. Also, we never had seen a white teacher of this literature address classroom questions like the ones our students posed to us. Admittedly, our classes in African American literature were primarily at the graduate level, in which a professor's authority is generally a given, regardless of race, and in which student comments are primarily textually rather than personally based. Since we were graduate student teachers, our experience was with freshman and sophomore students for whom the "ownership" of African American literature often privileges an experiential basis of knowledge over academic training. Teaching African American literature for the first time, we were largely unprepared to negotiate the disparity between the classrooms in which we had been students and the ones in which we were teachers.

While we believe that it was vital for us to be questioned by our students in ways that made us reference our white subject positions, we cannot ignore Kimberly Rae Connor's argument in "Can You Play? The Reconstruction of Instruction." Connor, a white teacher of African American religion, asserts that, in order to be a successful teacher of African American studies, one has to demonstrate a certain level of black cultural awareness to engender black students' trust in one's ability to teach. Amanda learned this need for cultural awareness during her second semester of teaching African American literature.

AMANDA: One day in class a student announced that a comic who frequently appears on BET was going to be in town for a show. Much to the class's surprise and disappointment, I did not recognize his name and confessed that I really didn't watch that channel. Several students disparagingly wondered aloud how I could be teaching African American literature and not keep up with BET. Several weeks later the question of my cultural awareness came into play again when the university sponsored a lecture by Chuck D. When I started talking about his lecture in class and obviously had some knowledge of not only what he had spoken about but also his music and rap in general (I had followed both for years), I thought I detected a change in the students' perceptions of me as a teacher. There was no demonstrable connection between the texts I was teaching at that time and the politics of rap, but simply knowing that I "spoke that language" seemed to open up the classroom discussion. At the time I thought I perceived a sense of new

> connectedness with some of the students, both black and white, and I concluded that the students then viewed me as more of an authority on African American literature. I felt imbued with a sudden credibility that my knowledge of the subject and academic credentials alone seemingly could not provide.

There is no way to know if the changes Amanda thought she saw in her students' demeanors were real or perceived. Certainly, her anxieties about perceptions of her credibility and thus her authority as a teacher of African American literature informed her interpretation of the students' responses. Because their earlier reaction to the fact that she did not watch BET established their belief that black popular culture is an essential interpretive tool for African American literature and that knowledge of one would imply knowledge of the other, Amanda felt that her authority was more validated when she demonstrated her familiarity with rap. Her satisfaction with presenting herself according to the students' criteria might also have been an extension of concerns that had been raised in her first African American literature class. Because she felt that she had not given an answer that sufficiently positioned her as invested in black culture the first time, she was eager to present herself as a valid authority according to the students' criteria this time.

The issues of authority Amanda was grappling with in this instance were not the same as those she had experienced when she first began teaching six years earlier or the same as those most teachers experience when they begin teaching a new course. Normally, she would not have allowed students' criteria for what constitutes a "good" teacher to influence how she viewed herself as an authority figure. She did so in this case, however, because she was eager to present herself as sensitive to the realities of race outside of the literature the class was studying.

We do not question the importance of acknowledging that this literature holds special significance for many students who identify with texts through common experience. Still, we accept duCille's point that privileging an experiential access to literature "both delimits and demeans those discourses" by "[restricting] this work to a narrow orbit in which it can be readily validated by those . . . for whom it reproduces what they already know" (30). Given, however, that students expect teachers to have intellectual knowledge as well as lived knowledge, how do you balance the two factors when discussing African American texts in the classroom? Indeed, how can a teacher ensure that this expectation for lived experience does not translate into an acceptance of experientially based knowledge as the sole source of authority? As Christie Farnham, a white teacher of African American history, asserts, "Although I have devoted many years to reading and researching in the field of African American history, white students want to hear the views of the black students on the issues raised. This is not simply a matter of being interested in the input of students from the group whose history is under discussion, as important as that is. It is also the belief that, no matter that the interpretations I present are often the results of black scholarship, what African American students have to say is the 'real truth' on the subject" (108).

The problem of who has authority to speak about a particular subject can potentially undermine a teacher's credibility as well as create a feeling of inequality in the classroom that can silence those without such lived experience. Perhaps the place to begin a dialogue in class is in fact with a kind of self-referentiality that not only "races" us as white but also races all of our students. We do not advocate this position only to make our black students more comfortable with our position as white teachers—to justify our presence to them—though that is a legitimate concern. We advocate this kind of self-referentiality because we also see how uncomfortable many of our students are when discussing issues of race. If we can make everyone aware of their racial positionality, then maybe we can have a more inviting and safe learning space in which everyone is examined and no one's cultural and lived experience trumps another's simply by virtue of the corporeal body that all of us see represented in the classroom. This kind inclusive of environment allows students to feel empowered as readers of this literature so that they feel like they have access to the text, even if they have not had that particular experience.

The complexities of racial positionality make this classroom vision idealistic, but we still believe that it is a vision that we should strive to achieve. DuCille concludes her article with the idea that a new generation of students may be the hope for transforming the way we approach this literature and its criticism (50). Therefore, in order to assist this new generation of students as they approach teaching and specializing in this literature, we advocate that graduate training should include some practical suggestions for creating classroom settings in which racial issues can be discussed openly and productively. Lisa M. Gonsalves outlines a model for establishing cross-racial communication in "Making Connections: Addressing the Pitfalls of White Faculty / Black Male Student Communication." Her proposal for dialogue between faculty of various levels of racial consciousness that takes place in "supportive environments, where faculty might feel less inhibited about revealing their vulnerabilities around race" is useful for thinking about graduate training (463).

We support a similar model of mentoring as a possible step toward providing graduate students with practical approaches to teaching African American literature. This mentoring would take place primarily through informal conversations between a cross-racial group of graduate students and experienced teachers, instead of in a formal setting such as a workshop or class, in which the pressure of grades might influence what is said. These conversations should address issues of power, authority, trust, and comfort in the classroom. When led by experienced teachers of African American literature, informal discussion groups can provide a forum for new teachers to share their own experiences in a productive environment. This seems particularly germane given that graduate students in this field already talk to one another about their feelings when they teach texts for the first time, often focusing on their anxieties. Having an experienced teacher moderating these discussions would assist graduate students in moving beyond the panic that can occur when young scholars first encounter the difficulties of teaching African American literature in their own classrooms. We acknowledge that this model cannot completely do away with the painful professional/psychological negotiations most of us go through when we first teach African American literature, and we certainly do not suggest that this model replace the kinds of quality mentoring that graduate students currently receive. We do see it as one possible way to continue the kind of discussion that this book will begin. Nellie McKay's vision for the future of African American literary studies can be better realized through a process of dialogue that teaches us not only to know our stuff but also to know ourselves.

# At Close Range

## Being Black and Mentoring Whites in African American Studies

BARBARA McCASKILL

In December 1988 I earned a Ph.D. degree in English with a concentration in African American literature. Sixteen years later I am a tenured associate professor at a very large, historically white, Tier One public research university in the sunny, post–civil rights era, southeastern United States. I was born in 1960, just as the baby boom started to nosedive, Vietnam was beginning to be a problem, and Kennedy's election ushered in an American Camelot. I was born "up nawuth," as my people bend our syllables to say, in an industrial town and military base just off the New Jersey Turnpike, but I am as alien and unaccustomed to the culture and climate there as the polar bear and the penguin are to the Sahara's sandy drifts. My parents are two black Southerners. Children of the Depression and the "Greatest Generation," they came of age in Dixie in the 1930s, 1940s, and 1950s, well before Atlanta reinvented itself as the City Too Busy to Hate yet not far enough after the Civil War for the hearts and minds of whites around them to let go of old grudges and resentments about Yankee carpetbaggers, their suspicions in regard to "uppity" Negroes, and the racial and sexual violence that stippled the former Confederacy like menacing images in a midsummer's nightmare.

So, I am not one to take where I am for granted. Inez Owens McCaskill of west-central Georgia, a descendant of slaves, slaveholders, and Creek Indians from just across the Alabama line in Hurtsboro, and John Lansdon McCaskill Jr., a descendant of Geechee slaves and free persons of color from Hartsville, South Carolina, saw to that. Up north, out west, overseas, regardless of where we lived and traveled, they often bore the haunted expressions of Holocaust victims. My sister, brother, and I inherited their trauma, and we grew up steeped in their stories of chain gangs and flaming crosses; "Whites Only" restaurants, restrooms, schools, and swimming pools; and downcast eyes and buckled shoulders to shield black bodies from the scornful gaze and wilting stare of Miss Ann and Master Alfred.

"That school" where I now am employed, as Mom sometimes contemptuously calls the University of Georgia, which raised beautiful brick and granite buildings and nobly instructed bobby-socked and Brill-Creamed white students, disdainfully sneered and denied us admittance when we qualified "colored" students applied. No string of honors or tribute of money from us was ever enough, even as it relied upon our taxes and toil to keep its gates swinging open for the state's white citizens. I do not think that Mom and the other women and men her age may ever truly believe that, fifty years after integration, that school has genuinely changed and sincerely desires to connect to and serve the dynamic black and Hispanic communities around it. And why should she? I am her youngest daughter, and I was the first black person in my department who was hired as an assistant professor and stayed long enough to earn tenure. That happened on 13 May 1998, thirty-four years after the passage of the 1964 Civil Rights Act. Mom and I know all too well that in my everyday professional world the struggle for civil rights continues.

Yet sixteen years into academia, with a whopping fifty theses and dissertation committees behind me—and counting—three-fourths of the students I have prodded and praised have been white Americans. And happily so. I enjoy mentoring for mentoring's sake, not out of some ulterior motive to clone myself in the classroom or to create my own entourage of sycophants. And if the awards and recognition I have earned in support of my work with students across races, genders, and classes are any indication, I am very, very good at what I do. I make no pretense, however, that my mentoring is casual, color-blind, or apolitical. I definitely subscribe to a politics and a plan. I think it benefits all of my students and energizes the discipline when I expose them to discussions of African and African American literature and culture from the enlightened and progressive perspective of both a professor and an insider.

And this also is my politics: to train all the students I mentor to become enlightened and progressive mentors themselves, a small gesture to turn what in this century has become a tsunami-like tide in our profession. As a coauthor of the *Women in the Profession 2000* report of the MLA Committee on the Status of Women in the Profession, I researched and reported about the diminishing numbers of people of color and women aspiring to or remaining in careers as tenure-track professors. Our report documented how women of color as a group were still "alarmingly underrepresented in PhD programs in English" and still lagged behind white women in gaining English and foreign languages doctorates (195). Mainstream or commercial publications additionally have noted increasing discrepancies between the overall college enrollments of African American men and women. A 3 March 2003 issue of *Newsweek* reported, for example, that, reflecting an overall increase of women in general obtaining university degrees since the 1970s, 35 percent of black women compared to 25 percent of black men went to college (Cose 49). We used to complain about the dearth of blacks in the pipeline; now, for growing numbers of black men, the pipe itself has burst.

Charlayne Hunter-Gault, who with Hamilton Holmes and Mary Frances Early integrated the University of Georgia in the early 1960s, returned to campus on 9 January 2001 from her post as a Cable News Network bureau chief in Johannesburg, South Africa. She had been invited to deliver the school's prestigious Holmes-Hunter Lecture, to commemorate the fortieth anniversary of the school's desegregation. On 9 January 1961 she and Hamilton Holmes had ended 160 years of racial discrimination at the university by walking through the university's landmark arch entrance and registering for classes in the Academic Building, which has now been renamed the Hunter-Holmes Academic Building in their honor. When informed that, forty years later, the undergraduate population of African American men in 2001 had dipped to an all-time record low of 1.9 percent, she said, "If I had known in 1961 that this would happen, I would have sat down under the Arch and cried."

A March–April 2002 *Harvard Magazine* article entitled "Faculty Diversity: Too Little for Too Long" traces the attrition of women and people of color in academia to a variety of factors, including lack of mentors and inappropriate or inconsistent mentoring, the difficulty involved in adjusting the tenure timeline to have children, the lack of a critical mass of supportive administrative policies, low salaries and less prestigious appointments, and the burden of additional, multiple service at departmental, college, and university levels that sabotages their potential for promotion and advancement. But mostly, the study concludes, women and people of color are earning doctorates and finding other careers to pursue besides teaching and research because of "an unaccommodating culture" (Trower and Chait 8).

The bottom line, as Nellie Y. McKay reminds us in the *PMLA* essay that stands as the inspiration for this book, is that "the alternative to having a black professor of African American literature should not be not having a professor of African American literature" (23). So, I do not plan to argue in this essay for the exclusion of whites and the one-sided ascendancy of people of color in black studies disciplines, even though calls for "balance" and "even-handedness" in hiring policies related to African American studies ring hollow at a university like mine, where faculty of color have become a precipitously shrinking minority and the percentage of nonwhite students in the undergraduate population—a single-digit figure to begin with—has taken similar plummets in recent years.

My purpose, instead, is to air the frustrations, conflicts, occasional misgivings, and triumphs that have come from my regular forays into the white side of African American literature. I have been a black mentor to white graduate students for what feels like some time now, but this is a discussion I have rarely launched with even my closest mentees and a difficult internal dialogue with myself. But, if my generation of black women professors wants another generation of women and minority professors to seek careers within the ivy walls and if we want our work conditions to improve enough that our colleagues and students who are already present remain, I think it is high time we are honest with ourselves and one another about airing the challenges of mentoring, another too long undervalued "domestic" or service task we do, and about discussing in particular the challenges and rewards of mentoring white students in a field that no longer exclusively "belongs" to us. So, in the following pages I will present my personal history as a kind of case study of the complexities of being black and mentoring white graduate students: how my own history as an academic and my sense of calling distinguishes my professional work from the careerism of some white students I have mentored, the connection between the racial logic (or illogic) of the current job market and my relationship as a black mentor to white students, and the ways in which mentoring white students has influenced my professional commitment to teaching African American literature at a historically white school. Finally, I want to call for more dialogue between black mentors like me and white mentees on the energies all of us should bring in equal portions to transforming outmoded pedagogies and the current academic status quo, both within ethnic studies disciplines and in traditional departments and fields.

To mentor white students effectively, I have had to come to terms with how my own history as a graduate student has shaped me. During my six years of graduate studies at a competitive, elite "Southern ivy"—six years!—I was one of only two African American students in the program. While I made a few friends and my seminars were phenomenal, my overall graduate experience simply was not very fun. As the first woman in my large, mostly working-class family who had ever attended graduate school, the only one besides my great-uncle Robert Whittlesey (he had earned his Ph.D. degree in education at night while working by day as a high school principal), I made more than my share of mistakes in selecting classes, friends, and mentors. I found my feet all too often after the School of Hard Knocks had smacked me and sent me tumbling to the floor. It sometimes felt that my life consisted exclusively—relentlessly—of teaching classes, taking them, composing my dissertation, and working in dead-end, subsistence-level, part-time jobs to avoid interminable decades of student loans. So, I did not take too much notice of the harbingers and advance warnings of the aforementioned limpid numbers of African Americans, Hispanics, Asian Americans, and other minorities electing to pursue academic careers as humanities professors. As I kept my head in my books, doleful demographics and dire predictions were bar-graphed, color-coded, and pie-charted with increasing ferocity and frequency in *Blacks in Higher Education*, the *Chronicle of Higher Education, Profession,* and other national publications. In fact, when I earned my doctorate in 1988, Duke University Press published a volume called *The Academic's Handbook*. Emily Toth's essay on women in academia (146–152) and Nellie Y. McKay's piece on the racism, classism, and sexism faced by "minority faculty in [mainstream white] academia" (46–60) offered sound advice for encountering the glass ceiling, tokenism, gate-keeping, and other workplace issues.

Yet the light at the end of the tunnel was finally shining for me, so I paid little regard to a fair number of these trends. In her essay on the impact of race in/on the college classroom Virginia Whatley Smith discusses "the racial pairings of white English majors with white faculty" and the absence of white English majors in her courses on African American literature at a historically white Southern institution (155). Having witnessed the same pattern in my undergraduate and graduate career, I think I was primed for more of the same self-exclusion of white students in my professional career. On another level I think it was as a self-protective measure that I kept my eyes on the prize and my mind on the goal—getting finished—and tuned out the depressing demographics. In other words, even though my graduate school experience gave every indication that the profession I was entering was very white and getting even whiter at all levels, I simply and ironically did not think too much about the prospect of spending a significant portion of my career as a mentor to a majority of white students. Instead, I imagined myself as a younger black, female, and feisty version of Lucy Craft Laney, Anna Julia Cooper, or Mary McLeod Bethune, one of the pioneering black women educators of the post-Reconstruction and Harlem Renaissance eras. My harvest, young students of color, would sprout miraculously before me like the next wave of black consciousness revolutionaries. Or, shoals of cresting and dipping clouds on a clear spring day, they would trail exuberantly in my inspirational wake and follow my lead in redefining outworn curricula and redefining the field.

For another part of me saw—and always has seen—my academic destiny as an evangelical as well as professional one. In spite of my isolation in graduate school, I knew that there were other African American students earning doctorates in my field and similar ones around the country. I dreamed that we would one day constitute a critical mass that would attract more students of color into our ranks and keep them there through our enthusiasm, altruism, competency, and dedication. This perhaps sounds saccharine or pie-in-the-sky to younger, postfeminist, post–affirmative action students. But it is at moments like this, when the students I engage do not understand my position that the civil rights struggle is ongoing and incomplete in academia, when they want to close the books on the movement and move on, that I run into the most difficulties in my role as mentor.

I came of age a beneficiary of affirmative action and proudly so. My earliest teachers were Peace Corp and Vista volunteers, bra-burners and NAACP members, civil rights marchers. Growing up, my parents banned Barbie dolls from the home, even the black "Christy" knock-off, and insisted that in the afternoons after our homework was done we read African American history books about leaders such as Harriet Tubman and Frederick Douglass, Rosa Parks and Dr. Martin Luther King. My siblings and I also attended Catholic schools for most of our childhood, back when it was the sisters and not the lay instructors who were still doing the lion's share of teaching. So many of the white nuns who taught us, however, were leaving the Sisters of Mercy or so openly and militantly challenging the pope and church hierarchies that one was hard-pressed to see the appeal of what they called their "vocation." Yet the dictionary definitions of the term—"a type of work demanding especial commitment," "a strong feeling of being destined or called to undertake a particular type of work"—were inclusive ones that transcended any particular religion or race, and they were also meanings modeled by virtually every African American adult around me. In the Baptist and Holiness churches that nurtured the older women in my extended Southern family, they subscribed to what black feminists Roseann Bell, Bettye Parker, and Beverly Guy-Sheftall have called (borrowing from the poet Carolyn Rodgers) the image of "sturdy black bridges." These are African American people, especially women, who have made a commitment not only to modeling respectable lives but also to implementing a dynamic self-help philosophy: to lovingly mobilizing their everyday energies and resources in order to assist individuals and communities in need.

This was really the old "race uplift" agenda of the turn-of-the-twentieth-century black women's clubs and female benevolent societies gussied up in a more contemporary guise. In 1892 Anna Julia Cooper had written, "Only the BLACK WOMAN can say 'when and where I enter, in the quiet, undisputed dignity of my womanhood, without violence and without suing or special patronage, then and there *the whole Negro race enters with me*'" (31). So, between Sunday school, grammar school, and home, I very passionately internalized a sense of obligation to design a vocation, not "just" a career, to be a bridge, to enter a profession that filled my soul and lifted my people and did not merely give me a job and a paycheck in return. Somewhere along the line I decided that fulfilling this idea of vocation in my particular life meant holding the door open for more black people like me to enter, find inclusion, and thrive in the halls of higher education.

After obtaining my first tenure-track appointment and real-world job, however, the gap between what I actually encountered and what I had previously imagined forced me to revise this vision. While the majority of graduate students I mentored in my very first years were women of color—African American, Latina, Asian—the tables quickly turned, just as the statisticians and prognosticators had predicted. What a painful reminder my new role mentoring white students was of the assistance and guidance I had generally failed to obtain from white professors when I had been a student! For every experience I had had with a white faculty member who went beyond the call of duty to show me how to write a proposal, critique an essay, compose a fellowship application, or prepare a persuasive conference paper, there had sadly been so many more at whose hands I encountered derision, contempt, indifference, and/or condescension. When the tables are turned, in other words, just how consistently can graduate students of color find committed white faculty in areas such as Renaissance literature or early American studies available to volunteer as their mentors and committee chairs and then to guide them beyond graduation through tenure and promotion? That is a rhetorical question, of course. The answer is that, all too often, we don't.

One disconnect I regularly experience with my white students is their sense of careerism and my aforesaid notions of vocation or calling. Regardless of racial or ethnic identities, my students aspire to job security, competitive health benefits, child-care programs and pension plans, access to libraries and computers, compensation for professional travel, stimulating classes, and supportive colleagues, as only several of myriad career goals. No group does or should have a monopoly on these dreams. And we have thankfully arrived at a place in our profession where to discuss these goals is no longer to dismiss ourselves or our colleagues as pseudo-intellectuals. If anything, we ensure that we will attract and keep the best and brightest undergraduates by holding public conversations in our advanced degree programs on such issues that once may have been considered indelicate, mercenarily corporate, or just plain incompatible with the nonmaterialistic and academic enterprises that the majority of us scholars of literature and lovers of culture engage in.

So, in invoking the careerism/vocation dichotomy, I have a different meaning in mind. I am referring to the absence of a sense of *obligation* to African American communities that sometimes seems to accompany the white students I encounter. I came along one generation too late actually to march in the civil rights movement or to otherwise earn my activist stripes by holding teach-ins or sit-ins in protest against the war, so perhaps I am on one level overcompensating for a loss I cannot regain. But what does it mean that the prospects of such "invisible" tasks as recruiting students of color from the high schools, mentoring student groups that focus on issues of diversity and race, or merely offering that bright black or Latino/a student that no one else wants to talk to some attention and guidance meet resistance from some white students I train who are rightly mindful that doing what "counts" consists of teaching, researching, and serving on a visible, officially sanctioned department or college-wide committee?

By investing my time, advice, and experience in white scholars who are slow to respond to the obligations I think the stories of segregation and Jim Crow require—especially in this place and on this ground—I worry that I am betraying both the sacrifices and gains that my parents' generation made and I benefited from. Don't *all* of us who enter African American studies owe more to their struggle than that? And what, then, does my involvement in this process make me? Am I really the wiser counselor passing the baton in a relay more diverse than ever before through the presence of women, American minorities, and international students? Or am I merely preparing some (white) students more than other (nonwhite) ones for succeeding in a different kind of race? How fair is it to my black mentees if I hold higher expectations of collaboration and community service for them without demanding the same from white students? Am I really helping to build an even playing field, or, co-opted and disingenuous, am I just repaving the same old warped and turbulent one? These anxieties, along with the other stresses and tensions of being a middle-aged black female professional in a racist, classist, ageist, and antifeminist society, have contributed at times to real physical problems for me—among them, insomnia and bruxism (teeth grinding).

I try to make the best of where I am by pushing my white graduate students to stay alert to and avoid mistaken assumptions and stereotypical generalizations about the students of color in their classrooms. I try to stay true to the activist roots of black studies in general and African American literature in particular by inculcating the necessity and importance of introducing discussions of race, sexuality, class, and history—as well as symbol, rhetoric, theme, and other literary critical devices—for a balanced approach to the discipline. And, while I cannot literally transfer my own visceral connection to an Afro-Southern past to my white mentees, I can encourage them to contemplate and articulate how earning their degrees in literature will be spirit enhancing as well as lifestyle improving, how to hear their calls and find their paths to their own lifelong vocations.

The racial politics of the job market, including the assumptions faculty search committees have about the kinds of jobs white and nonwhite students should take, is an issue that also very strongly affects my relationship as an African American mentor to white students. With dread and anticipation my students and I await the annual telephone interviews and campus visits that shape the winter rhythms of English departments. My program, like programs everywhere these days (in the time-honored spirit of launching a good defense as the best offense), organizes mock interviews for our students, vets their cover letters and curricula vitae, alerts colleagues at other institutions to the fine candidates we are preparing to send out in the world, and offers nerve-steadying conversation or coffee and consolation between busy MLA conference sessions. If the phone does not ring around New Year's Day or the mail carrier's bag runs thin, we know exactly what to say. Yet neither graduate school nor years of service have made me any better at responding when the inevitable student asks what to say when a search committee raises the question: "How do you justify being a white scholar in African American literature? How dare you?"

Part of me wants to ask these committee members, "How dare *you*?" Regardless of the cultural or social histories that inform it, the bottom line is that their assumptions about who should teach black studies assumes fixed, impervious, unadulterated genealogies of scholarly entitlement. African American researchers have no place in eighteenth-century British literature; Native scholars can make no claim to teaching the works of South African authors; and so on. Like rungs on the Great Chain of Being, some larger and longer than others, to each race or nation his or her literature. Too many of us doing African American disciplines in predominately white departments have discouraging stories to tell about the unspoken agreement that the only appropriate entry for scholars of color is through the occasional line advertising ethnic studies research interests. The inversion of this syllogism is that white students should step aside when an ethnic studies position comes up for grabs (particularly in the Eastern states, Hawaii, and California, where the undergraduate populations often have high proportions of students of color) and leave African American, Chicano studies, and similar area studies fields to be the ghettos for scholars of color that they were "meant" to be.

Black studies still remains synonymous with black people, and our colleagues researching the history, literature, and culture of nonblacks too often possess large doses of skepticism that black scholars can do the work of their fields equally as well as they can or even better. While lingering issues of political empowerment and institutional influence, competition for funding and other resources, salary and compensation inequities, and consolidation of power may still influence many departments' decisions to hire a black scholar in a black studies area instead of a more qualified white one, this practice ultimately contravenes the spirit and intent of the intellectuals and activists who created the field in the 1960s. Johnetta B. Cole, the president of the historic all-woman Bennett College and the former president of Atlanta's Spelman College, writes:

> As committed as Black Studies advocates were to the concept of African Americans rediscovering ourselves as a people in the context of world history and events, I think I speak for many of my colleagues when I say that we were not as myopic as critics made us out to be. We spoke out against what could be called "White Studies" occupying front and center in American curricula while Black Studies was "ghettoized" for minority students. Importantly, we also spoke out against the reverse. The goal was a balanced (and accurate!) curriculum that would include the studies of all people. Usage of the terms "Eurocentric" and "Multicultural" was not

as widespread as it is today, but the criticism of the former and the call for the latter was what progressive educators and students were essentially about in the 1960s. (27)

Nevertheless, the old question of who "owns" black studies is still being enacted at interview time. Over the years I have realized there is little I can do to prepare the white students I mentor that I do not already assist all my students in accomplishing: developing an innovative and well-written dissertation, gaining a wide variety of instructional and research experiences, updating their technological skills, soliciting detailed letters of recommendation, practicing for the interview and the job talk.

Sometimes this racial profiling of job candidates is too much for me. Then I send my white students elsewhere for advice on how to answer questions of authenticity from search committee members, to another white student or faculty member who has been there and done that. Part of me is quietly angry. Part of me, in all honesty, is also vindicated that my white students have also confronted the racial politics of the academy. At least they cannot pretend and fool themselves that the academy, and the United States by extension, is the color-blind "racial utopia" that the sociologist Robert Staples accuses post-1990s Americans of imagining. "The color-blind theory," Staples writes, "ignores the reality of . . . America: that race determines everyone's life chances in this country. In any area where there is a significant racial diversity, race impacts on where people live and go to school, whom they vote for, date, and marry, with whom they do business, who they buy from or sell to, how much they pay, and so on. This does not sound like the racial utopia Martin Luther King dreamed of" (231).

What the students I mentor can learn from their experiences on the job market where they are "profiled" as unsuitable for black studies or ethnic studies positions because of their whiteness is how changing an untenable system that reinforces racism and privilege is as much as part of what I am training them to do as discussing the spirituals or tracing the theme of double consciousness through three centuries of African American literature. And, ironically, their difficulties in the job market based on skin color also makes visible to some white students for the first time how they benefit from what Peggy McIntosh calls "white privilege," the advantages white Americans historically have gained by virtue of their race while denying that such benefits are predicated upon the systematic subjugation of other groups.

My response compensates for, though by no means remedies, the lack of entitlement I seem to have of a research field, that of all fields, I think I should be able to claim. For, regardless of the fact that more black professors of African American literature are tenured than ever before, this accomplishment does not so easily translate, I have found, into power. At the university level promotion does not automatically grant privilege to make decisions about development and funding where these affect us, to appoint hires, or to represent ourselves in the national and university-level bodies that influence our field's direction and growth. Now, to add insult to injury, after long sustaining the open secret that the only appropriate point of entry for black academics is through some people-of-color studies, it seems that some whites are dissatisfied with even this inequity. I am reminded of my Mom's conversations when I struggled to obtain tenure and promotion: Did black people's blood tint the bricks of the University of Georgia just so white students could get jobs teaching African American literature? At least, in the context of this history, the white students I mentor can understand a little more clearly what it is like when you receive an invitation to the party yet no one asks you to join him or her on the dance floor.

Being black and mentoring white students at a predominately white university also forces me to face uncomfortable professional realities about myself. I have a research collaborator and very good friend teaching at Tuskegee University in Tuskegee, Alabama, one of the premiere historically black institutions in the country. I visited her upper division African American literature class a few years ago in order to recruit for my graduate program (there is no master's or Ph.D. program in literature there, and the school is only a few hours down the road), and one of her undergraduates asked me why so many black professors like me taught at majority white schools. I told her that a large, historically white, public research institution like mine can afford to offer its faculty higher salaries, more travel and sabbatical support, smaller teaching loads, a larger library, and other benefits. With a shrinking pool of black applicants across academic areas, particularly as one moves up the ranks of a predominantly white university, it can and will energetically outbid the competition from smaller, private, often majority black schools. Because I was single, with an elderly, widowed mother suffering for the second time from cancer, an expensive disease, I needed and chose the money. So, what does this make me? A pragmatist? A race traitor? Complicit in my own destruction? A victim of a conspiracy to send white scholars to the historically black colleges and universities (HBCUs) and black scholars to the historically white colleges and universities (HWCUs)—depriving many black students of role models—that I fearfully and selfishly persuade myself not to notice? Or who can blame me if I hesitate to recruit African American students away from the nurturing environments of HBCUs to my institution? In exchange for the attractiveness of more instructional and research resources, lighter teaching loads, and better pay, these students face an environment characterized by isolation, role strain, and white privilege. The old stories of my parents return and make me squirm.

Some requests I simply no longer tender. Always eager to grow the field and nurture collegiality across the disciplines, I used to mentor white teaching assistants, write letters of recommendation for white students, and serve on white students' dissertation committees no matter how marginal their interest seemed in the field. When a student of British literature indicated that she wanted to work with me so she could score more MLA interviews and a wider range of tenure-track job offers, she inadvertently struck my last nerve. I want my students to earn terrific jobs, but I also want them to possess a sincere attraction to and passion for this literature. I want them to stay in the field and not abandon it like yesterday's paper once it has leveraged them to that plumb position in British literature, classical literature, or wherever they *really* wanted to go. I do not want to wind up one of those professors students can rely on to give them a crash course on the Middle Passage, civil rights, and whatever else they need to know in between so that they can nail an African American literature course to tide them over to the next semester without ever giving real black people more than the time of day. Not while I face frequent pressures to prove my ability and eligibility not only in my own field but also in general American literature, ethnic American literatures, survey courses, honors classes, freshmen seminars, senior seminars, and everything in between. I will not be so willing a participant in what I call the "*chic*-ening" of black studies.

What I also do not do is to prohibit myself and other scholars from talking about African American literature from an exclusively black perspective. In encounters with graduate students trained in the traditional "Great White" canon, white students in particular, I experience a different kind of version of the anxiety of influence. I have been impressed by the comparisons and allusions they easily draw between African American writers and the "classics," from Yeats to Faulkner. As more white scholars enter black studies, however, and as more qualified applicants across the board compete for fewer jobs, I worry that, in spite of the wide range of excellent scholarship to the contrary, the classics will once again become the most valued, and only, standard by which to compare and evaluate African American literature. I thus make it an expectation that my students will discuss the merits of black writers through the lenses of both African and African American culture with as much facility as they can note attributions to Shakespeare and Dante therein.

So, here I am, holding the door open. And I want my position as a mentor to white students ultimately to mean more than being their bridge into the world of black studies. My effectiveness requires a two-pronged approach in which some of my students study to become professors and researchers of African American literature and some of them take what they have learned and use it to talk about canonical British and American literature in new and transformative ways. If how we teach ethnic American literature makes no difference in how we teach the canon, then why bother? If I prepare white students for success only as critics in black studies and ethnic studies fields and not to use their training to think differently about the literature in an American Modernism or British Romanticism seminar, then I am just replicating the same old systems that poison the academy now. If we truly are committed to making the academy both accommodating to people of color and honest about the importance of their cultural contributions, then myth-shattering scholarship such as Timothy B. Powell's theory of "cultural aporia" in *Ruthless Democracy*, which conceptualizes American literature as a dialogic between multicultural identities and monoculturalism, and the work of historians Ronald Takaki and Gary Okihiro to place the legacies of "marginal" groups at the center of how we define American identity, is research that the white students I mentor should introduce in all kinds of classrooms, *especially* the mainstream ones.

Is all of this worth it, I sometimes wonder, or is it time to bow out now and find a school like Tuskegee, Hampton, Howard, or Fisk that would have me? In her *Academic's Handbook* essay for faculty of color in the academy, McKay advises: "Our jobs depend on having students, and we owe it to minority group students to be even more available to them than others. . . . At the same time, you may be the only minority group authority figure that many Anglo-American students come into contact with at close range. You have a good deal to teach this group as well" (55).

I am where I am in the academy today as a consequence of a confluence of movements, attitudes, histories, and opportunities that I could not control, a little bit of luck, and my own creativity, discipline, and ambition. I enjoy working with all of my students at graduate and undergraduate levels, and I often have been called "gifted" and a "natural" at mentoring and instruction. To prove it, I have stellar student evaluation scores, teaching awards, and a stream of requests for directed readings, recommendations, talks to student groups, and individual advisement sessions. I plan to continue to go that extra mile as a graduate mentor, to encourage my own people to represent themselves honestly and critically as knowledge producers and teachers and to train whites and other nonblack students to teach and research African American literature in an enlightened, politicized, and rigorous fashion. But I will never pretend to be color-blind about it.

## NOTE

I would like to thank my wonderful friends and colleagues in the Department of English at the University of Georgia, Timothy Powell and Sonja Lanehart, for their excellent critical comments on matters of tone, emphasis, organization, and style in earlier versions of this essay. Thank you for the outstanding work you do in taking theories of race, gender, language, and culture to new revolutionary levels.

PART THREE

# Beyond Black and White

# Faulty Analogies

## Queer White Critics Teaching African American Texts

SABINE MEYER

In her 1998 *PMLA* guest column Nellie McKay suggests that the continued scarcity of African American literary scholars and the reality of growing numbers of white scholars teaching African American literature ought to be discussed in conjunction. McKay advocates the need for African American scholars and scholars of African American literature—both black and other—to come to terms jointly with the academic spaces they can carve out for themselves. She foregrounds the need for these scholars to take collective care of the health and growth of the field of African American literary studies within an academy that, in spite of much theoretical effort to the contrary, still often relies on the questionable notion of "authenticity" as the foundation for teacherly and scholarly authority. McKay discusses three major problems as undeniably intertwined: "the insufficiency of the black PhD pipeline, the efforts to discourage white graduate students from exploring black literature, and untrained white scholars' undertaking of scholarship in black literature" ("Naming" 21). "The alternative to having a black professor of African American literature," she cautions, "should not be not having a professor of African American literature." Moreover, McKay highlights that modest numbers of newly appointed faculty members who are trained as African Americanists currently coincide with a drastic increase in scholarship authored by untrained white academics who "assume authority to teach, write about, and serve on panels that review black literature." While she specifically addresses disturbing developments within the field of African American literary studies, McKay also asks larger questions of an academic community that has yet to claim responsibility for the field's "willful continuing marginalization" (23).

I came to McKay's column after several years of intensive undergraduate and graduate training in African diaspora literatures and cultures that left me with a sense that I had learned—rather than ignorantly trespassed into—African American literature. While I was aware of the fact that there would remain gaps that I would never fill, I was also confident that I had attained both competence and training. That said, however, the degree of relief I felt when I first encountered McKay's column causes me to suspect that, perhaps a bit like Phillis Wheatley in her attempt to be fully accepted and acknowledged as the creator of (her own) poetry, I was always also "in search of authentication" (McKay, "Naming" 18). Did I need for someone of "social and political esteem" to confirm that I was eligible for a niche within the field of African American studies? Did I expect to rely on McKay, a prominent black scholar, to validate my location within the field? Was I intent on borrowing authority from her? At last, I remember thinking, a prominent African American scholar is taking issue with a condition that has loomed over much of my academic training: "Too often," McKay states, "one sees the same position advertised and readvertised from one year to the next, while the most-qualified non-black candidates are turned away, important work is left undone, and the crisis is allowed to continue unabated" (22). This assessment, I felt, acknowledged my own frequent encounters with the notion that no matter how knowledgeable I may have become in the field, no matter how thoroughly immersed I might be in the history of its emergence and the study of its persistence, my work in African American literary studies will always already be fraught with tendencies of usurpation—hence, rotten at the root.

Obviously, McKay's column initially led me to ponder my own peculiar positioning on a grid of racialized and sexualized, as well as gendered and nationalized, axes of identification. It made me dwell once more on my graduate school years, when my resolution to focus on African American literature met with repeated reminders, each one of them well intentioned, that I might want to invest my primary academic energies in lesbian, gay, bisexual, transgendered, or queer (LGBT/Q) studies, instead. My teaching and scholarship in queer theory or queer cultural production, it was implied, would be endowed with immediate authority by way of my perceived authenticity as a native informant on queer issues. My scholarship on and teaching of African American literature, in contrast, would forever lack such authenticity and, as a consequence, authority. By choosing African American literature and culture as the primary subject of my dissertation research, some cautioned, I would likely jeopardize my job prospects. I might end up making a career of defending my choices rather than moving swiftly toward establishing myself as a valued contributor to an academic discourse that still relies heavily on identity as the source of authority. Over time I learned to deflect these suggestions. I continued to struggle, however, with the realization that I may be a part of the pipeline problem McKay theorizes: if I—and others like me—had not been so readily available, there might have been more pressure within academe to make bigger, better investments in the recruitment and retention of black Ph.D. candidates interested in teaching African American literature over the past few decades. By now there might be less of an "imbalance between the number of minority PhDs entering the pipeline and the demand on the other end;" African American candidates might "materialize" more readily ("Naming" 22). Or would we simply see even more untrained white scholars claim license to assert themselves as ready and able to "cover" the field?

A related issue that demands attention in this context is the fact that it has become rather common, in both academic and general public discourse, to theorize white queers as "disadvantaged whites," inhabiting a space of "counter-whiteness," perhaps even of "discursive blackness," as Robyn Wiegman has phrased it ("Whiteness" 119). It is especially troubling to see the frequency with which such representations enable visions of supposedly "nondominant" white teachers as more suited to teach racially or ethnically minoritized literatures than other trained white academics. Building on McKay's stress on the degree of preparation rather than the "identity" of white scholars attempting to teach African American literature, I would propose that narratives of "disadvantaged whiteness" are inadequate as a means of boosting white queer teacherly and scholarly authority in the field. There seems to be no need, nor much authoritative space, for ready analogies between our own marginalization and our assumed ability to offer an informed commentary on African American literature. Instead, such analogies need to be scrutinized as both theoretically suspicious and politically ineffective. Most obviously, they conflate two forms of oppression that are not nearly as similar as they may appear on the surface. Moreover, they tend to hinge on faulty representations of all white queers as not only more disadvantaged but also more trustworthy and politically responsible than other whites, and they simplistically suggest that all African Americans are always already less advantaged than all others. What is often lost in this process is the importance of accounting for what George Lipsitz labels as the "cash value" of whiteness, the "all-too-real consequences for the distribution of wealth, prestige, and opportunity" that are attached to whiteness (vii). What is interesting also is the fact that assertions regarding the supposed compatibility of different minoritized lives and experiences do not usually lead to an assessment of heterosexual African American—nor other racially/ethnically minoritized heterosexual critics—as more prone to relate to or more equipped to teach queer literary and cultural production than straight white academics. Effectively, it appears that at the present moment non-queer license to read queers (well) remains mostly with progressive, "queer-friendly" whites, both within and beyond the corporate university.

One recent academic trend that contains more or less explicit representations of white queers as disadvantaged whites who can speak about matters of race—or on behalf of and in "natural alliance" with people of color—with heightened authority is that of so-called whiteness studies. For instance, while he initially states his discomfort with conflations of racial/ethnic and sexual minority status, film theorist Richard Dyer goes to great lengths to validate his teenaged sense of social proximity between himself as a marginalized queer boy and his "crush," a Jewish youth, who found himself relegated to a socially marginal position because of his ethnicity (5). He adds, "[Alt]hough I experienced making the connection between being gay and being Jewish or black as a purely individual perception, a glance at gay culture suggests that it is not a surprising one to make" (7). In these passages Dyer relies on degrees of likeness as the main vehicle for authorizing his self-positioning even as he questions his tendency to draw analogies between racial/ethnic and sexual "difference." Not only does he represent his "felt connection" with nonwhite others as rooted in his own marginal position within the realm of "white manhood," he also highlights similarities of cultural expression—namely, overlaps between disco and funk, camp and Jewish humor, or stories of "passing" (7–8)—when he narrates his attraction to nonwhite men.

Dyer's narrative of attraction to and fascination with the racialized other, intended as an honestly recounted element of his self-location "as a white man," adds up to a slightly different claim—that of a "naturally" proximate relationship, via experiences of both intimate personal connection and shared social marginalization, between his queer white self and nonwhite people. In many ways this is the logical continuation of his earlier assessment of white representational authority. "The point of seeing the racing of whites is to dislodge them/us from the position of power, with all the inequities, oppression, privileges and sufferings in its train," he states, "dislodging them/us by undercutting the authority with which they/we speak and act in and on the world" (Dyer 2). Yet by establishing himself as inhabiting a supposedly minor white location as a queer man and as intimately connected to other minor players in the game of race and sexuality—via "a felt connection between gays and ethnic minorities" as well as "romantic and sexual encounters with non-white men" (6)—Dyer actively counteracts his intention to bring about change by way of foregrounding the dominant racing of whites. He represents whiteness as internally split into minor and major locations then proceeds to assign epistemic privilege to supposedly disadvantaged whites. This attempt at drawing analogies and foregrounding links between white queers and nonwhites indeed questions the sociopolitical power and narrative authority of those whites whose positioning within the normative mainstream is difficult to dispute. It does not manage, however, to undercut or dislodge altogether white representational authority and sociopolitical power. Rather, within critical-theoretical constructs of this sort, whites who can claim distance from the assumed center find themselves authorized to "speak and act in and on the world" from an oppositional stance that is endowed with heightened epistemic privilege.

It is important to note that Dyer hardly stands out as peculiar in his attempt to foreground the assumed connectedness of white queers and nonwhite people. Similar expressions of connection are manifest in many white queer narratives of attraction, both public and ostensibly private. Such narratives frequently include asides on the deliciousness of "dark" bodies yet, unfortunately, focus far less on the desirability of the minds attached to these bodies. When critiqued, reductivist images of racial and/or ethnic others as consumable objects are commonly downplayed via claims of shared minority status. Too rarely are they identified as the product of a historical continuum that has required nonwhite people to learn about white people in order to thrive, or perhaps to survive, in a racist society, while it has provided white people with license to know little or nothing about nonwhite others even when they openly and eloquently express their desire for them.

Obviously, any attempt to scrutinize one's motivations for connecting with another person is laudable, even when it results in one's candid expression of sexual attraction as the first, perhaps the only, driving force. What is troubling, however, is the frequency with which such tales of "connection" are still being shared among white queers without immediate reference to a by now extensively theorized and documented history of unequal access to modes of expressing desire that has helped sustain externally imposed eroticized images of people of color as/and exotic strangers. Undoubtedly, "sex talk" is hip within both queer culture and queer studies. Efforts at importing such talk into the center of negotiations regarding representational authority across racial differences, however, frequently showcase a profound lack of immersion in the ongoing dialogue regarding the precarious nature of intersections between race and sexuality. In addition, whether or not a white queer has slept with, or fantasized about sleeping with, a racial/ethnic other is hardly the point when she or he attempts to negotiate whether she or he is literate enough to speak about this other with authority. Ready detours into talk about erotic attraction or sexual connection, I would suggest, often indicate the need to question the competence of a white queer speaker, for it suggests her or his inability to adequately position her- or himself vis-à-vis the oppressive history of the sexual appropriation and commodification of racialized others.

Assumptions regarding the epistemic privilege of marginalized groups and their social or political proximity to and responsibility for one another are also not limited to the representation of white queers as nondominant or less dominant white players in the arena of racialized discourse and representation. In fact, many straight proponents of what might fit under the awkward blanket of whiteness studies represent themselves and their contexts or motivations in this manner as well. While they may set the scene by explicitly self-castigating for inherited racial privilege, they often also highlight the "dark strain" buried within "minor" white positionalities, such as the often-cited "white trash" identity. Those who cannot claim white minority status foreground their willingness to function as "race traitors" intent on siding with nonwhite peoples in their struggles or prepared to abolish whiteness altogether.[1] They aim at establishing distance to a dominant white identity via solidarity with the nonwhite, less advantaged other. Yet, as Mike Hill points out, the libratory potential of such efforts is "compromised as white men reanimate their formerly normative status by developing a penchant for the margins" (183). It is important to keep in mind that, even as we assert our interest in or claim proximity to those who inhabit the margins, white critics of racial hegemony continue to profit from the discursive authority that comes with our undeniably easier access to and ready implication in the normative white mainstream. We may consider ourselves marginalized within that mainstream because of our gender, sexuality, class, nationality, or the like. Or we may choose to express our profound disgust with white privilege and attempt to live in solidarity with those who are refused access to such privilege. We cannot deny, however, that even our most passionate denunciation of whiteness is facilitated by our whiteness.

The final passages of Hill's *After Whiteness* draw rather extensively on Toni Morrison's immensely successful nonfiction prose text *Playing in the Dark*. In fact, it could be said that Hill relies on Morrison's widely celebrated words to function as the authorizing force behind his parting thoughts. Or should we argue, instead, that it is impossible, at present, to discuss adequately American constructions of whiteness and their complex interaction with images of racialized others without extensively referencing this frequently read, taught, and cited text? Likely, there is some substance to both statements, for it is certainly tempting, but perhaps also unavoidable, for those who wish to theorize racialized discourse to tap into the authenticating force that references to the Nobel laureate and her text(s) carry at this point in time. Along similar lines Hill himself reminds us that "the temptation upon reading certain passages of *PD* is to seek a false continuity of oppression between nominally black and white American dreamers." "But its materialist challenge," he adds, "is to come to terms with the unevenness of how racial categories position us in different ways, in different times and places, and with local, and inconsistent, effects" (214). If that is the case, what remains essential is a collective commitment to continuously questioning "false parallels" between black and ostensibly marginal white subjectivities as well as the overall readiness with which white academe has summoned prominent nonwhite voices as an authorizing force behind its own musings on "minor" white locations within present-day discourse on difference (214–215). To avoid or bypass such introspection, individually or as an academic community, I would argue, is to facilitate the presumptuous claims to representational authority that characterize the teaching and theorizing of those whose actual literacy in minoritized American literatures and cultures is profoundly lacking.

In addition, critical self-scrutiny requires that we attempt to reach beyond dominant confessions of the guilt of othering the other as well as the fear, or fantasy, of being or becoming the other. At the center of this process lies the need to separate power and authority—whether sociopolitical, epistemological, or narrative—from myths of dominant versus nondominant corporealities and perspectivities. Any such effort needs to build on placing "individuals in interaction with one another in ways that modify their observations, theories and hypotheses, and patterns of reasoning"—as feminist philosopher Helen Longino points out in "Subjects, Power, and Knowledge" (111). Equally central to this effort are questions about the commonplace assumption that a particular identity demands a particular politics and, maybe more important, that a particular politics requires a particular identity. At a time when, according to Judith Roof and Robyn Wiegman, "too often, the minoritized subject who has sought to speak from the specificity of its cultural position has been recontained through a new, deafening 'authenticity,' one that disturbingly reduces the complexity of social subjectivity" (ix–x), this stance needs to be seriously interrogated. If McKay is right to state that "repairing past damage will be difficult, but following along the previous path will make life worse for all of us" (26), we need to look ahead toward collaborative modes of making meaning and conveying such meaning to generations of scholars and teachers of African American as well as multicultural literatures that are yet to come. While we need to maintain that all knowledge is situated, or perspectival, we can no longer rely on the notion that some social locations are, by definition, more suited as starting points for the production of knowledge within the field—and, by implication, for "speaking" this knowledge—than other social locations.

It is also important to realize that, whether we retreat into speaking for ourselves or venture into speaking for others, we always already participate in specific power relations and discursive contexts through which, as Linda Alcoff argues, our "own and other selves are constructed" (109). Therefore, the act of speaking for somebody, whether self or other, necessarily implies effects on others; the speaker is, by definition, part of a network of intersecting and interrelated discourses. To claim that one cannot or will not speak for others—as well as to claim that one will "only" speak for oneself—does not guarantee that less harm is done. In fact, it might well signify a lack of solidarity and concern if it is true that "the declaration that I 'speak only for myself' has the sole effect of allowing me to avoid responsibility and accountability for my effect on others; it cannot literally erase those effects" (Alcoff 108). It is undeniable, however, that speaking for others often spells misrepresentation, silencing, and appropriation. Additionally, the question why it is that one chooses to speak for someone else—and also why some claim the privilege to "let Others speak"[2]—is often left uninterrogated or obscured. Alcoff responds to the former argument by stating that she is not "advocating a return to an unselfconscious appropriation of the other but rather that anyone who speaks for others should only do so out of a concrete analysis of the particular power relations and discursive effects involved" (111). Equal access to speaking and being listened to are necessary prerequisites for the kind of radical democratic dialogue that Alcoff envisions. Social proximity, on the other hand, whether to the margins in general or to a specific minoritized group or identity, does not suffice as a base for speaking for or about others with authority.

In spite of concerted efforts to move beyond this notion, the college classroom and the corporate university at large remain prime locales for ready analogies between identity and representational authority of the sort that I lament. Fairly consistently, students put forward the assumption that queer white teachers or scholars are "naturally" more authoritative than their straight white colleagues when working with racially/ethnically minoritized literatures and cultures. In addition, many hiring committees, curriculum development committees, and administrators in charge of allocating teaching assignments seem to subscribe to this view as well.[3] Finally, entire college and university curricula continue to reflect a preferred placement of minoritized literature and cultures within the frameworks of what Dennis Allen describes as an "identity course."[4] Inspired by a postindustrial consumer logic, courses of this sort are conceptualized and taught in ways that "allow the participants to consume themselves" (Allen 26). To stretch beyond the generic goals of such a course, then, means to switch the course focus from the study of identities to the investigation of intersections between normative discourse and modes of cultural production. It requires effort to invite students to read minoritized literatures within frameworks that interrogate the construction, dissemination, and instrumentalization of normative logic; it also entails a constant questioning—both individual and collective—of our own motivations for making consumable, and consuming, these literatures. Accordingly, Lauren Berlant and Michael Warner argue that "queer commentary provides exactly what some fear it will: perspectives and archives to challenge the comforts of privilege and unself-consciousness" in their fittingly entitled "What Does Queer Theory Teach Us about X?" (347). Queer theory and queer cultural production are attractive within academe today, it appears, partly because of the simple fact that they aim to "unpack" monolithic constructions of so-called primary identities and the normative assumptions these identities are (ab)used to shore up.[5]

Queer commentary, by means of its resistance to the politics and practices of "enforcing normalcy,"[6] undoubtedly lends itself as a tool that can enable white queer scholars and students alike in their efforts to position themselves vis-à-vis racially/ethnically minoritized social locations without having to resort to shared minority status as the source of speakerly and teacherly authority.[7] Much akin to other post-identity theories in its approach to such terms as subjectivity, agency, and social normativity, queer commentary foregrounds that notions of the deviant, the aberrant, and the minor are not merely modes of describing—or discriminating against—marginalized others; they always also function strategically to position the supposedly "different" in order to shore up dominant constructions of "the norm." It highlights that the revalidation of identities that have been relegated to the margins does not, by definition, lead to a remapping of either dominant ideologies or ideologies of dominance. Based on this premise, students in my African American and multicultural literature courses have begun to utilize queer commentary as theoretical "back-up" for their resistance to the terms of reduction that characterize the identitarian logic upon which many of their diversity requirements or cultural literacy courses continue to rely. Doubtful of a "civil rights for all who have been excluded" agenda, these students accede, as Dennis Allen has phrased it, that we need to "examin[e] sets of so-called categories of identity and at the same time realiz[e] that categories are inadequate" (23). As a result, they may find it easier to highlight the naturalized social configurations of gender and sexuality that exist in the folds of a text that appears to foreground primarily oppressive constructions of race or ethnicity. Much like the approaches championed by critical race studies and gender studies, queer commentary enables students to reposition themselves more generally vis-à-vis the politics of legibility and unambiguous identification that remain at the core of the curricular and pedagogical text that is supposed to frame classroom experiences for which they can earn diversity credit. It emerges as a mode of cultural production, critique, and reception that offers students much-needed pathways into the in-between and difficult-to-frame, into those fluid nonspaces that are increasingly present and permissible in their lives and that they expect to see reflected in their educational contexts as well. "Queer" is an invitation to stretch—*past* the normative, *past* conventional boundaries, *past* oneself. Such stretches into the realm of ambiguity and malleability are highly attractive to many students today, both across categories of identification and for a set of complex and, at times, complicated reasons that demand further interrogation.[8]

When imported into the discussion regarding the relationship between white scholars and nonwhite texts, the anti-identitarian stance queer theory promotes complements McKay's underlying suggestion that a teacher or scholar's training and motivation to continue to learn about and thoughtfully contribute to collaborative conversations within the field of African American literary studies may ultimately matter more than her or his identity. Because of ongoing fears of and resentment against "interlopers," however, it is critical that we continue to highlight the need to avoid new alliances of supposed insiders within the field. Such alliances would do little more than solidify further territorial claims to epistemic privilege based on minority status and shut out those who are unable to establish sufficient distance to the normative center to be allowed to partake. If competence and training are the pillars of our commitment to promoting the health and growth of the field, the degree of established expertise and ongoing immersion, not perceived distance from the normative mainstream, should be regarded as the prime source of teacherly and scholarly authority. Rather than bestowing an honorary insider status onto white queers or other allegedly nondominant whites who want to engage with nonwhite literatures and cultures, we need to hold these individuals to the same standards we would employ when considering the preparation of "dominant" white scholars and teachers interested in entering the field. A dialogue based primarily on the confirmation of shared marginality, in other words, would surely fall short of the potential of a cross-generational and global interaction across identities and affiliations that might promise the brightest future yet for the field.

## NOTES

1. A good example of this trend is Garvey and Ignatiev, "Toward a New Abolitionism," first published in the *minnesota review* in 1997 and reprinted later the same year in Mike Hill's edited volume, *Whiteness: A Critical Reader.*
2. The paradox of "letting Others speak" has been addressed by a wide variety of critics and within various (intersecting) minoritized discourses. For additional—relatively recent—pieces, see, for instance, duCille's article "The Occult of True Black Womanhood," Spivak's pieces in *The Post-Colonial Critic,* and the work of African American cultural critic bell hooks.
3. Queer scholars, in contrast, have alerted us to the fact that efforts to incorporate queer subjectivities into university classrooms that are increasingly governed by institutional responses to so-called market forces might force them into complicity with a dominant, normative logic that disavows the contradictions and counternarratives that "things queer" cultivate and thrive on. Similarly, other queer theorists have rejected attempts to discipline things queer into institutionalized locations such as the multicultural literature classroom that might force them to yield to the politics and aesthetics of define-ability, even applicability, in ways that would render them no longer fully productive or disruptive.
4. Allen borrows this term from a presentation by Judith Roof that has since been published as "Buckling Down and Knuckling Under: Discipline and Punish in Lesbian and Gay Studies."
5. Rosemary Hennessy describes queer theory as already representing "an effort to speak from and to the differences and silences that have been suppressed by the homo-hetero binary, an effort to unpack the monolithic identities 'lesbian' and 'gay,' including the intricate ways lesbian and gay sexualities are inflected by heterosexuality, race, gender, and ethnicity" ("Queer Theory" 86–87). Is that, however, really "true" (yet)?
6. This term is Lennard Davis's in *Enforcing Normalcy.*
7. In addition, several scholars interested in intersections between (queer) "identity" and collectivity have recently suggested that there is no inherent promise that those inhabiting different minoritized locations can or want to form alliances with one another or, more complicated yet, claim the authority to know one another and speak for one another. See Phelan, *Getting Specific.*

8. In addition, many young people today struggle with the sluggish acceptance of a category of "multiracial" as their mode of self-reference. Mostly, they appear to have little patience with those who appear to cling still to the infamous "one drop rule" when it comes to categorizing people's racial/ethnic identities. Yet they are willing to engage in dialogue about this issue. Queer theory—especially when it is introduced alongside (trans)gender theories and critical race theories—can foster such dialogue in classes that focus on nonwhite texts. As part of a "pool" of theories that focus on the inadequacy of solid notions of identity and the subjectivity/agency attached to identity, it can help facilitate the still rather timid but much-needed academic discussion of present-day racial ambiguity.

# The Color of the Critic

## An Intervention in the Critical Debate in African American Theory on Interpretive Authority

NITA N. KUMAR

This essay seeks to make an intervention in the black critical theory concerned with racial difference and interpretive authority. The claim of the essay is that the dominant framework of this question in black theory has been preoccupied with a binary opposition between black texts and white readers, thus causing a gap, a silence, in the theorization of interpretive authority across color boundaries. Racial difference has been constructed as a duality of black and white, and the critical effort has to some extent replicated the fixity of racial division rather than taking into consideration the presence of a range of positions from which the black text can be interpreted, thus minimizing/obliterating the presence of other identities and locations. This has in effect excluded as nonexistent all but those who are either self-evidently "black" or "white." In the interpretation of black texts the black reader has often been assumed to be an insider, hence privileged. The white reader is implicated in the history of subjugation, hence involved. Where, then, is the "brown" situated? How does the postcolonial other relate to the racial other?

The question "Who is best situated to read the 'black' authored texts?" perhaps rests on the assumption that there is a clear, unambiguous agreement about the nature of "blackness." There is evidently no consensus on the "essential" or "constructed" nature of blackness, which, like all identities, includes a range of differences within it. Yet the question already posed regarding the relationship between race and transmission of literary meaning is no mere tautology. It is a concern that has been pervasive in the development of African American writing in multiple ways. The question of a valid interpretation of black literature is crucially linked to how the concepts of "blackness" and "race" are understood. If blackness is seen as residing in the pigmentation of the skin, biologically determined, then a certain advantage could be seen as lying in the color of the critic as well. If, on the other hand, blackness is seen as a sociopolitical category and a black text as a linguistic construct, then being born black carries no inherent value as a reader of black texts. Such a constructed view of blackness leaves the field open to negotiations across the color line. Further, if race is understood not in terms of essential identities but as the operation of modes of domination and oppression, then the colonial and racial subjects can have access to shared lines of communication as the others.

As racial and postcolonial subjects, one of the major insights black and brown identities share is that the process of the definition of identity and subjectivity is crucially marked by the dialectics of the "self" and the "other" and that subject positions are constructed through an interplay of subjectivity and objecthood. Both postcolonial and African American theories face a challenge to constantly redefine their subjectivities not only against the other but also in terms of the hybridity within themselves. Hence, as a brown reader of black texts, what is foregrounded for me is the dialectics and the process of the definition of subjectivity that I read in the text and in which neither the other is unproblematically the other nor is the self, howsoever constructed, unambiguously the self. It is this dialectics between the subjectivity of the postcolonial reader and the subjectivity of the ethnic text that can be generative of new meanings.

This essay demonstrates that, while a constructed, dialectical view of identity has been inherent in the theoretical understanding of black subjectivity, the discourse about the identity of the "black critic" has not always benefited from these insights because it has remained locked in a monolithic racial dyad of black versus white. Consequently, theoretical perspectives on the question of interpretive authenticity have tended to invest authority in the black critic as a given category rather than postulating seriously about the "critic of black literature." Radical and insightful advances in African American theory toward understanding the nature of identity and of the literary text have often been arrested by rather conservative and essentialistic responses by black critics that betray a need to retain control of the discipline within the black community. While this may be strategically justified in the context of historical and continued racism, there is perhaps nothing to be gained by excluding those whose histories and current positions reflect similar struggles with power equations with the dominant cultures. The great promise shown by black theory in breaking out of the stereotypes has been subverted in the real domain of scholarship by the critics falling back on the white/black binary structure that gives a privileged position to blacks, is suspicious of whites, and is oblivious of all other identities. In the following section I examine some of the defining elements in the development of the idea of the black critic and the struggle for interpretive authority in black studies. This is done from a deliberately "outside" point of view with the vested interest of discovering the spaces, or quite frequently the lack thereof, where I, as a nonblack, nonwhite person may situate myself in a meaningful and acknowledged relationship with the body of black literature. The final section goes on to highlight the complexity of my identity in terms of location and argues for critical cross-cultural endeavors between black and postcolonial theories on the basis of the non-essentialistic, pluralistic views of identity within both these groups.

Certain structures clearly exclude me in the very terms of their theorization, such as those that emphasize biological or sociological essentialism in a binary structure and, further, do not see any viability of cross-cultural transactions. The black aesthetic theory in the 1960s assumed the existence of an "irreconcilable conflict between the black writer and the white critic" and vested the authority for the interpretation of black texts in the hands of black critics (Fuller 7). Hoyt Fuller, in "Towards a Black Aesthetic," warned black critics that the "white readers and white critics cannot be expected to recognize and to empathize with the subtleties and significance of black style and technique." He therefore entrusts to the black critic the "responsibility of rebutting the white critics and of putting things in the proper perspective." The specific task of the black critic was to "isolate and evaluate the artistic work of black people which reflect the special character and imperatives of black experience" (Fuller 11). The sociological context of the division between black and white preempted the black aesthetic theoretician from seriously interrogating the possibility of negotiations across the racial difference of which color was the definite manifestation. Interpretive authority clearly lay in the hands of the black critic.

This fixity of racial division and critical authenticity was not, however, always the norm, and some theoreticians did allow space for what Houston Baker calls "earned participation" (Baker and Redmond 3). For Larry Neal critical competence in evaluating African American works did not lie in the pigmentation of the skin but was to be gained by academic endeavor into the literary and cultural conditions of the works of art. Neal does not ask black critics to reject the readings of white critics but, rather, encourages them to provide leadership and guidance to them. "Instead of having the white critic get out of his area, the black critic is supposed to take upon himself the job of writing strong criticism and establishing the pace" (Rowell 23). Neal admits that the critical competence of the critic does not lie in the race or the color of the critic but is something that can be acquired. This represented a less deterministic view of racial identity and a possibility of negotiation across the color line academically through research and reading. Unlike Fuller, Neal is opening the field to interpretive mobility, but, like Fuller, he is also tactically retaining the privilege of the authority of experience.

From the other side of the fence Eric Bentley, a white critic, also puts the question of cross-cultural pursuit in terms that invite interpretive mobility. In an interesting essay entitled "Must I Side with Blacks or Whites?" Bentley praises Amiri Baraka's *Slave Ship* as among the strongest pieces of theater he had seen (138–142). Analyzing the play's effect on him in terms of its race message, he asks: "What is the White theatregoer to do? Stay away from Jones' play? Play at being Black? Enjoy being put down by such a fanatic down-putter?" All these alternatives Bentley finds ineffective with regard to Baraka's play. Bentley resolves the dilemma of siding with blacks or whites by de-essentializing identity and turning race into a metaphor and the struggle of blacks into "an image of all such struggles" that creates space within Baraka's play for other communities. Referring to his response to *Slave Ship*, he says: "I did identify myself with the Blacks but for me they weren't necessarily black. They were yellow, and from Vietnam. They were red, and from Manhattan. They were white-skinned and black with the coal-dust like the miners of Lancashire, England, where I come from" (Bentley 141). Bentley thus appropriates the black space for himself and for other "races" across the globe by defining *blackness* as an experience that can be shared.

Without wanting deliberately to misunderstand Bentley's insightful remark here, one would wish to ask if the mere fact of oppression of any kind would serve as the common denominator for the transmission of meaning? Do arguments such as authenticity and specificity of experience count? Bentley's rather easy conflation of the various groups with vastly different historical, social, and political experiences is theoretically open to question, particularly in the context of Baraka's play with the passage on the slave ship at its center. Bentley's claim that it is not the black critic who would be privileged to interpret *The Slave* but all those nationalities and peoples who have been oppressed and have struggled is liberating for the play as well as the audience. My discomfort with this position, however, lies in that it rests on a minimalist approach to shared experiences of oppression and marginalization, without taking into consideration the specificity of any particular group. What did open up the field of cross-ethnic communication in black theory was not the blurring of differences but a proliferation of differences within black identity that came to be seen as non-essentialistic and constructed by multiple spatiotemporal factors. The exploration of the plurality of the black identity, just as of the gendered and postcolonial identities, reconstitutes the field in such a way that correspondences and interventions can take place without the need to undermine individual histories and circumstances. The recognition of differences also disables the binary structure by bringing in a multiplicity of positions. Bentley's response reflects the ground reality in which readers from diverse cultures would read and make sense of the black texts without being trapped in essentialistic, color-coded reactions. What was, and perhaps is, needed is a theoretical conceptualization that would accommodate the various identities without erasing or minimizing the precious histories that they carry. What is important for me, for instance, is that I understand the black text *from* my position as a postcolonial reader in a specific place and time.

Contemporary African American criticism has made radical advances in theorizing the issues of identity in terms of its differences and specificities. Critics such as Henry Louis Gates Jr., Houston Baker, and Michael Awkward and feminist theorists such as Barbara Christian, Deborah McDowell, and Valerie Smith, among others, have in various ways redefined the identities of the readers and the nature of the text. They have been concerned with the need to study the formal workings of the text in order to go beyond reflexive responses and distinguish the personal and social experiences of being black from the language that defines a black text. There has also been a significant shift in African American studies from seeing blackness as a biological category to figuring its constructedness in sociopolitical and linguistic forms. Henry Louis Gates Jr. has engaged with the poststructuralist theory in African American study in terms of revising and expanding the notions of blackness and race in an attempt to diffuse their essentialist connotations. In "Writing, 'Race,' and the Difference It Makes" (1985), reprinted in *Loose Canons,* he observes that race, in the absence of any basis in biology, is best understood as "a trope of ultimate, irreducible differences between cultures" (Gates 49). He has vigorously pursued the concern to shift attention away from blackness as a sociological and biological experience to its literary, metaphorical construction and to replace "my experience as an Afroamerican" with "the act of language that defines a black text" (Gates, *Loose Canons* 79). He has also extensively investigated the relation of the black interpretive and critical practices to the Western postmodern theories. This has far-reaching implications for de-essentializing the color of the critic of black literature, and, commenting on this, Elaine Showalter articulates the broadening of the field made possible by the theoretical shift: "the black critic and the critic of black literature have been joined by the Third World critic and the critic of the Third World literature" (356–357).

In practice, however, this theoretical promise of egalitarianism expressed in Showalter's words has not often been realized, and the authority of criticism has remained monopolized and color-centric for various emotional and tactical reasons. Even in Gates's work, for example, there are traces of tension between representing blackness as accessible to critics of all shades and a certain privileging of the biological and sociological blackness as innately more authentic. His essay "Talking Black: Critical Signs of the Times" (1988), also included in *Loose Canons*, serves to illustrate my point here. The essay examines the relationship of the black critic to white theory and the black writer to white tradition. He emphasizes the need to read the black text both in its black and white matrices. "Race" he says, "is a text (an array of discursive practices), not an essence." Race and the black text, according to Gates, need to be "read with painstaking care and suspicion." It is this construction of blackness and race as text that allows Gates to argue that the tools of Western critical theories can enable the critic of black literature to reveal the complex workings of the black text. The black body of the writer and the critic is distinctly dissociated from the body of the text, and he calls for the necessity of creating "distance between the reader and texts in order to go beyond reflexive responses and achieve critical insight" (Gates 79).

As the essay progresses, however, a new voice begins to resound stridently and without warning. Protesting the attribution of naïveté to black critics, Gates begins to evoke a community of critics, represented here by *we*, an in-group bound by unseen forces. "We are the keepers of the black literary tradition. No matter what theories we embrace, we have more in common with each other than we do with any other critic of any other literature. We write for each other, and for our own contemporary writers. This relationship is a critical trust" (80). Who are "we" here, and what is the commonality? It is very hard to resist the connotations of an innate connection based on the facts of biology. The lines brook no openness, no crossovers, privileging the black critic over the more loosely construed "critic of black literature." Arguing for nonessentialist understandings of the black text, black critic, and black identity, Gates suddenly lapses into a polemical argument that assumes an in-group of black critics bound by unchallenged connections of birth and biology.

This politics of theoretical inclusion and practical exclusion belies and frustrates the advances made in African American theory toward truly meaningful exchanges across colors, cultures, nations, and ethnicities. The gap between theory and practice is particularly jarring in the case of critics who have shown exceptional sensitivity and acumen in redefining racial and gendered identities and thus expanding theoretically the scope and boundaries of critical enterprises. At the cost of some elaboration I trace here the conservative subtext beneath the liberating theory in Michael Awkward's deeply engaging book *Negotiating Difference: Race, Gender, and the Politics of Positionality.* Awkward, in *Negotiating Difference*, is concerned with the many aspects of crossovers and boundary crossings across racial and gender differences. Rejecting the "fictions of critical objectivity that marred previous interpretive regimes," he attempts to study "interpretive movement across putatively fixed biological, cultural, or ideological lines" (4). He calls our attention to an extremely important aspect of the boundaries by suggesting that the borders could be seen as putative rather than fixed and that there is need for negotiation not only between blacks and others but also within the African American cultural spaces across various figurations of blackness. Even as he acknowledges the constructed, partly fictive nature of racial, gendered, and other identities, he also points out that it is merely a "utopian fantasy that the essential meanings of race can be transcended in America" (3). Having made the nuances of the problem explicit, Awkward addresses the question of who has the authority and authenticity of the representation and interpretation of the black text. The answers, he suggests, might range from the view that the experience of a group belongs to the native, indigenous members, to a notion that "cultural forms should be utilized by people from every conceivable location who take an interest in them." Rejecting the argument that "location is destiny" and that interpretive border crossing is doomed to failure, Awkward says:

> What insiders and outsiders, artists and scholars alike, must attend to in discussing this matter is the fact that complex cultural forms are not available to anyone simply by virtue of geographical location, gendered or racial situation, sexual orientation, or other putative markings of experience. . . . What critics of the American borders especially cannot lose sight of is that regardless of our origins, neither we nor artists whose work we examine exist as reflections of untainted "whiteness," "blackness," "asianness," "maleness," "gaiety," or "femaleness." (14)

Of interest to me in this argument are a premise, a conclusion, and an absence/silence. The premise concerns the basis on which Awkward separates a white critic from a black critic: the distinction here is not an essentialist one and is based by Awkward on the domination-oppression divide. As is evident, the shift in the terms of definition has far-reaching implications for liberating the discourse from the black/white dyad and acknowledging identities in multiple contexts. The use of the domination/oppression framework is particularly amenable to linking the fields of race and postcolonial studies. But this premise is completely erased in Awkward's conclusion, in which he lapses back into the binary and sociological argument that "for the foreseeable future at least, Afro-American literary scholars would do well to maintain a degree of skepticism" about "even the most apparently self-conscious and self-referential white investigation" (Awkward, *Negotiating* 91). The silence in Awkward's thesis is regarding all other identities. Not only is the field of criticism not thrown open to all identities irrespective of birth; even the premise on which the difference between white and black is constructed in his account and the permeability of the boundary between the two are not sustained through the argument. If difference is constituted as relations of dominance and oppression or marginalization, then, by extension, one can postulate a possibility of constructing privileged readers across color boundaries. Given this premise, it is disappointing that Awkward does not theorize about the possibility of developing perspectives whereby conditions of marginality, plurality, and perceived otherness have possibilities of linkages. The essay remains locked in a black and white logic, thus excluding the entire range of other identities, even when the basis of distinction is not biological but sociopolitical, which includes categories such as class and ethnicities that replicate across nations and cultures.

Valuable perspectives on these issues have also emerged from black feminist criticism, which from the beginning has had to define itself in multiple contexts taking into consideration the factors of race, gender, and class. It is evident that neither the binarism of male/female nor of black/white racial difference could serve as useful models in the black women's figurations of their identity. In exploring their subjectivity, black feminist critics have therefore foregrounded the ideas of multiplicity and differences within their selves. In "The Race for Theory" Christian aligns the black woman in the United States with women of color in the Third World, arguing that the multiplicity calls for caution in abstract theorizing. But, again, such problematization of the subject position in black women's writing has not always and naturally led to liberalizing of the discipline itself or the position of the reader-critic. Deborah E. McDowell, in her essay "New Directions in Black Feminist Criticism" (1980), defines the term *black feminist criticism* as referring to "Black female critics who analyze the works of Black female writers from a feminist or political perspective" (191). McDowell does pose a question about the viability of black feminist criticism remaining a separatist enterprise and insists on the need for white feminism to become more accountable to black and Third World women but does not integrate these ideas in her discussion of black feminist theory. Deliberating on the agenda for this criticism, she advocates a contextual as well as a rigorously textual approach. If the constitutive terms of reference of black feminist criticism are contextual (the critic's knowledge of African American history and culture) and textual (a study of "thematic, stylistic, and linguistic" structures of works by black women writers), it follows that the discipline could be practiced by people other than black women.

This is the direction McDowell's answer takes when nearly ten years later, in 1989, she poses the question again in her essay "Boundaries: Or Distant Relations and Close Kin": "*What* is black feminist criticism and *who* does it?" (52). In her answer the black woman is still very much there, but there is less certainty about exclusions. Admitting that "it is widely assumed that a black feminist critic is an Afro-American *woman*," she says that the premise stands challenged in the presence of perceptive contributions in the field of black feminist criticism by black men such as Henry Gates, white women such as Barbara Johnson, and white men such as Robert Hemenway (McDowell, "Boundaries" 52). She defines the relationship of black women with the other categories interactively: "As black women, we can develop and practice our critical approaches interactively, dialogically, just as we have lived / are living our lives" (54). Valerie Smith, in her essay "Black Feminist Theory and the Representation of the 'Other,'" argues for a similar distancing between the biological and literary critical representations of black womanhood. She says that it is not her intention to reclaim the black feminist project from those who are not black women because "to do so would be to define the field too narrowly, emphasizing unduly the implications of a shared experience between 'black women as critics and black women as writers who represent black women's reality'" (Smith 39). These are valuable insights and promising directions, but the groundbreaking conceptual frameworks offered by the theorists need to be matched by acts of critical endeavor across boundaries.

The point of the disquisition presented here is not only to argue that black theory has not concerned itself very much with nonblack, nonwhite critical positions but also, equally important, to demonstrate that this has been so in spite of the fact that the theoretical developments in African American theory in the last four decades or so are among the strongest arguments for the opening up of the field to interpretive mobility. Black theory has pioneered not only issues of hybridity, difference, and constructedness of identity but also contributed significantly toward articulating a concern with the need to retain a kind of strategic essentialism, an authority of experience of specific ethnic groups. This critical tension that is produced by theorizing racial and ethnic identity in ways that deconstruct and then reconstruct them allows the field to remain sensitive to the complexities of real-life experiences. The argument of this essay has been that, having liberated the discourse into dimensions of plurality and multiplicity, black theory has squandered some of its precious insights by lapsing back into binary structures.

How is the work of a nonblack, nonwhite scholar living in or outside the United States and working on African American and other ethnic literatures to be defined and labeled, and what value is to be assigned to her work? Rephrased in personal terms, the question posed at the beginning of this essay, "How does the postcolonial 'other' relate to the racial 'other'?" can also be asked as "How do I, an Indian, woman reader, read the black texts separated from me by multiple boundaries of nation, culture, color, and other factors?" The difference is significant, and there is an inevitable need to retain a self-reflexive awareness of one's identity as defined by one's location. But location again is a site marked by innumerable borders and bridges. More specifically, as an Indian, middle-class woman, educated and trained in the disciplines of English and American literature and now with access to the Internet and the World Wide Web, my location too is a complex site, partaking of many of the same ambiguities and conflicts that mark the various other ethnic identities. The negotiations with my own and others' cultures from such a position are also conducted within the structure of power/powerlessness, desire/denial, subjectivity/objecthood, marginalization, historical sense of displacement, and so on, frameworks that are operative in the fields of both race/ethnic and postcolonial studies. Whether it is DuBois's double consciousness, Ralph Ellison's invisibility, or Adrienne Kennedy's ambiguity about her relations with the white world, her fascination and frustration—all create patterns of both similarity and difference in my sense of selfhood and my ambivalent relationship with the white Western culture.

It is important to remember that the postcolonial reader, like all other subject positions, cannot be essentialized, as she has tended to be in terms of Bhabha's diasporic, migrant identities. The question about the connections between race/ethnic studies in the United States and postcolonial criticism is addressed by Amritjit Singh and Peter Schmidt in their book, *Postcolonial Theory and the United States: Race, Ethnicity, and Literature*. In their introduction, entitled "On the Borders between U.S. Studies and Postcolonial Theory," Singh and Schmidt observe that postcolonial studies and U.S. ethnic studies have interacted in a number of complex ways in the last decades and they mention "three (of many) instances of such cross-fertilization—transnationalism, feminism, and whiteness studies" (30). What interests me here is the issue of the dynamics of identity construction, which is briefly hinted at by the writers under the rubric of transnationalism, in which they talk about significant exchange of ideas "especially in the area of how exilic or diasporic consciousness poses a challenge to traditional nation-state narratives of identity and majority/minority dichotomies" (Singh and Schmidt 30). While agreeing entirely with their claims, I would wish to add that the modes of identity construction for non-exilic individuals and groups in the postcolonial context are also equally defined by hybridity and a certain degree of internationalism, if not transnationalism. Can the native, literally the one who did not migrate or go into exile, be postcolonial? Presumably, Bhabha's defining terms for the postcolonial, "diaspora and displacement," are to be taken metaphorically.[1] The position of the postcolonial reader, exilic or otherwise, of racial/ethnic texts is therefore marked by reflexivity regarding subject/object constructions.

To conclude the main argument of this essay, a simultaneous acceptance of the permeable nature of racial and ethnic boundaries in terms of the subject positions of both the literary text and the reader/critic is a crucial aspect of cross-cultural transactions among ethnic literatures. The theory of colored identity and the praxis of the critic position, however, as this essay has attempted to demonstrate, have not always kept pace with the insights gained in the context of subject positions. African American critical theory appears a little solipsistic in not being cognizant of other such critical perspectives and locations from which enriching reading can emerge. In its concern with authentic "black" readings and its skepticism for "white" readings, it ignores the possibilities of complex "brown" readings by critics located at crucial points of intersection of white and black experiences and by those who have insights into the power structures from both perspectives of dominance and repression in their own situations. Read from these positions, black texts and critical concerns can acquire new ramifications and larger contexts by enabling the experiences in one context to reverberate in others' contexts. The argument here is not one of basing insights on a minimalist approach without taking into consideration the specificities of identities and locations. On the contrary, it is the specificity, the "authority of experience," that belongs to every individual and collective identity that makes the venture across borders significant and rewarding.

## NOTE

1. I discuss this question of the postcoloniality of the native in another essay, "Patriotic Past." To quote from it, "For Bhabha, it is the hybrid, the transnational rather than the national that is the realm of the postcolonial. The inflexion that Bhabha's argument takes is apparent from his very well known statement: 'it is from those who have suffered the sentence of history—subjugation, domination, diaspora and displacement—that we learn our most enduring lessons for living and thinking' [Bhabha 6]. The shift from subjugation and domination to diaspora and displacement puts the burden of postcolonial condition on the shoulders of the displaced and the exiled. Thus it again pushes into oblivion those who stayed back, either because they could not leave or did not wish to do so" (315). In "Patriotic Past" I go on to argue, taking the example of Ngugi and Mugo's *Trial of Dedan Kimathi*, that the native is not necessarily an essentialist figure, seeking a simplistic, aboriginal condition, and that this identity is also constructed out of multiple elements on the axis of, if not geography, certainly history.

# Between Rome, Harlem, and Harlan

ALESSANDRO PORTELLI

A few years ago I had the opportunity to see a video interview with Cornell West, in which, among other things, he discussed some aspects of Antonio Gramsci's political thought. Cornell West is an African American philosopher; Antonio Gramsci was an Italian political leader and theorist. They belong to different countries, races, languages, and generations. From the interview it was clear that Cornell West had not done a systematic study of Antonio Gramsci's all-important Sardinian background, of the context of class struggle in Turin from which Gramsci emerged as a leader, of the somewhat Byzantine and yet dramatic debates that were going on around him in the international Communist movement. Indeed, apparently he had read Antonio Gramsci only in translation, did not speak his language, had not read most of the authors Gramsci discusses in his *Prison Notebooks*, and could have only a faint idea of all the resonances that vibrate in every word he wrote.

Yet what West had to say about Gramsci was absolutely correct, indeed brilliant, within the context of his argument. Indeed, as someone who tries to locate himself in the tradition of which Gramsci is such a significant part, I was proud that this Italian Communist made sense to a philosopher from another country and culture. By looking at Gramsci from a relatively alien point of view, West provided me with some insights on aspects of my own tradition I might otherwise have taken for granted. Culture and ideas travel away from their original ground and often come back enriched.

Back about thirty-five years I was a teenager, not interested in politics at all. One night I saw the news from Little Rock on television. It was a turning point: I realized that politics could be not just about power and money but also about ethics, equality, dignity, freedom, participation. Those African American children in Little Rock taught this message to the whole world (I am not satisfied with Ralph Ellison's claim that what they stood for was "American"—on the one hand, they were no more or no less American than the people who pelted them with rocks and insults; on the other hand, both stood for values and attitudes that are much wider than just the United States). Later, after I had spent a year as a foreign exchange student in an all-white (now mostly black) high school in Los Angeles, this teaching was reinforced by Martin Luther King and by the freedom movement (as well as by the peace movement and the folk revival). It was only later that I connected to the radical tradition of struggle in my own country and to our own working-class cultural tradition. I owe my first political and moral motivations to Little Rock, to Martin Luther King, to Fannie Lou Hamer.

It was only natural that in 1969—at a time when air travel was still expensive and there was yet no flow of tourism from Europe to the United States—I should invest much of my savings in another visit to the United States, in the effort to find out more about what was going on in the African American struggle and culture. It was during that month of January 1969, in New York, that I read *The Autobiography of Malcolm X*, and it turned me around—as did hearing and recording the activist music of Frederick Douglass Kirkpatrick, Mable Hillery, Matt Jones, and Barbara Dane.[1]

At the time nothing was farther from my mind than an academic career. I had finished my degree in law and was working in a government office. But I came back to an Italy in turmoil: the student movement was brewing, and the "hot autumn" of the working class was not far behind. Imbued with the political passion I had gained from my American experiences and the African American example, I couldn't help but join in. The humanities schools in the university, especially in Rome, were the hotbed of the movement. My office was across the street from the university, I could sneak out to classes and meetings, so I enrolled again—as an English studies major (one could not major in American studies at the time—this was to be one of my battles and small victories later on).

In Italy at the time there was a good deal of attention directed toward the African American movement. As is often the case with the approach to another country's politics and culture, some of it was stereotyped and superficial, though generous—can you imagine thousands of white kids, marching down the streets of downtown Rome screaming, "Black Power"? I thought it was ironic, but at least it showed a willingness to listen.

At least I had been there, had come back with a suitcase full of books, records, tapes, and poems. My mentor in the university, Professor Agostino Lombardo, was also aware of the need to learn and teach more about the African American tradition, so he encouraged me and gave me space. For the first time in any Italian university, our department started a two-year required seminar in African American literature. I am sure it was often superficial, paternalistic, sectarian. We were learning. But dozens of Italian students read dozens of African

American books, and a generation of scholars was shaped. How much of this was going on in American universities in 1969? When Carole Tarantelli and I edited and translated *Frederick Douglass's Life and Times*, it was out of print in the United States. I published my first essay on James Weldon Johnson in 1969 (it's been revised over and over since) and a book on passing in American literature in 1975.[2]

Another small victory of those years is that I had no difficulty persuading Agostino Lombardo to make *The Autobiography of Malcolm X* required reading for all courses in American literature. For a while I was *the* African American studies "expert" in the department, which grew to be an increasingly uncomfortable role for a number of reasons. One is that, thirty years later, my academic colleagues still have trouble recognizing that I also teach and write about other American authors (which is why I titled my recent collection of essays *Canoni americani*—American canons—to stress the fact that it has all the standard "canonical" names, from Melville to Pynchon, from Hawthorne to DeLillo, though it defeats some of this purpose by starting with Phillis Wheatley and Olaudah Equiano and closing with Spike Lee).[3] The other, of course, was that it became untenable to be the authority of something on which I knew I had no authority at all (although it must be observed that, given the demographics of Italy at the time, there were no black candidates for this role either).

There were a couple of epiphanies that made it all come clear. The first was when I realized that my students spoke about "whites" in the third person—as if they weren't white themselves, as if their color was just the default hue of the human race. An anecdote. After passing with flying colors an oral exam for which *Native Son* was required reading, a (white) girl student confided, "You know, Professor, I just got engaged to an African boy." I congratulated her, and she went on to tell me the classic "guess who's coming to dinner" narrative: she had introduced her fiancé to her parents, and it was great; they loved each other, and the future was bright. As he closed the door after the young man had left the house, her father turned around and said (remember: he was passing the test of "letting his daughter marry one"!), "Anyway: they're a race, and we're not."

At that time Italy had no significant African or non-European population; therefore, Italians tended not to define themselves in terms of color—they're a race; we're not.[4] Even the Italian colonialist discourse was not about blacks and whites but about blacks and Italians. This self-deceiving color blindness in turn fed into the persistent myth that there was no racism in Italy. Of course, Italy had the infamous anti-Jewish race laws from 1938 to 1944—but that was "the Fascists," somehow othered from the national identity (plus, there is no perceived color factor in anti-Semitism). The same applied to Italian racism and Italian crimes in Africa, not only explained away in terms of the Fascists but also taking place so far from Italian territory as to preserve our self-image from being touched (it took the Ethiopian flag among the belongings of the evicted Harlem couple in *Invisible Man* to make me aware of how those events were perceived in the rest of the world).

The other epiphany came from listening to the students talk about their reading of *The Autobiography of Malcolm X.* By the mid-1970s I realized that what had been urgently contemporary figures and issues to my generation—civil rights, the black liberation struggles, Malcom, Martin Luther King—were faint figures in a distant historical past for the new generations of students. They had not been taught anything about them in school (the teaching of history never went farther than 1922 in Italian schools at the time; besides, this is not Italian history anyway) and were not familiar with them other than as vague media icons. On the other hand, the political scene was dominated at the time by armed underground groups such as the Red Brigades and their practice of political murder. Thus, the meaning of Malcom X's discourse on revolutionary violence was lost in the context of contemporary terrorism, and he was flattened into a generic, ahistorical icon of good feelings.

At this point, rather than contribute to these misunderstandings and also pressed by an awareness of identity politics in African American studies (and by an excess of political correctness), I stopped teaching African American texts. It was not so much a matter of legitimacy as of adequacy: I just felt that I didn't know enough. It was a few years before I realized it was a mistake. In the first place, by not teaching black texts, I was giving my students a lily-white representation of American culture, and this was wrong. The second was that my silence did not prevent misunderstandings, misreadings, and stereotypes from being rampant in the media, in the press, in the minds of my students: I didn't know enough, but I knew a few things, and it was my responsibility at least to respond with what I had learned, pass on some information. In the third place the new immigration from Africa, the Middle East, and South America was creating in Italy a relatively multicultural society such as had never existed before, and we could learn a few things from the African American experience. For the first time I found myself in a situation described by several colleagues in the United States: a white teacher teaching black texts to a class that included one or two black students and trying to speak to the white students and to the black ones at the same time.

There is a scene in Woody Allen's *Bananas* in which he tells his girlfriend that he is majoring in black studies. She asks him what he expects to become, and he says, I don't know, perhaps I can become black. It's a spoof on the myth of cultural appropriation through academic learning—a variant of the idea that blackness, or any other identity, can be acquired by choice, rather than through lived experience. On the other hand, Woody Allen is Jewish and may also be alluding to this fact in this scene. There are significant similarities between African American and Jewish humor on the question of identity. One of the great stories of "passing," James Weldon Johnson's *The Autobiography of an Ex-Coloured Man*, has a number of passages that are identical to certain Jewish jokes or parables. The African American experience of passing, in fact, was preceded historically by that of Jewish *marranos*, who passed for Christians while holding on to their Jewishness. In Allen, Johnson, and in the traditional Jewish jokes, the story is both about how you cannot "become black" or "become a Jew" unless you have that kind of history behind you—and also about how, if you have that history, you cannot will yourself to stop being one.

The idea that you can wish an identity upon yourself is a recurring myth in an Italian mass culture that has not come to terms with its own whiteness. There are pop songs that say, "I wish my skin was black" (they ought to try being black after sunset in certain neighborhoods in Turin), pop groups of white musicians who call themselves "Negri per Caso," Accidentally Black. On the other hand: a rap group from Naples, Almegretta, had its first hit with a piece called "Hannibal's Children," based on a quote from one of Malcolm X's last speeches in which he suggests that the long Italian sojourn of Hannibal's African soldiers left a visible mark on the Italian people. Southern Italians were long stigmatized as being "African" by northern prejudice; as a response, they often took up this identity as a source of pride.

Rather than "becoming black," then, what the majority of my students were learning from African American texts was a recognition of their own whiteness. On the one hand, they were beginning to realize that we, too, are "colored," just as all other human beings, and that our color is not "normal" or "default" or "universal" but partial and specific (the passage in Olaudah Equiano in which he describes the first Europeans he meets as "horrible red faces" was very useful from this point of view). On the other hand, they also realized that, while they may see themselves as white in relation to some people, they may also be some other people's "blacks." (In the United States *Caucasian* is a euphemism for "white"; in Russia real Caucasians are derisively called "black" because of the color of their hair.) After all, Italians weren't always considered white in the United States, were we? In 1983 I was spending a semester in Lexington, Kentucky, and enrolled my six-year-old son in a public school. Kindly, the principal welcomed us and helped us fill out the forms—name, birth date, etc. When he came to "race," he looked up from the sheet and said, "White—I guess."

And then there were the one or two black students in the class. As opposed to the students of my U.S. colleagues, these were not African Americans but Africans, period. While the black students in the United States are U.S. citizens and born in the country, most of my black students were born abroad and were citizens of some other nation. As part of an oral history project on the historical memory of the student population, I interviewed some of them. Omar Nasser

Milhudi, part Italian and part Libyan, fully integrated in Roman society, saw his very integration as a sign of something wrong: "A black boy who speaks with a Rome accent is the sign of a violence, the sign of a course that has been deviated." "A course that has been deviated" is the literal meaning of the term *tropos*; the mother of all tropes is metaphor, and *metaphorein* means "being brought." Like Phillis Wheatley, Omar had been brought from Africa to Europe; both testified to the historical violence of colonialism and slavery and to the power and pain of syncretism and survival. The difference, of course, is that Omar can use Phillis Wheatley's precedent, while—as June Jordan says—she was the first.

Ribka Sibhatu, from Eritrea, was a refugee from war, had been in jail, spoke at least five languages, supported herself as a housekeeper for an old lady in Rome, and wrote stories and poems in her spare time. It was another epiphany. I recognized in Ribka the first stirrings of what, for lack of a better term, I was later to label as African Italian literature (though it also comes from the Middle East and South America): a literature written in Italian by multinational migrants, describing their experience of migration and their memory of their homeland. I found a publisher for Ribka's work (she went on to earn a Ph.D. degree and now works as an "intercultural mediator" for the city of Rome); with her help and that of some of her friends (and some of my white students) we founded *Caffè* (Coffee), a journal of migrant literature that I edited for a while.

African American texts were an important reference for these young people, yet they had to be *learned* just as any other text from any other culture. Beyond an emotional response to the fact of discrimination and racism, the fact that they were *African* did not give them any privileged access to the understanding of these *American* texts. In different ways, then, all of us were seeking, though African American texts a dialogue not with identity but with difference.

Difference is to me the key of all learning. With all respect due to native anthropology or identity politics, I come to an understanding of myself best of all through conversations with what I am not, through the way others' eyes look at me. Which is perhaps why the work of writers who are African Americans and women has generated for me the kind of self-scrutiny that the work of great writers who are Italian and white—even Calvino or Tabucchi—never could. None of these writers ever told me, "You can't trust a white schoolteacher." Which is who I am.

(On the other hand, when Toni Morrison generously came to speak to my class, my students and I pointed out to her a paradigm of liquid/solid metaphors in *Beloved* that she said she hadn't thought about and agreed was correct.)[5]

A couple of brief literary examples. Reading Frederick Douglass finally sent me back to a major Italian masterpiece, Primo Levi's *Se questo è un uomo*, his narrative and interpretation of the experience of Auschwitz. Both texts are an interrogation on what it means to be human ("is this a man?" is Levi's question), and both explore this theme, among other things, through animal imagery. This common ground, however, only brought into relief the differences. Douglass's animal imagery was mainly metonymical ("We were all ranked together at the valuation. Men and women, old and young, married and single, were ranked with horses, sheep, and swine. There were horses and men, cattle and women, pigs and children, all holding the same rank in the scale of being" [89–90]), while Levi's was based on metaphors and similes (to the other passengers on the train to Auschwitz, the deportees "are not *Menschen*, human beings, but beasts, swine") (*Il sommersi* 19). This is not just a difference in rhetorical devices: indeed, it helps us perceive a basic difference. Douglass's narrative is the story of how someone who was ranked as an animal discovers and creates his own humanity; Levi's is the story of how a human being begins to lose his own humanity. Douglass moves from "animal" to human; Levi from human to animal and thing. Metaphor, then, marks the awareness, the memory of having been human (Olaudah Equiano, born in Africa, also uses animal metaphors, not metonymies). In fact, after Douglass gains an awareness of his condition, he, too, replaces animal metonymies with animal metaphors: he is now in Levi's position, a human being whose humanity is endangered ("behold a man transformed into a brute!"). This distinction is reinforced by the fact that Douglass' imagery is one of familiar farm animals (sheep, cows), whereas Levi's is either generic ("beasts") or abstract (insects, parasites). When Douglass shifts from metonymy to metaphor, his animal references also change to the biblical and exotic (snake, tiger) and to the generic ("brutes"). Only in his final confrontation with Covey do metonymy and farm animals return (he is *with* the horses in the stable). Taken together, then, these two texts tell us different sides of the story of being human: both tell us how humanity can be lost, but Douglass also tells us how it can be gained and regained.

The other example is not from an African American author but from a Native American, Sherman Alexie, in *Indian Killer*. It also has to do with Woody Allen's joke about "becoming black"—in this case, "becoming an Indian." Alexie's metaphor is that of adoption: from captivity narratives to James Fenimore Cooper to contemporary "shamans," white people have been convinced that Indianness can be appropriated through an act of desire such as adoption. Now, in Italian academic terminology, when we include a text into the syllabus, we say that we "adopt" it. To me, then, Sherman Alexie's image was also a warning about what I was doing by "adopting" not Native or African American people but Native or African American texts. A part of Alexie's novel, in fact, places this in an academic environment. The Marxist professor (I have to admit that I am a Marxist professor of sorts, too) claims that, taking a line from Whitman, "every good story that belongs to Indians belongs to non-Indians, too" (the same applies to the land, I suppose); the Native protagonist (ironically named John Smith by the good white folks who adopted him) concludes, "let us have our own pain."[6]

I don't think this means white scholars have no right to read or even teach about those texts. It means, however, that they must not delude themselves that they are transparent. Just as John Smith does not become white because he is adopted by a white family and Natty Bumppo or Alexie's professor do not become Natives just by having Native tribes adopt them, the texts of the Native American or African American literary canon face white scholars with a resistance, a darkness, in which lies much of their meaning for them. The white scholar's task is to negotiate the boundaries of this darkness ("the outlines of a night," as Rebecca Harding Davis, writing as a middle-class man about a working-class man, puts it) and learn from it ("Life" 23).

It's the mistrust, it's the diffidence, it's the no-trespassing signs, in African American (or Native American) texts that reveal to me crucial aspects of who I am and where I stand. I resist the interpretations of Malcolm X that insist that in the end he was revising his attitudes to white people—not because to some extent he wasn't but because his greatest gift to us was that he never told us he loved us. No matter where he was headed, he would never have made us feel good about ourselves. I opened my book on figures of passing in American literature with Nikki Giovanni's poem in which she hopes no white person ever has cause to write about her and went on from there (I never wrote about her—yet I assumed hers was not an act of censorship but, rather, a warning to remember the difference always and teach it). One of the great moments in my oral history work was my first interview with an African American lady in Kentucky—a coal miner and Baptist preacher's wife—who told me that what she had inherited from her slave ancestors was that, "although no white person has done anything to me, yet because of what I know of others—I don't trust you. There's gon' always be a line." And then for over two hours her narrative was an eloquent illustration both of why she couldn't trust me (I thought I would learn a lot more by taking it personally!) and of why she wanted, needed, to talk to me across that inerasable line (or, as DuBois put it, from behind the veil). I was reminded that Richard Wright's Mary Dalton paid with her life (and Bigger's) for thinking she could cross that line. I am sure the reason this lady talked to me that way was that I never attempted to ask questions that would intrude upon her territory or attempt to lift the veil. I just sat there listening and learning.[7]

Oral history has taught me that an interview is basically a learning situation. Likewise, my attitude toward African American texts (or Jewish texts or women's writing or so-called postcolonial authors) is that I am not *studying* but *learning* from them and that my teaching is a sharing of what I am still in the process of learning. Learning from otherness means accepting that you will never possess it, that you will never know all. It means accepting a space of inaccessibility, a limit to our imperial will to know. Yet, because learning is not an all-or-nothing game, it also means that there are things that can be understood and shared, messages that cross the line and speak beyond identity boundaries. And even insights, like Cornell West's on Gramsci, that may be granted to those who are outside.

Early in March 2004 I had the opportunity to speak at a college in Nashik, Maharashtra, India. In the discussion period the first question was: "You are from Italy. Can you tell us about Gramsci?"

## NOTES

1. My 1969 tapes from New York and Washington were published as a long-playing record called *L'America della contestazione*; they were also the basis of a book, a collection of songs with a long introduction, called *Veleno di piombo sul muro*. My first published article, based on the poems I brought back with me from that voyage, was on "Cultura poetica afro-americana."
2. Much of the work of the early seminars on African American literature at the University of Rome resulted later in a book, *Saggi sulla cultura afroamericana*, of which I was the editor. Frederick Douglass's *Life and Times* was translated as *Autobiografia di uno schiavo*; his *Narrative* (first published in Italy in 1961) was reissued with my introduction as *Memorie di uno schiavo fuggiasco*. I also have sections on Douglass, Ellison, and Morrison in *The Text and the Voice*. On passing in American literature, see *Bianchi e neri*.
3. *Canoni americani* came out in 2004. It includes essays, to which I refer briefly in this essay on Wheatley, Equiano, Douglass (and Levi), James Weldon Johnson, Morrison, and Spike Lee. A shorter version of the Douglass-Levi essay also appeared as "Who Ain't a Slave?" The essays on Wheatley and Equiano were based on my introduction to a book of early African American texts that I edited with my students, *Libri parlanti*. Part of the essay on Equiano appeared as "Tropes of the Talking Book."
4. On Italian racial discourse, see "Su alcune forme," also delivered as a keynote presentation at the 1998 Council for African American Research Conference in Cagliari, Italy.
5. On the imagery in *Beloved*, see "Blood, Milk, and Ink" and "Padri e figlie." On Morrison and Wright (and Hurston, Chesnutt, and others), see *La linea del colore*.
6. The essays on Douglass and Levi and on Sherman Alexie are in *Canoni americani*.
7. The interview with the African American lady in Kentucky is discussed in a chapter in *The Battle of Valle Giulia*.

# The Stepsister and the Clan

## When the Native Teaches African American Literature

NGWARSUNGU CHIWENGO

In the past years multiculturalism and the teaching of race and minority literatures, and African American literature in particular, have been some of the most popular pedagogical topics. As minority literatures were deemed scientific disciplines and minority faculty joined the ranks of European faculty in higher education, questions about the universality and the essentialization of literatures arose. Are European scholars competent to teach minority literatures, and are minorities capable of teaching only literatures of people of color?

In an academic context where multiculturalism is synonymous with ethnicity and identities with minority writings, do insider perspectives enrich teachers' interpretations of literature? Numerous works—among them, Katherine J. Maryberry's *Teaching What You're Not* (1996), James A. Banks's *Multicultural Education, Transformative Knowledge, and Action*, Bonnie TuSmith and Maureen T. Reddy's *Race in the College Classroom* (2002), and Nellie Y. McKay's "Naming the Problem That Led to the Question 'Who Shall Teach African American Literature?' or, Are We Ready to Disband the Wheatley Court?" (1998)—have examined the role of race in higher education and the teaching of minority literatures. The majority of essays on the teaching of African American literature explore the relationship between power and knowledge, the positionality and textuality of the instructor, and the interactions between colored or black/white and male/female faculty and students. Very few articles have sought, however, to break the black/white bipolar discourse on the teaching of race. Yet there is need to examine how "twilight faculty" who teach African American literature through the interstices of racialized America may shed some light on the black/white dichotomized dialogue on the teaching of race, race and knowledge, and the production of meaning within black texts. If race is what lends legitimacy to the reading of a black text, do Africans, those stepbrothers and sisters, read and teach African American texts better than their white counterparts? Do they have a privileged position in this debate because of their understanding of racial oppression, their race, and their ability to engage in a black-centered reading? Or are they, like their European counterparts, also incapable of probing these texts with the needed integrity, sensitivity, and understanding of the African American experience and the pain encoded within the literary oeuvre?

Numerous African and African American songs and writings suggest that Africans and African Americans have a common ancestry despite a long parallel history. The dispersing of Africans around the world has not completely severed the ties of the diaspora from the mother continent. Our racial or/and common oppressions do not always translate, however, into harmonious, fraternal relationships. Indeed, our different historical and cultural experiences and our respective alienations, aptly analyzed by Frantz Fanon, have at times fostered, in our search for the recognition of our subjectivity, ambivalent love and hate relationships between Africans and African Americans. The South African writer Peter Abrahams thus writes in *Tell Freedom* (1954) that it is not until he read the Harlem Renaissance writers Jean Toomer, Claude Mckay, and the Panafricanist W.E.B. DuBois that he understood his South African Apartheid world and his beingness-in-the-world. Through African American literature, he writes, "I became a nationalist, a colour nationalist through the writings of men and women who had lived a world from me. To them I owe a great debt for crystallizing my vague yearnings to write and for showing me the long dream was attainable." While Abrahams lauds the commonality between the African American experience and that of a young man in Johannesburg, South Africa, he nonetheless contends that his family remained indifferent to his discovery of African American literature, since Harlem, or America, was a remote location across the Atlantic Ocean. "And in Coloured terminology," according to Abrahams, "Negroes were black people whom both whites and Coloreds called Natives in their polite moments" (*Tell Freedom* 197).

Likewise, the African American Richard Wright, in *Black Power*, seeks to map the distance between African and American blacks, albeit their common historical suffering. According to Wright, he might be black, but he is foremost American, culturally and historically. Despite the similarities he perceives between Ghanaians and African Americans, he adamantly projects cultural and racial differences onto the African body and the environment. The African may laugh like the African American and might be black, but their different shades of brownness tellingly bespeak racial differences. The African, for Wright, is the other, unfathomable, distant, and primal. Where Abrahams sees similarities, Wright sees differences. The perceptual divergence of these two writers raises interesting questions regarding the ability of the African teacher to teach African American literature. If our ideological perspectives, cultures, and identities determine our readings of black texts, can the text of the other be read accurately? Do people of color read African American literature like their white counterparts? What is entailed in teaching African American literature for an African, and what spatial position does she hold within the academic debate and American racial history?

These seminal questions about race, culture, and knowledge need to be addressed because racial and cultural positions are at the core of this academic debate. Knowledge and competence are predicated on racial and cultural positions. Is it so easy to place people in defined cultural and racial categories? What happens when the instructor occupies an ambiguous border position? How does a hybrid African who has spent half of her life, as I have, within both American and African cultures read and teach an African American text? Having been nurtured on American racist discourses and having shared the American experience, can my insider and outsider position at the border enable me to teach African American literature with the integrity of an African American teacher, or not? Can I convey the pain of racism and the African American experience while I socially look at this community from white middle-class and middle-class African cultural positions?

I have never thought that culture was an impediment since race did not determine one's mastery of knowledge. The idea that African Americans alone could teach African American literature never crossed my mind. If I thought of race at all, it was as a means to social exclusion and to maintaining one's social privilege. When Belgians sought to maintain their monopoly in English studies in the Democratic Republic of Congo, Congolese intellectuals were deemed incapable of becoming lecturers because their thick lips would hinder them from pronouncing accurately this Saxon language, distorted by the Belgians' very affected speech. This explains why the English department of the University of Lubumbashi only appointed its first Congolese assistant in the early 1970s. This exclusionary practice went against the very colonial assimilationist ideology that alleged that knowledge and culture, albeit white and grounded in Western epistemology, could be acquired with perseverance as the colonial term *évolué*—designating Westernized Congolese—implies. To be an *évolué* during the colonial era was to have the ability to assimilate knowledge and Western cultural practices. So, reading and apprehending Western and African American texts, according to this logic, is a matter of training and not of racial perception, even though it also implied cultural integration. Accordingly, the Congolese students to whom I taught African American literature in the summer of 2004 never questioned their and my competence to understand and interpret African American literature. On the contrary, they empathized and sighed over the misfortunes of Frederick Douglass and the Invisible Man and cried and agonized over Cinque's pain and need to be set free. What did they see in the films we screened and the African American literature they read if not a racial extension of themselves, geographically located across the ocean, and a mirror for their own identity construction and understanding of their place within globalization discourses?

Knowledge, as depicted in the works of both African and African Americans, does not have racial and cultural boundaries. In *Carte postale* the Congolese writer Zamenga Batukezanga rightly depicts the Congolese literally appropriating Western magic—knowledge—through the possession of missionary objects and hairs. Similarly, the Americans Frederick Douglass and Phillis Wheatley achieved humanness solely by stealthily learning to read and write like whites, since Western culture has historically inextricably linked humanness to a "neutral" European knowledge. Hence, in Gloria Naylor's *Mama Day* Reema's boy associates knowledge with Western academic practices—notebooks and a tape recorder. The young student, it is said, arrives on the island rattling about "ethnology," "unique speech patterns," "cultural preservation," and "whatever else he seemed to be getting so much pleasure out of while talking in his little gray machine" (*Mama Day* 7). Assuredly, my American Peace Corps professors at the University of Lubumbashi in the Democratic Republic of the Congo also interpreted African and African American literary texts from a Western perspective that posited the universality of literary aesthetics and cultural values. These American teachers presumed, like the anthropologist narrator of Laura Bohannan's "Shakespeare in the Bush," that cultural particularities and race did not determine the reading of African texts, since Prospero's tools sufficed to sound their meanings. Because Western knowledge is central to the formation of both African American and African writings and modern thought, black intellectuals and critics are taught, within the Western, patriarchal, educational system, to read and see their respective literatures and societies as whites. After all, scientific inquiry is foremost legitimated by Western scientific and cultural paradigms and theoretical approaches. Joy James contends in "The Academic Addict" that whites who indulge in these practices get "white time," in which they are sent to seminars on diversity for rehabilitation. On the other hand, blacks who refuse to inject themselves into "white supremacy" have "black time," in which they are "likely caged, to be pimped by guards, . . . and to be profiled . . . when . . . voting or teaching. It is commonly argued, another truism, that those so held deserve to be imprisoned. How then do the racially different (read deviant) survive addiction" (James 265)? Unfortunately, there is no means to survive abnormality or deviance—being or thinking differently—since, according to Lewis Gordon, normality is becoming the other, or white.

Even though the assumption has been that Western literature is neutral and nonracial, Western literature has always been racialized. Nowhere is this racialization more apparent than in the Congolese educational colonial textbook project. Charles A. Gallagher contends in "White Construction in the University" that whiteness has lost, in our contemporary society, its invisibility and transparency and that "whites are viewed as simultaneously being privileged by their skin color yet unable or unwilling to recognize the cultural and institutional conventions and practices that continue to normalize white invisibility" (302). Yet whiteness never was raceless and invisible, since Belgian colonial texts, proscribing the behavior of colonizers in their efforts to construct whiteness, belie this assumption. What is lost, perhaps, is the keen sense of privilege, authority, and the ethical, normalizing, righteousness of whiteness but certainly not whiteness itself.

Yet, when Bohannan's anthropologist narrator in "Shakespeare in the Bush" tests the theory of the universality of knowledge, it is obvious that cultural particularities modify the content and determine textual readings, for Shakespeare's *Hamlet* becomes a new narrative with different character motivations once the play is interpreted by the African elders. Likewise, Reema's boy's ethnological study on Willow Springs fails to capture, despite his relationship to the community, the meaning of "18 & 23" because he lacks the authentic field experience and cultural perspective enabling him to apprehend this communal reality. He decodes the experience of the Willow Springs inhabitants through Western paradigms and theories, and thus, as one of the Willow Springs's community members accounts in *Mama Day*, 18 & 23 becomes 81 & 32, the lines of longitude and latitude on which Willow Springs is geographically located. They were so dumb, says the narrator, that, according to Reema's boy, they had inverted the meaning:

> Not that he called it being dumb, mind you, called it "asserting our cultural identity," "inverting hostile social and political parameters." 'Cause, see, being we was brought here as slaves, we had no choice but to look at everything upside-down. And then being that we was isolated off here on this island, everybody else in the country went on learning good English and calling things what they really was—in the dictionary and all that—while we kept on calling things ass-backwards. . . .
>
> If the boy wanted to know what 18 & 23 meant, why didn't he just ask? When he was running around sticking that machine in everybody's face, we were sitting here—every one of us—and him being Reema's, we woulda have obliged him. (*Mama Day* 8)

Although the anecdote of Reema's boy posits the significance of experience or cultural particularity in the production of meaning, textual interpretation is not racial, nor are cultural and racial experiences nontranslatable. According to the narrator, all Reema's boy had to do to decode 18 & 23 was to ask, listen, and experience.

Reema's boy, as stated by the narrator of *Mama Day*, could have learned more about the Willow Springs community had he had the ability to ask. Yet he would have failed to question the community because, as Peter Abrahams writes in *The Coyaba Chronicles: Reflections on the Black Experience in the 20th Century*,

> to grow up educated into such an environment is to grow up mentally crippled. You are effectively separated from your own roots without having any real roots in the dominant occupying culture. You are the classic outsider. Not the man of two worlds or two cultures as portrayed by the historical romantics, but the man trapped between two worlds and comfortable in neither, accepted by neither. To break free of this situation you must either tear down the structures of domination and control or take them over and reshape them to your heart's desire. (128–129)

The Western discourse Reema's boy acquired in college does not, as Abrahams's Jake in *The View from Coyaba* contends, exclude the discourses of thinkers such as W.E.B. DuBois and Marcus Garvey, unless science and technology "were a sort of exclusive copyrighted Western European character and quality" (*View from Coyaba* 201). Still, as Nellie McKay rightly points out, these discourses minimize Phillis Wheatley's intellectual abilities and disregard the Indians' knowledge of the impending tornado storm in Zora Neale Hurston's *Their Eyes Were Watching God.*

The Enlightenment concept of reason may stipulate universality, as Abrahams claims in "The Conflict of Cultures in Africa," but the power relations undergirding exclusive Western epistemologies brand non-Western knowledge inconsequential. This ideologically laden concept, and dismissal of non-Westerners and their knowledge, is most apparent in Charles W. Chesnutt's "Baxter's Procrustes," a short story about literary criticism and how the cover of a book informs the club members' interpretation of the book content, which is nonexistent. A book, according to this short story, is valued monetarily not for its content, fabricated on the basis of the supposed personality of the author, but for its cover. Ironically, Chesnutt, the author, embodies the cover through his literary marginalization when his readership declines once his racial identity is revealed. The eponymous character of Ralph Ellison's *Invisible Man* equally discovers the marginalization of gender and race even within the all-embracing Communist socialist discourse and W. E. B. DuBois's faith in the "talented tenth" is extinguished by their invisibility. This lack of intellectual credibility explains why my American students have reacted negatively to the presence of black authors on American and World Literature syllabi and perceived these African American texts as repetitive onslaughts on the Western reader. Blacks' supposed lack of intellectuality also explains my own frustration with interpretations of the Congolese political experience elided by Western experts who master it from the comfort of their offices and solely through their readings of other Western texts reaffirming Congolese tribalism. Accordingly, textual pleasure, for some white students, is possible solely through the reading of classic literature within the dominant Western canon, non-Western writers failing, after all, to measure up to Western stylistics and intellectual depth. Who can thus blame the Jean Toomers, Peter Abrahams, and the Ralph Ellison's for desiring to be just writers? And does this not explain why minority faculties are generally recruited to teach themselves?

Race, as shown obviously in *Mama Day*, is not the determining factor in the teaching of black texts, whether African or African American; it is the legitimacy and power to name reality and to own knowledge that fuels these debates. In "The Language of African Literature" Ngugi wa Thiong'o contends that he had no ownership in the production of technology until he discovered the Gikuyu word for "missile." "This may in part explain why technology always appears to us as slightly external, their product and not ours. The word 'missile' used to hold an alien far-away sound until I recently learned its equivalent in Gikuyu, ngurukuki, and it made me apprehend it differently," he writes (442). In writing this very essay on language and African literature, Ngugi attempts to wrestle African knowledge and power from Western domination in a foreign language. This discursive move to master language and to redefine science witnesses to the authority of Western technology and languages, defined as the superior norms. The continually changing names of non-Western literatures from Third World to postcolonial, Anglophone, and so on, is also the same power struggle to contain or naturalize the latter by obliterating cultural and racial differences.

Western literature is similar to what Georges Bataille calls, when he discusses social structure in "The Psychological Structure of Fascism," the homogeneous state that "fixes and constitutes as the rule" (139). African American and African literatures are the heterogeneous element in academia that "break the laws of social homogeneity." Within the general academic context Western literature is considered seminal and neutral. Conversely, African American literature is that other abject literature, the structure of knowledge, for a "*homogeneous* reality," according to Bataille, is "that of science," whereas "the knowledge of a *heterogeneous* reality as such is to be found in the mystical thinking of primitives and in dreams: it is identical to the structure of the unconscious" (143). Both African and African American literatures are excluded from homogeneous reality, both being irrational writings.

Despite the emergence of multiculturalism and anthologies such as *The Heath Anthology of American Literature* and the recent success in marketing books on black topics, African American literature continues to be a minor literature, relegated to obscure categories of ethnicity, identities, and multiculturalism. Despite its visibility in publications and in university curricula, it is not an equal voice among numerous other voices; it is always that other literature, marked by identity politics. It is, indeed, a voice that engages in the national dialogue with other minority voices, but it remains ethnic, notwithstanding the attempts of authors such as Toni Morrison who seek to challenge the racial neutrality or universalism of Euro-American literature. The value of this identity literature does not reside in its artistic form but in its expression of identity, and, hence, it is dismissable. After all, should ideological and political tracts be considered great literary works? Moreover, it is a literature that cannot be easily assimilated when, by its very nature, it seeks to deconstruct Euro-Western meta-narratives and cultural and literary values. And this, when the premise of some professors within academia is that just such Euro-Western meta-narratives are the foundation of the majority of non-Western literatures. To master Western literature is thus to master non-Western writings. Why give these literatures a preponderant role when knowledge of the Western tradition suffices and provides tools with which to decode these texts? African American literature—the heterogeneous element within the academic market, to use Georges Bataille's words—is difficult to assimilate because

> the object of science is to establish the *homogeneity* of the phenomena; that is, in a sense, one of the eminent functions of homogeneity. Thus, the heterogeneous elements excluded from the latter are excluded as well from the field of scientific considerations: as a rule, science cannot know *heterogeneous* elements as such. Compelled to note the existence of irreducible facts—of a nature as incompatible with its own homogeneity as are, for example, born criminals with the social order—*science finds itself deprived of any functional satisfaction* (exploited in the same manner as a laborer in a capitalist factory, used without sharing in its profits). Indeed, science is not an abstract entity: it is constantly reducible to a group of men living the aspirations inherent to the scientific process. (141)

For Euro-American literature—the homogeneous state that "fixes and constitutes the law" (Bataille 139)—African American literature, the heterogeneous element in academia that "breaks the laws of social homogeneity," is not an integral part of the structure of knowledge but that foster child that remains forever embedded in mythical thinking and dreams and, hence, easy (143). And, when its aesthetic qualities are overwhelming, it is the foster child of William Faulkner and other Western authors.

Despite the efforts of critics such as Henry Louis Gates Jr. who seek to liberate African American literature, mainstream literature continues to shape the orientation of African American scholarship. Surveying the literary and critical history of African American literature in *Figures in Black: Words, Signs, and the "Racial Self,"* Gates claims that the tradition emerged as a response to eighteenth- and nineteenth-century assumptions that blacks are incapable of creating a literature. Additionally, African American literary criticism has focused, Gates aptly demonstrates, on the ideological nature of African American literature (Addison Gayle) and thematic approaches privileging the discussion of blackness. In this critical work, Gates advocates the need to consider African American literature as an independent system and not just a Western form delineating a black experience. He also advocates the necessity of exploring the "black medium" for principles of criticism. But can the black critic develop a theory without "cutting monkeyshines, or can signifying monkeys decode the signs that comprise our black structures of literature?" he wonders (47). Gates contends that his own critical approach is one of repetition with a difference. He proposes his signifying theory—"a uniquely black rhetorical concept, entirely textual or linguistic, by which a statement or figure repeats, or tropes, or reverses the first" (49)—that he considers black specific as a reading technique. Yet some scholars question the racial specificity of the figure because it is simply construed as a parody of the Western concept of connotation and intertextuality. Paradoxically, even as Gates wills the affirmation of black texts, he once again validates Western knowledge and theory in *Black Theory and Literary Theory*. In its theorization of black literature *Black Theory* attempts to legitimate and elevate the study of black texts to that of Western texts through the critic's utilization of poststructuralist theories.

So, if both African and African American literatures are contestatory, or heterogeneous, why shouldn't the African literary critic be capable of interpreting African literature? The genesis of African literature, just like that of African American literature, is the result of Western desires to establish the abilities of Africans to write literature, albeit inferior, like René Maran's *Batouala*. And, if blackness is a central element in the interpretation and analysis of black texts, why shouldn't the African be capable of interpreting African American literature? The African American critic Houston Baker questions the ability of Africans to judge African American literature. He contends in *Long Black Song: Essays in Black American Literature and Culture* that "black folklore and the black American literary tradition that grew out of it reflect a culture that is distinctive both of white American and African culture, and therefore neither can provide valid standards by which black American folklore and literature may be judged" (qtd. in *Figures in Black* 35–36). According to Baker, an insider alone can understand this mestizo culture. If insiderness entails familiarity and if the African American critic has the vantage point of interpreting African American literature from an insider/outsider perspective, cannot an African critic such as I, who shares a common history of oppression and racism, have just as good an understanding of African American literature if she were to use African American paradigms and concepts?

Consequently, can an African teach African American literature? Can an African have the perspective of an outsider and yet capture the complexity and subtleties of language evoking the collective African American experience? Can the African see beyond Joel Chandler Harris's "Free Joe and the Rest of the World"'s perception of the African American as a lazy shiftless individual, especially when American society distinguishes the African from the African American? If the African American accepts the rhetoric of the browning of America that we were served during the 2004 presidential campaign, can the "pure" African feel, convey, express the distinctive "brownness" of the text while attending to the aesthetics of the literary work? If African Americans are culturally and racially estranged from the continent as the result of American miscegenation and feel that their ontological selves are more Western than African, can a supposedly "pure" African still understand and interpret the black experience?

Despite his desire to sever himself from the African, in *Black Power* Richard Wright reached the conclusion that, as long as Africans continued to be vilified and oppressed, the African American would be marginalized within Western society. Even though he was biracial, he was always impelled to acknowledge the blackness within; he was an American subject but an object nonetheless. Wright desires and yearns to cease being the heterogeneous, abject element within his society, but blackness is difficult to assimilate. While he assumes that his body is the very site of racial difference and demonstrates his kinship to Western Logos, Wright misreads Africa not because of his cultural and racial difference but because of his refusal to see and listen. Willing to create a Western African American essence, Wright fails "to perceive similarities between Africans and African Americans when he recognizes certain African American gestures and movements in the African women's 'snake-like, shuffling dance'" (*Black Power* 37). His inability to see and read Africa correctly is dictated by his desire to disclaim Africa.

Interestingly, Wright's perception of brownness in Africa fails to acknowledge that Africa, like the United States, is a dynamic society that has its share of diverse people and "brown" people because his reading is constricted by the Western ethnological grid he uses that perpetually fixes the continent in a primal context. So, despite this browning of America, the African teacher is still capable of understanding the condition of heterogeneity. Even the reluctant Wright is forced to acknowledge the similarities between the gestures of Africans and those of African Americans. After all, browning (mental, cultural, and physical) is not the sole privilege of African Americans. Try as he did, Wright discovered the impossibility of freeing himself from Africa, despite the geographical distance and cultural differences. Inextricably and arbitrarily ontologically also labeled black despite his brownness, Wright realizes that, if both the African and the African American are to be selves freed from stereotypes and oppression, they must of necessity walk into the twentieth century. This march, according to Wright, can materialize only by placing African personality at the center and reorganizing that personality (Chiwengo 44).

Wright's refusal to identify with the African is the result of years of Western misrepresentation and dehumanization of the African. While the African American has known her own dehumanization in the United States, the African is still lower on the evolutionary ladder. African anecdotes about what Westerners and African Americans wish to know about Africa generally reek with racism. This racism rears its head at the very border, marking the end of one world and the beginning of the next. Some Americans, both black and white, have innocently asked me whether I had bought my clothes upon arrival, actually lived in trees, eaten cockroaches, or seen giraffes from my backyard. While these questions express legitimate desires to know the other, they are, nevertheless, couched in racialist concepts that have been propagated and disseminated by American popular culture and Eurocentric colonial, missionary, and academic discourses. As a Congolese, I have, just like my American counterparts, my own memories and histories of violence and dehumanization. Our hands have been cut off; we have been called *Macaque* (monkey), *Musenji* (savage), *Sale Bête* (dirty beast), and relegated, in our own country, to *cités indigènes* (indigenous quarters). So, there is no question that I arrived at the border of this country with a strong awareness of my black essence and understanding of my peculiar place within the world, even though I never had to measure my being in the world in terms of my blackness. But at the very port of entry to the United States I was welcomed by a taxi driver, who immediately told me about the "lazy and shiftless African Americans" who, unlike the Africans, refused to take advantage of the opportunities of the country. In spite of and because of this history of oppression, some African Americans and Africans perpetually struggle to maintain their humanness in relationship to the other black.

Yet, even as the African is discriminated against and humiliated, I hold within the American racial structure a peculiar position. Although the African American is considered an American, she is still a special kind of American, for her identity continues to be interlaced with that of the African. Despite the recent American, assimilationist, political rhetoric separating the African American from the "pure" African, miscegenation does not resolve the subject/object position of the former. The African is "purely" black, and thus different, yet the same as the African American. Her history of oppression is, however, not American bred. American students can thus discuss African literature more easily with the objectivity of distance. It is nonthreatening as long as continental violence is self-inflicted and the result of ethnicity and does not reveal or condemn American involvement and complicity, impoverishment, and violence raging on the continent as in Ama Ata Aidoo's *Our Sister Killjoy*. Depending on the book selection, I can be construed an outsider or an ally by both African and Caucasian Americans. Or I can be an invader or a foreigner but negligible because of my lack of political power. The African is for the white American as she is for the African American, that other/same image within the American racial mirror. Her ontological difference can be obliterated through sameness, as is Tashi's when she eats "barbecue" in Alice Walker's *The Color*

*Purple.* After all, the stories African Americans continue to tell rely, as Donna J. Watson asserts, "on the cultural memories of [their] African past, living now in the context of slavery: Congo square, sugar cane, full moon, Jim Crow, sharecropping, and the blues are some of the things that reshaped our narrations, metamorphosed native tongues into Creole languages as a way of communicating. Teeth sucking, soft moaning, low grunting, eye rolling, head shaking, "Chile. . . ," non-verbal codes, and what we did not say were highly important subtexts flavoring the dullness of servitude" (311). The African's relationship to the United States is thus one of perpetual tension, one in which she is racially assimilable or marginalized within the interstices.

As an African stands at the interstices of racial politics, color and accent blur the boundaries between African and African American. The African teacher is a black text within the classroom, just like her African American counterpart. Because African American literature demands that the teacher courageously discuss racial issues elicited by the text, black teachers can inhibit and alienate students who fail to trust them. The black teacher, construed as the victim who imposes her values upon students, can limit class discussion. Yet the political and didactic nature of the majority of the literature demands that the black teacher address the representation of social and racial realities as well as form. The African teacher's accent can be empowering if it marks her as the other. She can, hence, be construed as an unthreatening outsider who mutually explores the painful history of American racism with white students. When, however, the students identify the latter with the threatening discourses of the texts she has chosen or marks her as an African/American who incriminates them for the wrongs committed against blacks in this country, she quickly becomes identified with the African American and is construed as the embodiment of white collective guilt. Or she possibly is considered incompetent to truly convey this literature, since the politics of accents is what legitimates knowledge. Accent is what explains why some of my white students have written on my evaluations that I know my material well because I am African American.

The white teacher might question her legitimacy to teach and discuss African American literature and issues, as evinced by frequent disclaimers of white interveners such as "I know I could never know what blackness means." Indeed, the white scholar and teacher may not have the legitimacy or credit of knowing racism and color oppression and disenfranchisement firsthand. But, regardless of her lack of racial experience, the factor that empowers the latter to teach black texts and issues is not, as Thomas Gerschick contends, in "Should and Can a White, Heterosexual, Middle-Class Man Teach Students about Social Inequality and Oppression? One Person's Experience and Reflections," the introduction of other voices and the decentering of his knowledge. While all teachers must win the trust of their students to obtain the legitimacy to teach, a white male generally walks into the classroom with the legitimacy of centuries of knowledge and racelessness trailing behind him. He might have to mitigate his inexperience of racial oppression and his ethnocentric readings, but he embodies for both white and black students knowledge and power. Indeed, Gerschick writes: "My experience has been that another reason for white males to teach such courses is that my personal characteristics tended to lessen some white students' resistance to discussing such issues. . . . white students may have difficulties relating to faculty who are different from themselves. While I am glad that I was able to reach these students, I am also troubled by the fact that my co-teachers may have been seen as biased" (205).

As an African teacher who addresses the social and racial realities reflected in literature, I often tend to make students uncomfortable because, unlike Gerschick, I am visibly different. White students fear to question and sound racial issues; the books, according to them, incriminate them and leave no space for dialogue. Thus, Toni Morrison's *The Bluest Eye* raised ethical issues in a Southern institution where I once taught and was the source of student and communal discontentment because of its indecency. "The Signifying Monkey," in *The Heath Anthology of American Literature 2*, has, likewise, generated an even greater outcry. The students and some members within the community automatically assumed that the indecent, violent language of the poem is a manifestation of the perverseness and immorality of African culture, rather than a sign of the violent, racist American history. It is Africa, the abject element, that had to be curbed and tamed. The morally and intellectually assaulted African teacher was thus dehumanized, and the African American's denigration and beastialization was repeated, reinforced, and rehearsed on my African body. Perceived as threatening the social and moral order, African American high school teachers who attended workshops I conducted in Alabama also expressed concerns about teaching African American literature, considered irrelevant, immoral, and lacking in intellectual depth.

The discussion of racial issues elicits fear in both African American and Caucasian students. Both student bodies are uncomfortable discussing slavery and racial oppression. White students generally are overwhelmed by what they call "in your face," "finger-pointing" rhetoric. African American literature, according to one white student, is indoctrinating and, hence, needs to be unheeded. To encourage class discussion, racial atrocities and injustice must be diluted so students can consume the texts. And, when students complain about the course, I am invited to present these issues in an unthreatening, comfortable manner. But what do *comfortable* and *unthreatening* imply? These words entail the decentering and silencing of black texts, allowing students to discuss what they assume to be of interest and to skirt sensitive issues. This refusal to examine and to see one's involvement in violent acts toward other groups and the desire to assuage the anxieties of the majority white students is why a white colleague told me that she only discussed the indecent language in Morrison's

*Song of Solomon*. Do we continue to teach when we fail to present and confront reality in all its starkness and when we cover textual mirrors with veils?

Similarly, African American students are afraid to look into textual mirrors. The pain and the atrocities are too difficult to bear (after all, we do live in a society in which we like happy and not grim endings). Foremost, since black texts are didactic and thus delineate what black students see as negative images, focusing on these points can also deteriorate faculty/student trust and dialogue. When I examine black stereotypes, I tread carefully lest some of my African American students construe my discussion of these issues as my projection of negative images of blacks, especially when I am read as a native. Worse, my pretensions of telling about black oppression, rather than speaking for it, can also dangerously result in misinterpretation of my discussion of stereotypes. Where I seek to tell of African American oppression as a shared experience, a black student who decodes me as an outsider may solely see herself as the object of a stereotypical gaze.

I must thus tread with caution for fear of being considered insensitive and racist, despite my blackness. I must tactfully introduce representations of blacks within texts, such as Toni Morrison's *The Bluest Eye*, Haile Gerima's *Sankofa*, and Maya Angelou's *I Know Why the Caged Bird Sings*. Because students are appalled by the rapes and incest depicted within African American texts, some black students feel that the books are windows that allow outsiders voyeuristically to take pleasure in the suffering of blacks—especially when white courses do not focus on books, such as Joyce Carol Oates's *Them,* that depict white violence and oppression as a racial trait. Moreover, since rhetorics of diversity and multiculturalism suggest that racism is a thing of the past, even when it functions in homes and off stage, both African and Euro-American students consider the racial concerns of African American literature *dépassé* and irrelevant. With our black students' increasing desire to be invisible by not "standing out," or not being "ethnic," can we encourage and afford to create monological classrooms that erase certain perspectives of history?

Can I, as an African, teach African American literature if I cannot comprehend the signifying within the texts? Can I understand the reversal of values in Morrison's works? Can I understand the mule episode in *Their Eyes Were Watching God*? Can I aptly convey what "cutting the monkey" and "playing the dozens" mean? Are these cultural particularities so mystical and esoteric that African Americans alone can understand their meaning? Virginia Whatley Smith states, in "The Question of Comfort," that "as a bicultural African American" she "reads the world double-consciously in black and white" (155). The African teacher is also biculturally white and African. She may read African American literature from a Western perspective or an African perspective, but, when she reads Gloria Naylor's *Mama Day*, it is Birago Diop's "Breaths" and the marginalization of blacks that permeate the text; in Morrison's *Sula* it's the "Tar

Baby" folktale. Jean Toomer's *Cane* evokes feelings and a common worldview that affirm Toomer's claim that the "the Dixie Pike has grown from a goat path in Africa" (10). The spiritual world of *Mama Day* only affirms Robert Farris Tompkins's theory, in *Flash of the Spirit: African American Art and Philosophy*, that African residuals persist despite centuries of separate history.

Despite this affinity or identification with African American culture, an African teacher must, however, learn to read both the literature and the culture as an African American. She must embrace African American culture and have an experiential relationship with the community, in addition to the textual. She must love and hear the melodies and rhythms of Ebonics and engage in dialogue with the community. This is the sole means of teaching the text with the perspective of an insider, one that sees from a participatory perspective and is capable of reading the signposts along the road. She must scrutinize her outsider gaze so that her language is not contaminated by Western stereotypes of African Americans, embedded within the educational system and acquired from American popular culture and society. After all, having gone to the same Western schools, both Africans and African Americans contemplate each other through Western eyes that alienate each from the other. Through love, understanding, and appreciation of African American literature and culture, an African teacher can, as the African American scholar, read African American texts through her cultural and aesthetic grids. This black-centered reading, focusing on the African American experience, is possible only through one's familiarity with the diverse black culture and one's ability to listen to multiple black voices, for, as Michael Dyson asserts in "Contesting Racial Amnesia," one should not presume to master the culture if one is not aware of cultural particularities and differing experiences (347).

An African teacher, I believe, can teach African American literature if she studies and respects the distinctiveness of the African American literary tradition. Questions of insiderness/outsiderness and issues of essentialized literatures dominate our discussions within the discipline at times of economic and academic crises; they are generally a reaction to the marginalization of minority literatures and power relationships. As long as our educational institutions continue to consider Western literatures, English and American (a contestatory literature also), as neutral bodies of knowledge, opposed to politicized and ethnicized literatures, black intellectuality will always be relegated to the margins. The legitimization of black intellectuality and scholarship is what our black authors and critics—Chinweizu, wa Thiong'o, Gates, Baker, Morrison ("Unspeakable Things Unspoken"), and others—seek to achieve. An African teacher might have a different cultural and historical experience, but blacks' common experience of blackness, humiliation, and suffering empowers Africans to cross the threshold of African American literature, unlike my white colleague, who can only surmise the threshold. Insiderness merely conveys blacks' need to be, speak with passion about who they are and their values, and engage the world as equal and significant interlocutors in the production of meaning. I am an African teacher perhaps, yet our common history of blackness and pain allows me to cross gently the threshold of African American literature. Yet, even as I stand on the other side, I know that my speech will always be contaminated and suspicious because I will never be totally "blood" and never be allowed to reach the intimacy of using the *N* word of endearment.

These reflections are those of one African—there are other African points of view to consider. Yet, as a voice among discordant voices, I continue to listen and to observe, so I can speak, unlike Reema's Boy, within the black tradition. After all, as a stepsister, when I speak, read, and interpret African American literature, I speak for others and myself. I sing with the chorus and also sing solo when I bring African historical and cultural experiences to African American texts. The Congolese accent is also marked by racism, oppression, and frequently threatened with silence. My speech, in this country, is forever interstitial, a voice reinforcing that of my siblings, forever suspicious though singing to the same tune. Through my utterances in class I affirm African American knowledge. And at the border I hope to be the site where the difficult American racial dialogue can be mediated and translated. I am another voice, another perspective, among Euro-American, Native American, Asian American, Hispanic, and African American voices. As I speak inside and outside the African American tradition, I hope to contribute to the scientific legitimacy of black thought and creativity and to make this tradition a valid universal participant, despite its cultural particularities, within the academic debate.

PART FOUR

# Case Studies

# Twelve Years with Martin Delany

## A Confession

ROBERT S. LEVINE

–A confession, because there *is* something personal about such a long-standing critical interest in a writer, and there are secrets.

My initial "meeting" with Martin R. Delany (1812–1885) occurred inadvertently in 1991, as I was attempting to throw myself into a second book project, which (I proudly thought) had developed coherently from my first, *Conspiracy and Romance* (1989). Having written about threats from without in a book that had examined the relationship between conspiratorial anxieties and the American romance, I now decided to turn my attention to threats from within in a book-length study tentatively titled "The Intoxicated Body: From Franklin to Twain." For months I had worked my way through the Yale Benjamin Franklin, and, on reaching volume fifteen (with many still to go and a seeming infinitude of volumes still to be published over the next several decades), I realized I hadn't a clue about what I wanted to say on Franklin. So, I decided to do something new for me: break with chronology and draft a chapter that would come much later in the study, "Frederick Douglass and the Black Temperance Movement."

The prospect of plunging into Douglass's writings excited me, for the simple reason that I knew very little about Douglass beyond his famous *Narrative* and very little about nineteenth-century African American literature and culture in general. At Stanford, after all, my late-1970s qualifying orals exam on American literature from 1620 to 1950 had included only two African American texts (Douglass's *Narrative* and Wright's *Native Son*). Although I had been inspired by my African Americanist faculty colleagues at the University of Maryland to begin to address this gap, I hadn't had the time to do much more than read (and teach) such newly canonical texts as Harriet Jacobs's *Incidents in the Life of a Slave Girl* and Harriet Wilson's *Our Nig.* What I really wanted to do was immerse myself in African American literary culture in the same way that I had immersed myself in more mainstream American literary culture. To that end, one morning in February 1991, I took the Metro to the Library of Congress and requested the microfilm for two of Douglass's newspapers: the *North Star* (1847–1851) and *Frederick Douglass's Paper* (1851–1859). My experience of reading those two newspapers can only be described as revelatory.

As anyone who has looked at nineteenth-century African American newspapers knows, these papers expose the reader to a panoply of voices, issues, and generic modes (of which the slave narrative is the least on display)—in short, to the relatively hidden world of black cultural debate. Accustomed to the measured sonorities of the *Narrative*, I found it a pleasure to discover a different sort of Douglass, one who mixed it up with white and black writers alike in aggressively taking on the big issues of the day: the Mexican War, the Fugitive Slave Law, African colonization, black emigration, voting rights and citizenship for African Americans, capital punishment, the peace movement, European revolutions, sectional conflict, and, of course, temperance. Although I dutifully took notes on temperance during my first few days with the microfilm, I found myself increasingly absorbed by the reception of *Uncle Tom's Cabin* in *Frederick Douglass' Paper*, for Douglass's enthusiastic presentation of the novel went against the grain of my expectations. Whereas much critical writing had emphasized African Americans' suspicions of Stowe, here I found arguably *the* major black writer of the time doing his best to champion the novel, even in the face of the scathing criticism directed at it by one Martin R. Delany, whom Douglass very responsibly and honestly, I thought, printed in his newspaper, along with his own rebuttals. Who was Martin Delany? I've got to say that at the time I didn't know and didn't much care, for his attacks on Stowe for her racism and colonizationism ultimately provided me with the critical occasion to celebrate Douglass's canny appropriation of *Uncle Tom's Cabin* in an essay that I quickly wrote up and later placed in *American Literature.* Proud of having made a sort of entree into African American scholarship when the essay appeared in 1992, I put a reprint in the office box of one of my distinguished senior African American colleagues at the University of Maryland, Mary Helen Washington, and then waited for the praise to come rolling in.

Things didn't go quite to script. A day or two later I found a three-page handwritten letter in my box from Washington congratulating me on the essay while at the same time raising questions about the motives behind my virtual elision of Delany. "What about Martin Delany?" she asked. Did I know who he was? Did I really understand his perspective? If not, then how could I be so sure that I was being fair to him and to the African American debate on *Uncle Tom's*

*Cabin*? What about the endemic problem of race and racism? What about the debate on African colonizationism? And so on. Washington's questions sent me back to the Library of Congress, back to the microfilm room, where I pretty much reread Douglass's newspapers from Delany's perspective. In the course of doing so, I discovered, among other things, that Delany had actually been Douglass's coeditor during the first eighteen months of the *North Star*, that in addition to his letters on Stowe he had published numerous travel letters and political essays in the *North Star* and *Frederick Douglass' Paper*, that these letters and essays were just as fascinating and engaged and perceptive as Douglass's letters and essays, that Delany had a wonderfully strong critical voice in his debates not only with Douglass but also with numerous other African American leaders of the time, and that during the 1850s he made particularly compelling arguments in favor of black emigrationism. Overall, I found something enormously attractive about his combativeness, his unwillingness to fall into step as an uncritical follower of Douglass.

My rereading of Douglass's newspapers from Delany's perspective was the beginning of a much larger reading project that moved me, serendipitously and fortuitously, from a study of temperance and American literature to a study of Delany and Douglass (with a chapter on temperance), and to an additional long-term project of editing a comprehensive Martin R. Delany reader that would examine the full sweep of his career: his journalism in 1840s Pittsburgh; his association with Douglass and the *North Star* during the late 1840s and early 1850s; his subsequent break with Douglass and emergence as the leading black emigrationist of the 1850s (signaled by the publication of *The Condition, Elevation, Emigration and Destiny of the Colored People of the United States* [1852] and "Political Destiny of the Colored Race on the American Continent" [1854]); his work on the novel *Blake* (1859, 1861–1862); his pursuit of an African emigration project and then surprising embrace of the Civil War as a war of emancipation; his Reconstruction work in South Carolina; and, finally, his renewed interest in African emigration during the late 1870s, before his death in relative obscurity in Ohio.

In making the move from a somewhat traditional study of temperance to a bio-critical study of Douglass and Delany, along with an editing project focused solely on Delany, I confess to having been troubled by questions of professional and racial identity. How appropriate would it be for a white, traditionally trained scholar to become a critic and biographer of one of the leading black nationalists of the nineteenth century? Nellie Y. McKay proclaims in her 1998 essay "Naming the Problem" that "there is nothing mystical about African American literature that makes it the sole property of those of African descent" (24). Nevertheless, in the early to mid-1990s there was certainly a feeling in the air (and in the halls of academe) that it was just a bit inappropriate for a white scholar to enter into this field. And, if I was troubled about a sense of myself as an interloper in a field in which I may not have "belonged," I have to say that I did not get as much support from Delany as I would have liked. Delany regularly voiced his suspicion of whites, arguing in both "Political Destiny" and *Principia of Ethnology* (1879) that blacks may well be superior to whites. More to the point, in his attack on Harriet Beecher Stowe in the 1 April 1853 issue of *Frederick Douglass' Paper*, he declared that "in all due respect and deference to Mrs. Stowe, I beg leave to say, that she *knows nothing about us*, 'the Free Colored people of the United States,' [and] neither does any other white person."[1] The pervasiveness of whites' antiblack racism and mendacity, Delany argued in his public letters on Stowe, worked to make cross-racial sympathy and understanding a virtual impossibility in the United States.

How could I work in productive ways on someone so "other" from myself, a black nationalist who insisted so strenuously at various moments in his career on his difference from and even hatred of whites? Working on Delany would obviously be very different from working on Douglass, who took a more "humanistic" and cross-racial view of human oneness. Could I research (and teach) a writer who might have said about me, as he said about Stowe, that he "knows nothing about us"? Could I research and teach a writer who, in the current parlance, I was not?

But what does it mean to say that I was not Delany? Of course I wasn't Delany, but neither was I, as such binary logic would seem to imply, a canonical white author of the sort I'd studied and taught for years. Mulling it over in the early 1990s, I said to myself that Delany was no more other than any of the writers I had been trained to write about, no more other, say, than Nathaniel Hawthorne. After all, both Delany and Hawthorne lived in the nineteenth century, and in certain respects Delany's family history had the more compelling parallels with my own family's history in the nineteenth century, given that my great-grandparents were Russian and Polish Jews who suffered through pogroms and eventually were forced (or chose) to emigrate. But of course there is something facile about such an argument, on the simple grounds that working on Hawthorne has typically meant working with predominately white critical communities (the professors I trained with, the colleagues I exchanged work with), while working on Delany would mean, especially at the beginning stages, working with a rather different community of scholars whose backgrounds, more often than not, were quite different from my own. There are (and certainly should be) differences between working on African American writers and working on canonized white writers, in part because the field of African American studies has had a long history of being marginalized in the academy. Given that history, and the field's historical mission of challenging the very racism that had contributed to its marginalization, the prospects for doing good work in African American studies, whatever one's race and ethnicity, cannot help but be enhanced by seeking out and learning from experienced African Americanists.

Such a desire to draw on a combination of expertise and institutional history was certainly one of the reasons I gave my Douglass/Stowe essay to Mary Helen Washington back in 1992.

But, even as I worried over questions of identity and authority, there had been an upsurge of compelling work on race during the mid-1990s that in effect urged me to stop my worrying. In the influential essay collection *Identities* (1995), for instance, the editors, Kwame Anthony Appiah and Henry Louis Gates Jr., presented essays that developed what they termed "anti-essentialist critiques of ethnic, sexual, national, and racial identities" (1). The idea that racial identity was contingent, constructed, and perhaps even fictional was of a piece with much critical writing of the mid-1990s—a time when, perhaps not coincidentally, more white scholars than ever before were engaging black texts. Echoing Appiah and Gates's anti-essentialism, Stuart Hall proposed a "strategic and positional" notion of racial and cultural identity, insisting that identities are "never singular but multiply constructed across different, often intersecting and antagonistic, discourses, practices, and positions" (3, 4).[2] A number of other writers, such as David Roediger, Matthew Frye Jacobson, Noel Ignatiev, and George Lipsitz, elaborated on such insights to develop what has come to be termed "whiteness studies," with its most clarion spokesperson, Roediger, calling for the "abolition" of whiteness as a "natural" category that somehow exists beyond race and outside of power.[3] Recent critical work on the subject continues to heed the anti-essentialist call, with some writers wanting to dispense not only with whiteness but with the concept of race altogether. In *Against Race* Paul Gilroy warns that essentialist notions of racial identity can close down "the possibility of communication across the gulf between one heavily defended island of particularly and its equally well fortified neighbors" (103), and in *Situatedness* David Simpson argues that we ultimately do not know much about who we are or where we are, and that fashionably self-conscious "azza" sentences (e.g. "As a white male middle-aged professor...") bespeak a reductive and overly confident conception of identity that needs to be contested (esp. 32–47).[4]

"Azza" white male middle-aged professor interested in African American studies and Delany, I find such rejections of racial essentialism liberating. At the same time, I don't quite buy the dismissal of race and identity with respect to our institutionally situated academic work, for such dismissals fail to take account of the history of white privilege in the academy. Moreover, even as I am willing to concede to David Simpson and other like-minded critics that it is difficult to know who "we" are, the fact is that it has never been all that difficult for white racist culture to identify who "they" are. As Katherine J. Mayberry points out, there are a number of pragmatic reasons for holding onto notions of racial identity, even as we concede the constructedness or problematic status of such categories. Efforts to "problematize identity out of existence," for instance, dovetail all too easily with the current assault on affirmative action and diversity in higher education (Mayberry 17). But here I must stop myself and ask, What does all this have to do with my scholarly work on Delany?

It is simply this: my scholarly turn to a Delany/Douglass monograph and a Delany reader could not proceed without a measure of self-consciousness and defensiveness about the *lack* of hurdles or barriers to my taking on these projects. Such are the privileges of whiteness, and such were the privileges that I wanted to explore as part of my work—in large part because Delany's writings themselves encourage such explorations. Central to Delany's critique of Stowe, for instance, was a concern that she would be regarded as having presented "objective" truths on slavery that somehow rose above the situatedness of race, and so in his letters to Douglass he took special pains to point out that Stowe in *Uncle Tom's Cabin* drew on black antislavery testimonies that hitherto had not garnered all that much attention. "I am of the opinion that Mrs. Stowe has draughted largely on all of the best fugitive slave narratives," he asserted to Douglass, declaring that these narratives are now "clothed in Mrs. Stowe's own language."[5] Part of Delany's frustration with the acclaim for *Uncle Tom's Cabin* had to do with his own investment in issues of authorship and authority. Published the same year as *Uncle Tom's Cabin*, his *Condition* was pretty much ignored both in mainstream and African American journals, not even getting a review in *Frederick Douglass' Paper*.[6] Was it not race and location, he asked, that gave Stowe an undeserved cultural authority at the expense of African American writers?

Without being overly self-conscious, defensive, and/or aggressive, I sought to make my own critical, historical, and racial location part of my work on Delany and Douglass. In hindsight I can now see that I was in sympathy with the 1995 call of Linda Alcoff to "interrogate the *bearing of our location and context* on what we are saying" (112). Elizabeth Abel's well-known essay "Black Writing, White Reading: Race and the Politics of Feminist Interpretation," also published in 1995, perhaps best captures my sense of the challenge of working on Delany. Abel addresses the hesitancy of some white feminist critics to work on black feminist texts and allows that such critical forays may simply "disclose white critical fantasies" (477). Her hesitations aside, she encourages white readings of black texts for the following crucial reasons: "If we produce our readings cautiously and locate them in a self-conscious and self-critical relation to black feminist criticism, these risks, I hope, would be counterbalanced by the benefits of broadening the spectrum of interpretation, illuminating the social determinants of reading, and deepening our recognition of our racial selves and the 'others' we fantasmatically construct—and thereby expanding the possibilities of dialogue across as well as about racial boundaries" (498). There is much that is attractive in this call for critical engagement and much that is relevant to my own work on Delany. For one, Abel makes the crucial point that white readings need to be located in relation to black criticism, and I would only underscore that this is crucial because historically it is blacks who produced the early work on African American literature in its precanonical days. For another, there is an implication here that all critical readings are to a certain extent "fantasmatically" construed. I understand Abel to mean by this that there are deep, generally unacknowledged connections between desire and interpretation, and it is along these lines that I wish to make another confession:

Harriet Beecher Stowe: *C'est moi.*

I make this confession in relation to my book *Martin Delany, Frederick Douglass, and the Politics of Representative Identity*, and, in making it, I would like to free from liability the particular mentor who once told me that all criticism is autobiographical. What my mentor meant by this is that we make all sorts of personal investments in our critical work and that our work would be all the better for facing up to this fact. Abel's notion of the fantasmatical seems to me of a piece with my mentor's understanding of the place of personal desire in the critical. It was my awareness of my initial outsider status in relation to Delany and Douglass, of my need to listen and learn, that led me to bring Stowe into the critical study as the very embodiment of the white who (like me) did not quite understand, did not quite get things right (witness my initial elision of Delany's perspective on the debate on *Uncle Tom's Cabin*), but who eventually moved to some sort of larger knowledge suggestive of the ability to communicate across the color line. To a significant extent, then, I invested in Stowe my own desires for cross-racial understanding, conceiving of her in allegorical terms as a surrogate for myself. Thus (so my skeptical readers might say), I made her into something that she possibly was not. How wrong she had seemed about so many things! And yet, though Stowe was attacked by Delany and other African American writers for her racialism and colonizationism, I saw in her a brave white woman who was trying to do good in her own time by speaking out against slavery with the conceptual tools that she had at hand (like most of us, she never did manage to "transcend" her culture). But, perhaps even more important (and here I may have been projecting my own desires), Stowe attempted to continue to do good after the publication of *Uncle Tom's Cabin* by making a strenuous effort to listen to and learn from African American writers. Thus, I presented *Uncle Tom's Cabin* not as the summa of her novelistic writing and not as her single statement on slavery. Rather, I presented the novel as part of her *process* of trying to understand the interrelated issues of race and slavery in U.S. culture by attending to African Americans' perspectives (Levine, *Martin* esp. 147–155).

In *Uncle Tom's Cabin*, then, as was analogously true for my own initial work on *Uncle Tom's Cabin*, Stowe didn't get things quite right. But, as a subscriber to *Frederick Douglass' Paper*, she would have read the debate between Douglass and Delany on *Uncle Tom's Cabin*, and she would have known of other critical

African American responses to her novel as well. Attending to these criticisms, she evidently rethought her support for colonizationism, sending a letter in May 1853 to the New York meeting of the American and Foreign Anti-Slavery Society that declared, as recorded in the proceedings, that "if she were to write 'Uncle Tom' again, she would not send George Harris to Liberia" (Gossett 294). Moreover, in her second antislavery novel, *Dred* (1856), she presented her readers with a black revolutionary (Dred) and a black reformer (Milly), neither of whom advocated colonizationism. Unlike in *Uncle Tom's Cabin*, Stowe ends her second antislavery novel not with a call for African colonization but with some of the black characters emigrating to Canada (which is precisely what Delany did in the mid-1850s) and with some moving to New York City, where they come to have a vital role in the life of what she presents as an interracial community. There is compelling evidence that Stowe in *Dred* also rethought her racialist conception of Uncle Tom's nonviolence in light of Delany's criticism of her novel. In one of his letters to Douglass published in *Frederick Douglass' Paper*, Delany lamented that the black men of *Uncle Tom's Cabin* didn't respond to their bullying white masters in the way that he imagined the rebellious former slave Lewis Hayden would have done: by burying a "hoe deep in the master's skull, laying him lifeless at his feet."[7] Perhaps inspired by Delany, Stowe in *Dred* imagines a dark-skinned black who, unlike Uncle Tom, does not fulfill the racialist script of being religious to the point of (maternal) nonviolence but, instead, deploys his religiosity to organize a violent slave rebellion. Would the changes in her colonizationist and racialist vision have occurred if she had not been aware of the criticisms of Delany and other African Americans of her first antislavery novel? My sense is, probably not.

Such was the revisionary force of Stowe's second antislavery novel that Delany himself was influenced by it when working on his own antislavery novel, *Blake*, in the late 1850s and early 1860s. Or so I argued in *Martin Delany, Frederick Douglass.* After all, *Blake*, like *Dred*, has a black revolutionary at its center who is conceived of in hemispheric terms as the Toussaint L'Ouverture of his people. Both novels celebrate a black revolutionary conspirator who strategically makes use of the swamps as a locale for black community; both link the situation in the United States to the situation in Cuba.[8] Significantly, Delany uses a stanza from Stowe's poem "Caste and Christ" as the running epigraph to all of the published chapters in the 1861–1862 serialization of *Blake* in the *Weekly Anglo-African*, and I see no evidence that he did so with ironic intentions. My study of Delany and Douglass, then, in addition to tracing the unfolding productive rivalry between these two great African American leaders, tells a second story of a white person who made an effort to understand the situation of the free and enslaved blacks in the United States, wrote a novel that got some things wrong, listened to the responses of African American writers (particularly Delany), and rethought her literary and racial politics accordingly, producing a novel that had an impact on the African American writer who had been among those most skeptical and critical of her initial effort. The submerged autobiographical allegory of my book on Delany and Douglass, then, its informing hope and desire, was that there *could* be a productive give-and-take between writers as different as Stowe and Delany (or myself and Delany), that writers were not frozen into completely differentiated, distant, and distinct racial selves, and that "fantasies" of desire could contribute to cross-racial dialogues.

A dynamic (fantasmatical?) sense of interracial give-and-take, of learning occurring on both sides of the color line, also initially helped to guide my long-term project of editing Martin Delany's writings. While working on the documentary reader, I wanted to think of myself not as a brute editor constructing a Delany to my own liking but, rather, as a pleasant conversationalist who was listening to Delany as he was listening to me. When, however, the edition became my main research project in 1997, I found it difficult to sustain the illusion of a frictionless conversation. Part of the reason for this is that Delany is a recalcitrant writer who deliberately tries to provoke, happy to hit the raw nerves of even his closest acquaintances.[9] There is no reason that an editor should remain untouched by Delany's free-swinging rhetoric. But what also intruded into the project was my decision in 1998 to assume a new administrative position, director of Graduate Studies in the Department of English, which brought me to take greater note of the harsh realities of the color line in higher education. Whereas my Delany/Douglass book had been framed with a sort of utopianist conception of cross-racial dialogue, my move into administration confounded that idealism, particularly as I found myself simultaneously editing Delany and dealing with the vexing issue of graduate recruitment of minority students.

For those who have worked in graduate recruitment, what I have to say will sound disturbingly familiar; for those who haven't, there is something eye-opening about the perspective that you gain as a graduate director on the situation of African American students in higher education. All deans charge all graduate directors to recruit minority students, but the reality is that there are not that many African American students to recruit. Thus, all graduate directors must compete to attract the same small group of candidates. If you recruit successfully, you get the student that everyone else wanted, but you don't make any changes in the numbers themselves. Compounding the problem of minority recruitment is the recent emergence in graduate programs throughout the country of field-based fellowship packages in African American studies as a way of sustaining financial support for black scholars at a time when race-based fellowships have come under legal challenge. The obvious consequence of linking a disciplinary field to race is to naturalize such links, and to reinforce the ultimately self-fulfilling notion that African American students in the humanities have little interest in subjects other than black studies. These new fellowships shrink rather than expand the space for African American students in English departments. We recently recruited a talented African American student working in British Romanticism who insisted, when she visited campus, on the political importance of blacks working in fields outside of African American studies. Despite her excellent undergraduate record, strong writing sample, and high test scores, she had no competing fellowship offers from other institutions, perhaps because graduate directors were reluctant to "waste" a fellowship on an African American working in a field outside of African American studies. I can't help but worry about her prospects when she enters the job market. As Nellie Y. McKay writes, "African American scholars seeking appointments in more-traditional fields for which they were trained confront an automatic assumption that they are better able to teach, say, Morrison, than Milton" ("Naming" 23).[10] These assumptions about the supposed fit of field to race, I fear, go back to secondary education, pervade undergraduate education, and reveal themselves most starkly in graduate recruitment, the academic job market, and the distribution of faculty across disciplinary fields.

As graduate director, I found it difficult not to be acutely aware of the privileges of whiteness in higher education and, more specifically, literary and historical scholarship. Although I continue to believe that whites should be "in" African American studies and that the best way of judging that participation is through the quality of the work, as an administrator I experienced a certain loss of innocence, which to some extent informs *Martin R. Delany: A Documentary Reader*. While my Delany/Douglass book tells a relatively upbeat story of cross-racial conversation and influence (a story, as I have confessed, generated in part by desire and in part by my sense that such desire led me to the "objective" truth of the story), my Delany reader offers a more sobering picture of what Delany termed the "American colored patriot," who "lives but to be despised, feared and hated, accordingly as his talents may place him in the community."[11] One of the recurring motifs of the documentary reader, then, is the failure of cross-racial conversation, even as Delany refuses to give up on its possibilities. Thus, we see Delany during the 1840s working with white abolitionists, only to find himself ejected from Harvard Medical School because of his blackness. He attempted to work with Canadian and British whites in the late 1850s and early 1860s to establish an African American community in Africa but was ultimately undone by the machinations of British missionaries. Alienated by what he regarded as the hypocrisies of Reconstruction, Delany chose to support Southern Democrats in the South Carolina elections of the mid-1870s, only to find himself once again betrayed by racist whites who promised to do well by blacks. The final entry in the documentary reader is a heartbreaking letter of 1880 from Delany to William Coppinger, the secretary and treasurer of the American Colonization Society, asking for his assistance in getting him the job of Door Keeper in the U.S. Senate. There is no reply, no closure to the conversation, and Delany dies in relative obscurity, unhonored for his work as a Union officer during the American Civil War.

What survives, of course, are Delany's writings, which continue to have much to say about race and racism in the United States. As I worked on the documentary reader from my graduate director perspective, I found his comments on education to be particularly worth listening to. Again and again, Delany assailed a white supremacist society that was doing its best, through slavery, black codes, and class inequities, to keep education beyond the reach of blacks and thus to type African Americans as beyond the hope of education. As he tours the Midwest during the late 1840s, he finds that black children in the public schools "have learned comparatively nothing," receiving "a very bad education" because their white teachers assume that all they can do is perform by rote. In his 1852 *Condition* he therefore enjoins African Americans to pursue as best they can a practical education that will allow them to participate in the economic life of the society: "Let us have an education, that shall practically develope our thinking faculties and manhood; and then, and not until then, shall we be able to vie with our oppressors, go where we may." Women, too, he insists, need a solid education if they hope to contribute to the project of black elevation: "Let our young women have an education; let their minds be well informed; well stored with useful information and practical proficiency, rather than the light superficial acquirements, popularly and fashionably called accomplishments."[12]

Sifting through the over two thousand pages of Delany's writings that I needed to whittle down to around five hundred pages and listening extra-attentively to Delany's thoughts on education, I found myself drawn to a Delany whom I was also in the process of editorially shaping, who, as an "American colored patriot," was committed to the antiracist struggle in the United States, even as he explored transnational projects, experiments, and commitments. The Delany who emerges in the documentary reader, then, is a Delany who had been helping me to think about my own jaundiced perspective on race and class inequities in higher education and a Delany who saw as his life mission the need continually to challenge such inequities. He is a pragmatist trying what he can to improve the situation of blacks in the United States and, consequently, resisting being pinned down to any sort of racial essentialism or political foundationalism. This Delany is rather different from the popular image of Delany as a fiery black nationalist and separatist whose life was guided by an "African dream."[13] If Delany dreamed of Africa now and again, it is because the white racist society he was seeking to reform regularly thwarted his U.S. dreams. My editing reflected my interpretation of Delany as race leader who moved nimbly betwixt and between nationalisms and transnationalisms, and thus I placed great emphasis on what could be termed the "phases" of his career (his black emigrationism of the 1850s, his Reconstruction work of the 1860s and 1870s, and so on) while rejecting a more thematic approach that would have isolated the "African" or some sort of black racial chauvinism as the key to a complex and ever-changing and -adapting career. Even so, I have to confess that I was just a bit more responsive to the Delany who brought me back to the cross-racial utopianism of my Delany/Douglass book than I was to the Delany who undercut that utopianism. I could imagine another editor who would want to give even greater weight to Delany's black separatism while cutting back, say, on his celebratory references to now-obscure white philanthropists or on the presentation of his misguided support for the Democrat Wade Hampton's run for the governorship of South Carolina in 1876. Still, in light of the overall career, in which Delany did work with whites and did express his hopes of a multiracial United States, I think I got things right in the reader by accentuating his U.S. commitments.

One of the benefits of having had such a long gestation period with the volume (from around 1992, when I submitted a proposal to a publisher, to 2002, when I submitted the manuscript) is that that period allowed me to listen to and learn from, and continue to appreciate the otherness of, Delany. And he *is* other, just as every object of study is other, though what I came to realize in working on Delany is that I, too, am other—the raced white who has been privileged to work on Delany for so many years.[14] So, why am I passionate about Delany? There are numerous reasons, ranging from his literary bravura to his bold political engagements. I admire his tenacity, his improvisatory skills, his pride, and his pragmatism. I'm moved by his belief in the power of the word, even in the face of an intractable white racism, and, Hawthornean that I am, I am moved as well by his failures (in *The Blithedale Romance* [1852] Hawthorne's narrator remarks that "if the vision have been worth the having, it is certain never to be consummated otherwise than by a failure" [10–11]). Delany is someone who sought to make his life matter every day and who creatively addressed the biggest issues of his time even at the risk of failure. He's someone, I am convinced, who took great pride in his blackness but was nonetheless prepared to listen to and negotiate with whites; thus, I have tried to make listening and negotiation central to my work on Delany.

## NOTES

1. Delany to Douglass, letter of 20 March 1853, in *Frederick Douglass' Paper*, 1 April 1853, rpt. in Levine, *Martin R. Delany* 224. Under attack from Douglass, Delany quickly modified his views on the ability of whites to understand the situation of blacks, conceding the following in a letter of 18 April 1853, printed in the 6 May 1853 *Frederick Douglass' Paper*. "In saying in my letter of the 22d of March, that 'Mrs. Stowe knows nothing about us—"the *Free* Colored People of the United States"—neither does any

white person,' I admit the expression to be ironical, and not intended to be taken in its literal sense" (Levine, *Martin R. Delany* 232).

2. See also Powell, *Beyond*.
3. For a critical overview of whiteness studies, see Kolchin, "Whiteness Studies."
4. David Simpson's main point is this: "We do not know much about our situatedness" (33).
5. Delany to Douglass, letter of 15 April 1853, in *Frederick Douglass' Paper*, 29 April 1853, rpt. in Levine, *Martin R. Delany* 231.
6. For Delany's complaint on this matter, see his letter to Douglass of 10 July 1852, in the 23 July 1852 issue of *Frederick Douglass' Paper*, rpt. in Levine, *Martin R. Delany* 221–223.
7. Delany to Douglass, letter of 15 April 1853, in *Frederick Douglass' Paper*, 29 April 1853, rpt. in Levine, *Martin R. Delany* 231. During the late 1840s Delany regularly complained in the *North Star* that blacks' religiosity was making them overly subservient to the masters. See, for example, his three-part essay "Domestic Economy," printed in issues of 23 March 1849, 13 April 1849, and 20 April 1849, rpt. in Levine, *Martin R. Delany* 151–156.
8. One of the characters in *Dred* warns that the leaders of the Southern slave power "are going to annex Cuba and the Sandwich Islands, . . . and have a great and splendid slaveholding empire." At Dred's death Stowe compares him to Toussaint L'Ouverture (470, 516).
9. See, for example, Holly's 1886 overview of Delany's career ("In Memoriam" 117, 124).
10. DuCille similarly writes, "Black scholars on predominately or overwhelmingly white campuses are rarely authorized simply as scholars. Rather, our racial difference is an authenticating stamp that . . . often casts us in the role of Caliban in the classroom and on the campus" (33). In a thoughtful and disturbing essay Gîtahi Gîtîtî talks of how he's distrusted in the classroom when he works outside the field of African American studies, given that student and faculty expectations are "colored by a departmental ideology, the internalized 'fittedness' of black people to teach black courses" ("Menaced by Resistance" 184).
11. Delany, "True Patriotism," *North Star*, 8 December 1848, rpt. in Levine, *Martin R. Delany* 140.
12. Delany to Douglass, letter of 20 May 1848, in *North Star*, 9 June 1848, rpt. in Levine, *Martin R. Delany* 95; Delany to Douglass, letter of 18 November 1848, in *North Star*, 1 December 1848, rpt. in Levine, *Martin R. Delany* 124; Delany, *The Condition, Elevation, Emigration and Destiny of the Colored People of the United States* (1852), rpt. in Levine, *Martin R. Delany* 212.
13. See, for example, Griffith, *African Dream*.
14. Abel remarks that self-conscious considerations by white scholars about their practice of reading black writers can prove to be a useful strategy for what she terms the "racialization of whiteness," in which otherness is seen to exist on both sides of the color line ("Black Writing, White Reading" 269).

# Master Thoughts

DALE M. BAUER

One of my first assumptions about teaching Emma Kelley-Hawkins's novel *Megda* (1891) in an undergraduate class devoted to nineteenth-century American fictions, from *The Coquette* through "The Jolly Corner," was that the students would hate it. (Why teach a book that I imagine my students will hate is another question entirely.) I assumed, wrongly it turns out, that students, first at the University of Wisconsin–Madison and then at the University of Kentucky (UK), would object to Kelley-Hawkins's preaching the lesson of Christian salvation and material renunciation. To my surprise, I discovered that most of them loved it, and they did so precisely for the reason I most distrusted—the novel's didacticism. While I was teaching the novel as a cultural and historical challenge to racism, they read it as "more real" than the critical and psychological realism by Henry James and William Dean Howells. Why did I never suppose that students would *not* reject a decidedly Christian and conservative novel about overcoming one's worldly vanity in favor of Christian submission? Focused as I was on delivering the news about racial uplift in the 1890s, I forgot about the spiritual component of the question. This is no doubt an example of the professorial blindness to student values that critics of cultural leftist teaching such as Mark Edmundson denounce: I missed the "universal"—that is, Christian—for the specific paradigm of the novel in its racial dimension.

Clearly, I was blind to my students' religious convictions. But what were my other blindnesses, especially about teaching African American texts to white students primarily? This question is a necessary one for the purposes of this essay in particular—and this volume in general. *Megda* is a controversial novel insofar as it erases the race of its characters, though most critics agree, following Claudia Tate, that the novel is a version of *Little Women* written for the black middle classes. In it Kelley-Hawkins omits almost all references to the characters' race and focuses instead on their religious and educational communities, relying on what Tate calls "racial indeterminacy" (*Psychoanalysis and Black Novels* 120). *Megda*'s heroine, Meg Randal, moves away from the worldly pleasures of drama and dancing and toward religious conversion and teaching rhetoric: she is employed at the same school where she was taught and begins instructing young women based on her own "rare elocutionary powers" (312). As Carla Peterson notes in her reading of Kelley-Hawkins's novels in relation to modernity, "The novels posit a raceless world of characters who are not racially marked, in which the category of whiteness refers most immediately to skin tone; narrator and characters alike repeatedly remark upon the white skin of the elite female protagonists, which is contrasted to the brownness of the male characters and the more working-class women." Peterson argues that Kelley-Hawkins deliberately offered her Baptist readers "a vision of what it would be like to live in a modern world in which racial difference no longer existed" and suggests that "whiteness was a notoriously unstable signifier" for Kelley-Hawkins ("New Negro" 113–117), though I am not sure that my students see it that way.

Peterson's reading leads me to ask: what if students like reading the novel because of its dream of a "raceless world," even though they are not of the world of black Baptist readers for which Kelley-Hawkins intended her novel? Students may more readily assume that such a raceless world is possible than I might believe.[1] I like to read and assign Kelley-Hawkins's novels, *Megda* and *Four Girls at Cottage City* (1898), for arguably dubious reasons: her rendering of the post-Reconstruction United States, the 1890s black middle class, and educational capital. In both novels the status of the teacher/professor reflects a great deal about the possibility of class transcendence of racial prejudice, especially in this historical nadir of race relations when racial segregation after *Plessy v. Ferguson* became further entrenched. My assumption has been that becoming a professor—for Kelley-Hawkins as for me—means respect and admiration; working in the academy means entering a race-blind world. The classroom seems to me to be a mirror world for Kelley-Hawkins's novel, where students can focus on character rather than color. Another of my assumptions is that professors are the ethical authorities of her novels, as they so often are in realist fictions. I am dedicated to this idea of teaching as calling, despite my often better judgment. (This may amuse those of us who have grown accustomed to thinking of ourselves as mere parts of the Professional-Managerial Complex and our students as consumers, of both avid and passive varieties.) Perhaps my engagement with this novel is a fantasy of fulfillment: that the academy and professorial training have always led to a kind of moral victory over the forces of evil, racism among them.

In part I am drawn to Kelley-Hawkins's work because of its vision of racial uplift through the model of the professor. I turn to *Megda* as an apt novel to teach because it raises questions of personal and communal values, including the moral use-value of education. What I thought my students would respond to—the value of education in changing social classes and overcoming racism—was not as crucial to them as the transition from worldly student to Christian believer. For me, however, the most crucial transition in this novel is based on the move from student to professor, a move that I believe represents the "true" epiphany through intellectual conversion. As a white scholar, I approach the novel through education, the common ground Kelley-Hawkins's characters share with my students reading this book for a course assignment. I see now that this assumption about education is mediated through my own ethnic heritage and assumptions about class mobility. As the grandchild of Polish immigrants, I also cling to the idea of an educational meritocracy and hold that the raceless world that Peterson holds as the novel's promise can be found in the academy, or in the learning communities that both novels represent.

While I willfully, even utopianly, want to read the heroine's education in rhetoric as the mode of her transcendence, my students read education more suspiciously. Kelley-Hawkins's novel imparts a different message for them altogether: that professors are to be distrusted, though eventually they might be redeemed. Perhaps all academic study is a lesson in cynicism and distrust—including white privilege and institutionalized racism—but some American realist novels depict teaching as violence or aggression, and teaching English especially. In confronting Kelley-Hawkins, I have had to turn not only to the history of white privilege in the academy but also to the violent history of American universities. For, just as white, middle-class male and female students learned to distrust their professors, so too do African American novels at the turn of the century distrust the black professoriate. Kelley-Hawkins's depictions of disciplinary intimacy lead her to embedded lessons of disciplinary violence. These depictions challenge both my own supposition about professors in the black middle class and the assumption that the academy could ever become a race-blind or gender-blind world of equal opportunity.

Thus, my entry as a white scholar into the 1890s and African American fiction is through the figure of the professor, what I had heretofore assumed was a benevolent, or at least race-neutral, figure of moral authority in both black and white novels. Yet, in tracing this literary and educational history, as I do in the pages that follow, this figure is more vexed than neutral, a vessel of both racism and sexism in late-nineteenth- and early-twentieth-century novels alike. White, male privilege is so entrenched in the models of the professoriate that it is virtually impossible to find a neutral way to discuss education as uplift, so much so that I began to question whether it is possible in any professorial relation—to students or to texts—to escape this history. Both actual and symbolic violence is embedded in our educational history; in order to put white scholars teaching black texts into context, we must also ask whether professors of any identity can ever teach texts or teach students without tracing that violence and thereby encountering resistance and invoking wrath. Neither the students' assumptions about Christian transcendence nor mine about educational uplift proved tenable. As this volume shows, teaching always invokes a history of contested relations between professors and students, professors and texts.

## Women, Whiteness, and the Nineteenth-Century World of Letters

The suspicion with which white male and female students encounter their professors has its analogue in Kelley-Hawkins's novels, in which the black professors are vaguely suspicious, even part of the systemic racism and violence against African Americans that haunts her fictions.

I turn here to my historical and personal presuppositions about education in order to unpack—one by one—my claims about intellectual and academic life. What follows is the narrative of academic violence, both in its historical and fictional forms and in women novelists' fascination with the professor as a mysterious, perhaps even dangerous, figure. This fascination emerges from the hope that many women invest in academic uplift but also in the ambivalence about that desire. Yet the academy is no haven for women or male minorities, who have much to fear from the white male professor; even if the professor were benevolent, women and male minorities may have more to gain from agonistic combat rather than happy union with him.

We know from the history of nineteenth-century American colleges, as Robert Connors has taught us in "Women's Reclamation of Rhetoric in Nineteenth-Century America," that between 1800 and 1875 "violent rebellions of students against faculty" took place at an impressive list of schools: Princeton, Miami, Amherst, Brown, the University of South Carolina, the University of North Carolina, Williams, Georgetown, Harvard, Yale, Dartmouth, Lafayette, Bowdoin, City College of New York, Dickinson, and DePauw. These rebellions were marked by violence directed against professors' bodies, in which professors were publicly whipped, shot at, stabbed, wounded, maimed, and stoned. As Connors reports, "One paradigmatic episode occurred at Davidson College, where the students rioted because their mathematics problems were too difficult. They barricaded themselves inside a dormitory and threw rocks at the faculty members who came to investigate" (73). Connors documents these anxieties about performance that arose when the teaching of oratory, based on agonistic rhetoric, was dominant in colleges and before written communication—the essay—became the predominant form of baccalaureate expression (see Berlin 87–88). The difference between these modes was crucial: oral performance gave students a greater sense of audience and participation in public life. In moving from oratory to written composition in college, students lost the sense of public voice once embodied in their rhetorical training for citizenship

(Berlin 88).[2] This violence occurred at the same time that coeducation became part of the college scene, insofar as women were discouraged from studying elocution and rhetoric and, instead, were forced to master the essay and other written, more private forms.

This turns out to be a crucial distinction in the turn-of-the-century African American novels that I routinely teach. Agonistic rhetoric was, as Connors writes, "concerned with contest" (67)—ritualized argument and debate, based on "personal display" (71). The cultural anxieties associated with coeducation—and a major shift in the content of English classrooms—led to a residuum of violence. One of these fears was tied to women studying rhetoric, since learning public speaking might lead them to take to the pulpits and streets. Writing was supposed to keep them immersed in their private thoughts. The novels by American women writers to which I will soon turn reveal how little this scheme worked as well as how aggressively, even ruthlessly, women pursued their professors for knowledge. Women students were eager to pursue rhetoric, starting with recitation and moving on to elocution, but the question for women students and male professors remained the same: what to do with the agonistic rage, the rhetorical violence, with which they were invested when taught rhetoric? In general, as many nineteenth- and twentieth-century novels show, this was the rage of the professor, to which students responded in kind. The agon was supposed to be subordinated to the act of persuasion, ostensibly to some ethical good. Classical rhetoric was taught in school as an aid to the citizen's future in the public sphere, especially for use in political discourse. No wonder, then, that, as more and more black students entered college (see Gatewood), rhetoric became central in African American fiction. By the end of the nineteenth century this violence against the professor turned from the literal (campus revolt) to the affective (distrust of the professor). Indeed, the cultural distrust of professors and their motives fueling numerous plots in Kelley-Hawkins's novels (among others) leads us to ask: what does the figure of the master-teacher that we have inherited from American literature signify, especially for women writers? Another way to ask this question is to figure when teaching moved from the idea of content to the idea of method, from authority in the texts to the authority of the teacher—because this key move, from content to method, then opened up questions about the authority of teaching to its embodiment, both for white women and African Americans. American education changed dramatically in embracing the idea of teaching as mastery of students rather than mastery of texts. Teachers became invested with a new force of disciplinary authority, so much so that students came to fear retaliatory violence resided in college teachers.[3]

Alcott's *Little Women* is a prototype of the kind of disciplinary teaching that gets replicated in African American women's fiction. Jo March's future husband, Professor Bhaer, represents the ultimate patriarch—Berlin-educated and nearly forty, as Jo describes him (412, 432). His intellectual force emerges from the highest category of taste, as his profession is meant to bestow. But in America the poor professor is reduced to teaching the daughter of the Frenchwoman who does the laundry (415). As Jo March records in her journal, "Cast away at the very bottom of the table was the Professor, shouting answers to the questions of a very inquisitive, deaf old gentleman on one side, and talking philosophy with a Frenchman on the other. . . . [H]e had a great appetite, and shovelled in his dinner [. . .] the poor man must have needed a deal of food, after teaching idiots all day" (414–415). Even Jo becomes one of the "idiots" he must teach, when he comes to see that she writes sensational stories for the newspapers. Teaching has become a dirty job, something that brings the professor in contact with the baser orders from whom he must protect himself. While Jo comes to save Professor Bhaer, teaching in the United States is far from the intellectual standards of his standing as "an honored professor in Berlin" (432). He is the epitome of the acculturated, well-bred white professor—with his "Plato, Homer, and Milton" (423)—but teaching women, in particular, is a degraded act.

Anzia Yezierska's *Bread Givers* provides a further example of this cynicism about professorial authority. Sara Smolinsky comes to grasp that her professor is starving, disrespected, overworked. When she wants to recite the new book on psychology to her professor, as a residue of the old days of rhetorical learning, he tells her he is too busy. She launches into a characteristic rage: "How I had dreamed of college! The inspired companionship of teachers who are friends! . . . Was the college only a factory, and the teachers machines turning out lectures by the hour on wooden dummies, incapable of response? Was there no time for the flash from eye to eye, from heart to heart?" (Yezierska 223–224). Sara Smolinsky's reaction reflects the split that Graff explains in *Professing Literature* between the generalist's "inspirational style of teaching" and the scholarly researcher's self-cultivated "dry, impersonal teaching style" (86–87). But the inspirational style she expects comes into conflict with the low regard with which the "lecturer" is held. Soon she overhears him complaining, "Maybe I was a fool to take this job. No sweatshop labour is so underpaid as the college instructor" (Yezierska 225). The nature of Smolinsky's suspicion is that the professor is just in it for the money and is no more reliable than a sweatshop boss or a shift manager. Only when she comes to see her teacher as another factory operative does she understand the emotional violence of teaching: the students' wooden responses and the factory-like aspect of the modern university are just the secondary sources of the professors' and students' rage against the devaluation of intellectual capital in the United States.

From the 1860s through the 1920s the culture struggles to define what intellectual capital would mean for women and whether white women, in particular, could attain the intellectual heights Laurie does in *Little Women*. Laurie, the other ascendant male in the novel, shows his maturity by graduating with honors and being elected to recite the Latin oration, which he did "with the grace of a Phillips, and the eloquence of a Demosthenes" (Alcott 443). Without the problem of poverty, Laurie achieves the stature of the rhetorician, with all of the privileges that his fortune allows. He doesn't have to dirty his hands with teaching, as Bhaer does. No moral high ground exists for the professor. Even in my own desire to see education as a utopian place of intellectual elevation, the women authors I study see teaching as a humiliation to be borne and even as a source of rage. Moreover, the agon invested in rhetorical education is crucial to my students' doubts about educational uplift. This uplift involves too much anger.

## Race and Intellectual Capital

What happens when African Americans become professors? How does race make a difference in the context of the ambivalence about teaching in the United States? Rather than charting a decline in rhetoric, the African American novels I teach from the 1890s rehabilitate rhetoric as key to African American education. In *Contending Forces* (1900) Pauline Hopkins especially suggests how important rhetoric was for advancing the cause of racial uplift. Mrs. Willis's sewing circle focuses on the speeches about "events of interest to the Negro race which had transpired during the week" and which serve in the narrative to anchor discussions about how best to uplift the race (143):

> After these points had been gone over, Mrs. Willis gave a talk upon some topic of interest. . . . She could talk dashingly on many themes [related to "the evolution of true womanhood"], for which she had received much applause in by-gone days, when in private life she had held forth in the drawing-room of some Back Bay philanthropist who sought to use her talents as an attraction for a worthy charitable object, the discovery of a rare species of versatility in the Negro character being a sure drawing-card. . . . Thus she became the pivot about which all the social and intellectual life of the colored people of her section revolved. (146–148)

As Hopkins illustrates, Mrs. Willis is able to effect uplift—including a recovery of "virtue" for sexually assaulted black women—by lecturing about black women's sexual integrity. As Anne-Elizabeth Murdy argues, Hopkins shows how women must work "outside the apparatus of traditional educational structures" with a pedagogy based on "intimacy" (118, 120). Willis's rhetorical performances elicit a renewed sense of struggle and agonistic violence in the heroine, whereby Sappho is able to redefine her "duty" in terms of "race and womanhood," but not without a moral struggle, during which she responds "in spite of herself, by the woman's words" (Hopkins, *Contending* 156–157). In short, Mrs. Willis's words bring out the heroine's fight by invoking her resistance to the racial status quo. The resistance, not the acquiescence, is crucial to racial uplift.[4]

As *Megda* also demonstrates, oratory and public performance were central to the rise of the black middle class. In a dynamic similar to that of *Little Women* Kelley-Hawkins's novel invests cultural capital in the professor, a repressive figure who evokes not sympathy but fear, even antipathy. *Megda*'s early scenes are not so much based on evangelical allegory as an educational one. The heroine Meg's first crisis occurs when her essay assignment goes missing and her teacher, the headmistress, refuses to believe Meg's excuse that it was stolen. Eventually, the teacher blames the poor "dark" little girl, Ruth Dean, and suspends her from the female academy. It turns out that a rich rival of Meg's hid the essay, but one of Meg's friends found it in their dressing room. In losing her written composition, however, Megda finds her voice. Like most of the other symbolic moments in this highly figurative novel, losing the essay is a trope for abandoning the repression of writing and discovering the pleasures of speaking. It is a symbolic victory over the teacher, with whom the heroine is locked in the agon of competition.

At the end of the novel the once-maligned Ruth herself becomes a teacher. One wonders what sort of lesson she herself has internalized and perpetuates by being singled out for discipline. The very person ostracized and punished by the educational system ends up reproducing it by working in it. Like Ruth, Meg had professed to wanting to become a teacher so that she could continue to study elocution (Kelley-Hawkins, *Megda* 302). She does so for a few years, working for Professor Weir, who falls in love with her and proposes. Yet, finally, she becomes a preacher's wife, while Ruth takes up being a "professor," which means ambiguously both teacher and Christian witness. But only with the authority of religion do rhetoric and teaching regain their cultural value. The novel's one moment of cynicism stems from the treatment of Ruth Dean, when she is singled out by her color and class as the likely scapegoat.

In 1898 Kelley-Hawkins published her second novel, *Four Girls at Cottage City*, which also employs another shadowy professor, Mr. Wild, "whose authoritative title of professor is undercut by the 'wildness' of his surname" (Peterson, "New Negro" 123). As in *Megda*, the four girls are middle-class African American women (two are mulattas, whose most telling reference to their race is their reference to sitting in "nigger heaven") but this time on vacation in Cottage City.[5] The professor they encounter on holiday resembles "Uriah Heep," Dickens's evil presence, and is employed as a professor of phrenology in Boston. He comes to the lodgings that the four girls have rented and disrupts the happy six-some of the girls and their two male companions. Explaining his profession as "the science of the function of the parts of the brain" (Kelley-Hawkins, *Four Girls* 253), he proceeds to analyze the girls' mental faculties and their futures. One of the male companions suggests that his type is more "Oscar Wilde," a suggestion that recalls the well-known trial of the 1890s (263). When Wild starts to mesmerize Jessie, the girls break down in fits and beg him to stop (328–329). He then proceeds to examine their heads, delineating their natures and desires.

All of the professor's science is set against the long, embedded narrative of Mrs. Hood, whose conversion to Christianity came after the deaths of her husbands, all but one of her children, and her family. Mrs. Hood's conversion occurs as a result of a dream of middle-class heaven, in which she encounters her children and family happily playing and praying together. Thus, the lessons of conversion and science are set against each other. Despite the girls' immediate distrust of the professor, he eventually proves to be helpful in their mission to raise money for little Robin's (Mrs. Hood's last child) spinal operation (yes, that's Robin Hood). He gives them ten dollars, which gets them started toward saving the five hundred dollars they need (350–351).

This negotiation between the myth of Robin Hood and the middle-class black professor indicates a major transition from earlier African American novels and their support of Christianity over science. More important, however, it indicates the shift between women giving over authority to Christian fathers and the transfer of authority to educational/head masters. The professor is made to prove the benevolence of his practice—that is, to justify the benefits, however indirect, of his science. (Soon enough, American women's fiction will adopt the authority of the master teacher, the professor, without question.) Perhaps even more important is the fact that Kelley-Hawkins turns a racist pseudoscience—phrenology—into a tool to legitimize African American authority. That John Wild is a moral and philanthropic professor of phrenology wrests the power away from white ethnologists and racial scientists and revalues it as a potential claim to black authority. Phrenology, rhetoric, and science all become instruments of the new black professoriate, even as they do in Pauline Hopkins's *Of One Blood* (1903).[6]

In that novel, too, the black professor Reuel Briggs becomes the hero but only after a significant trial of his moral authority. Briggs is a doctor of psychology and authority in "brain diseases." He begins by deceiving his patient, Dianthe Lusk, into believing she is a white woman so that she won't draw attention to his own racial passing at Harvard, where he works. That Hopkins focuses on the white-privileged world of Harvard gives even more credence to the doubt she casts upon Briggs as a harbinger of the "race man" that the novel eventually offers. In short, this doctor must first relinquish the privilege that being a Harvard professor confers, in order to accept his destiny as the ruler of the lost African world. Hopkins does not let us lose sight of how being a professor means, for Briggs, denying his race. For Hopkins's audience, and I suspect also for Kelley-Hawkins's, the danger in becoming a professor lies in forgetting one's ties of kinship to the black community. It may even be that Hopkins sees the process of educational uplift as a process of "whitening"—a deracination linked to the erasure of identity.

## Teaching Race, Religion, and Rage

In teaching *Megda*, I had wanted to teach educational uplift *as* racial uplift, but my students preferred religious uplift. Their interest and resistance lead me to ask whether it is possible, given the examples I have included, to teach educational uplift in the twenty-first century in the face of professorial frustration and student rage and thus to wrest educational uplift from its legacy of conflict and violence. Or are we still playing out a legacy of the nineteenth-century rage against professors, documented by Connors? Perhaps there is something irreducibly dystopian in the very scene of teaching itself. If so, it may be a reaction to the failure of a "raceless world," as Peterson's reading suggests.

In reading Kelley-Hawkins's novel, my students and I return to the dystopian world in which we live, where race does not disappear and where being a professor does not confer moral authority and respect but often evokes cynicism and suspicion of political and cultural values. Perhaps my students' acceptance and my own resistance to the Christian vision of raceless equality emerge from a displaced anxiety about the place where we are working together, the classroom, and the profession that is supposed to offer this transcendence, teaching. Like most college teachers, I have always assumed the classroom to be the space of transcendence and freedom. It is clear that many students do *not*, preferring instead to see the church as the primary source of that possibility. In offering us different utopian visions of racial freedom via religious or educational uplift, *Megda* reminds us how far we are from Kelley-Hawkins's vision of racelessness and educational meritocracy.

*Megda* is not *Native Son*, and Kelley-Hawkins does not want to posit race as so central a cultural determinant as Richard Wright does. At least that is the message that the students avidly grasp. Perhaps I cluelessly ignored the religious message or felt it should be refocused so that students understand that race is more centrally meaningful than religion. What the students may be responding to is the middle-class vision of black uplift, and the Christian conversion puts the lie to the vision of middle-class transformation. They don't see transformation as a result of education; religion is a more tangible version of transformation for them than for me, granddaughter of immigrants as I am. Instead, Christianity is the "universal," the screen that keeps us from seeing that race may be less central a determinant than progressives and pluralists want it to be. So, the students' rejection of my vision of uplift in favor of a Christian vision is not solely because they are good Lutherans and Methodists (at Madison) or good Baptists (at UK)—but because they are good believers in bourgeois individuation. Race and class seem too large to tackle, and so they prefer the individuating vision of religious salvation. Race and class are rationalized systems, Weberian "iron cages," which can only be eluded by the promise of individual redemption.

The pedagogical task then becomes how to return to race, and not education or religion, as the concern of Kelley-Hawkins's novels. This means asserting the communal model and rejecting the individual paradigm, supported by the Protestant ethic that Weber has articulated and our students often live out. We must leave behind Kelley-Hawkins's utopian dreams of racelessness and return to the everyday violence that occurs in communities, classes, colleges. My pedagogical hope is to teach students how the universal of Christian uplift was implicated in the adoption of racial segregation, white supremacist ideologies, and white racial privilege. In so doing, I will also have to teach how the educational system has been implicated in the same white supremacist and privileged spheres. Within both institutions that my students and I see as modes of racial uplift are violent histories of suppression. In acknowledging this history, we can also believe in the project of white scholars teaching African American texts, especially if it provokes us all into rethinking our assumptions about the universal value of religion and education. Teaching these texts within this institutional critique can help us reclaim professing as an ethical act.

## NOTES

My thanks to Andy Doolen, whose spirited response to my essay made all the difference.

1. And what if I have chosen to include Kelley-Hawkins's novel on my syllabus because it poses her ambivalence about racial categorizing and allows another instance of white erasure of black culture? Once you start on this path, the "what if" questions mount.
2. Or, as Peterson argues, elocutionism was an acceptable female profession and "performative mode" for women, balancing as it did the emotions with the performance of them ("New Negro" 125).
3. Consider Mark Edmundson's 2002 memoir, *Teacher*, which analyzes pedagogy as inspirational authority: his teacher turned a thug like him into a Bennington College student, a Yale Ph.D., and an English professor at the University of Virginia. Perhaps this is less a transformation than it is destiny? English majors are attracted to the profession precisely because it allows aggression to find a legitimate outlet. Edmundson's agonistic relationship with his teacher, Franklin Lears, is a case in point of the kind of psychic violence we have come to expect from master teachers.
4. As Eldred and Mortensen remind us in *Imagining Rhetoric*, Charlotte Forten experienced great despair and became dispirited when trying to reconcile her teaching life with the unrest in the "unsatisfactory" world of the 1850s challenges to slavery (qtd. in Eldred 211). When she joins the teaching force on the South Carolina Sea Islands, she is able to unite her rhetoric with her teaching life.
5. As Peterson documents: "The town was originally known for its Methodist camp meetings held every August; Baptists were welcomed from the 1870s on, and there is evidence showing that African Americans did attend meetings. Significantly, in the

1870s Cottage City did become a summer resort for middle-class Americans, so that religious practice and leisure activities came to complement one another. Well-to-do blacks visited Cottage City as well, although Oak Bluffs did not become a specifically African American resort until the early twentieth century" ("New Negro" 115).

6. Keep in mind that the turn to the middle-class and civic identity came as a result of the failed history of U.S. Reconstruction. These new professors of science, in turn-of-the-century black novels, are scientists of the body, professing the voice, the organs, the mind. This is a significant shift, given the complexity of making the black body a subject worthy of study. By presenting the African American body as both the source and the professor of its own knowledge, Kelley-Hawkins reinvents teaching as a "master discourse." Moreover, especially with oratory and elocution, professors teach *control* over the body and its functions. All of this control goes toward persuading an audience of the usefulness of the speaker's place in the public sphere and civil discourse. *Special note*: When this essay was in press, Holly Jackson's research revealed that Emma Dunham Kelley-Hawkins was a white woman (*The Boston Globe* February 20, 2005). As Jackson points out, this discovery complicates, if not invalidates, readings of the racial hopefulness of *Megda* and *Four Girls at Cottage City.* Henry Louis Gates replies that her novels will be taken out of the Schomburg Series of Nineteenth-Century Black Women Writers. My own reading of Kelley-Hawkins depends on the mistaken racial identification, but the pedagogical situation of my students's goals and professorial desire is still my main argument.

# Writing about Gwendolyn Brooks Anyway

JAMES D. SULLIVAN

Since the publication of Gwendolyn Brooks's first book, *A Street in Bronzeville*, in 1945, white critics have generally received her work warmly, but their attempts to address its racial politics have not always aged well. By the late 1960s she was fed up with us: "Whites are not going to understand what is happening in black literature today. Even those who most sympathize with it still are not equipped to be proper critics" (Brooks, *Report* 176–177). Critical comments that devalued her subject matter of urban African American life indicated to her that critics from other backgrounds often just missed the point of her poetry. She therefore said in another interview, "I am absolutely free of any fear of what any white critic might say because I feel that it's going to be most amazing if any of them really understand the true significance of what's going on" (Garland 56). Portrayals of angry responses to white racism seemed to make white critics respond with defensiveness or hostility.

By that time her sympathy with the black arts movement had also led her to think of African American readers as her main audience, and she ridiculed white critics who felt excluded, resentful that she was not speaking to them. "They will probably look at the blacker products," she said, "and disapprove of them because, naturally, they have to disapprove of disapproval of themselves" (Garland 56). This was a moment of African American cultural independence, with a desire for cultural self-sufficiency that did not need and—in this moment that Brooks saw as a decisive break—did not want white critical feedback. She insisted, therefore, that African American culture was changing in ways that white audiences simply would not appreciate, and so their response—hostile, sympathetic, or whatever—would be irrelevant:

> There is indeed a new black today. He is different from any the world has known. He's a tall-walker. Almost firm. By many of his own *brothers* he is not understood. And he is understood by *no* white. Not the wise white; not the Schooled white; not the Kind white. Your *least* pre-requisite toward an understanding of the new black is an exceptional Doctorate which can be conferred only upon those with the proper properties of bitter birth and intrinsic sorrow. I know this is infuriating, especially to those professional Negro-understanders, some of them so very kind, with special portfolio, special savvy. But I cannot say anything other, because nothing other is the truth. (*Report* 85–86)

Younger, more militant African American poet Don L. Lee (Haki R. Madhubuti) apparently considered this paragraph of Brooks's so important that for his preface to her 1972 autobiography, *Report from Part One*, he opened his own remarks by quoting it (13). Brooks's autobiography, therefore, effectively begins by warding off white readers.

Yet, aware of her warning, I have continued to read her work, to teach it, even to write about it and publish that criticism. Perhaps this is a form of colonization, an unwelcome appropriation of African American literature. Perhaps, on the other hand, it is not a problem at all. After all, with publication, any work leaves the author's hands, and readers encounter and use the work in all sorts of settings and contexts that the writer cannot control. Removed from its previous context, it interacts with new contexts to produce sometimes different meanings. Claude McKay, for example, wrote "If We Must Die" as a response to racist white mobs attacking African American neighborhoods in the riots of 1919, but Winston Churchill later found that sonnet the perfect expression of British fighting spirit during the Battle of Britain. The poem was available for meanings McKay could not have anticipated when he wrote it. Mid- to late-twentieth-century African American culture and experience, therefore, need not, perhaps, under such a de- or recontextualizing reading practice, be the ultimate referent for all of Brooks's poetry and fiction. Certainly, someone coming to these accounts of African American experience from a different cultural background would understand them rather differently from the way Brooks herself did. Yet, though such an understanding might have its own coherence and aesthetic delight, the poet herself might notice that it emphasizes different aspects of the experience than she would; some of the outsiders' recontextualized readings might be so different from an insider's that she might even consider them misreadings.

But that procedure requires isolating the text within some new reading context, the moment of reception slewed off from the moment of production—easy enough to do, especially if one knows little about the author or about the text's history. After all, how many English people listening to Churchill on the radio knew much about the Jamaican McKay or about American racial politics circa 1919? How many suburbanites had spent much time in Brooks's South Side Chicago Bronzeville? That lack of connection could create what Brooks may have considered unwelcome shifts in emphasis or aberrant readings.

When I first started reading Brooks (back in college, after hearing her perform her poetry), I did not know about her statements rejecting a white readership's understanding, but, once I learned about them, that rejection became, paradoxically, part of the context within which I read her work. Amusement, for example, at the condescending charity of "The Ladies of the Ladies' Betterment League" in "The Lovers of the Poor" (Brooks, *Blacks* 349), or schadenfreude at the fall of self-absorbed John Cabot, "all whitebluerose below his yellow hair," in "Riot" (470), proceeds, therefore, not to smug certainty that one is surely better, more sensitive, than they but to a self-questioning about the extent to which they are a portrait of me: the white reader. To what extent, after, say, reading "In the Mecca," does the white reader better understand the tenement life recounted there, and to what extent does that reader still remain out of touch with it? Awareness of Brooks's rejection thus introduces an awareness of cultural distance into a reading of the work. Therefore, the author's rejection of my understanding is, after all, indeed a problem, and I need to justify my scholarship and criticism of her work—either by rejecting her rejection as perhaps some form of noxious cultural intolerance itself or else by exploring the reasons for that rejection and then finding a critical strategy that both accepts and includes the cultural gap in the critic's knowledge and that also evades those errors that so annoyed her in the work of some earlier white commentators.

It would be easy to isolate Brooks's pronouncements about who might and who might not understand her work as an expression of a past historical moment, the political enthusiasms of the black power movement of the late 1960s and early 1970s. That approach of historically isolating the hostility to white critics, however, would suggest that my own historical moment, in the early twenty-first century, has somehow transcended the political and cultural concerns that provoked her statements. It would suggest that those concerns are no longer an issue, that we have (and clearly we have not) found our way out of the history of racism. Certainly, we are at a different moment in that history, but, unfortunately, that history continues. From the vantage point of the following century I can look back now on the moment of Brooks's declarations of white irrelevance (which she never, by the way, retracted in later decades), but I cannot look back on it from a position entirely beyond it, as though the problems that provoked her comments are things of the past. Taking Brooks's rejection of white critics seriously, therefore, means not just isolating them in a distant historical context. Her remarks usefully remind me that I am still working from within the history of racism. They make me question to what extent my own historical and intellectual perspective leads me to readings preferable to those of the white critics of earlier decades and to what extent my frame of reference still resembles theirs.

A more successful approach to Brooks's comments may, therefore, proceed through an examination of how that history has been manifest in the writings of even some of the most well-meaning white critics. What did they write that led to such sharp rebukes from a poet whose work they admired? White book reviewers in the 1940s through the 1960s saw themselves as endorsing her work in perfectly good faith—indeed, in a progressive and antiracist spirit. Yet by the late 1960s it became possible to see that praise as shot through with unfortunate assumptions about what they saw as the limitations of African American literature. Rereading those old reviews in the light of later insights and concerns reveals how implicated they were—though certainly not consciously—in the continuing history of racism. In the midst of their own history those reviewers could not—as, of course, no one ever can—see all the limitations of their own perspective, limitations that might burn with blazing clarity when exposed to the light of a different historical moment.

Harper and Row (now HarperCollins), a major publisher, had sold Brooks's work, from her 1945 *A Street in Bronzeville* through her 1968 *In the Mecca*, to a general reading public that is and was, after all, mostly white. Reviewers for such publications as, for example, the *Chicago Tribune, Poetry* magazine, and the *New York Herald Tribune Book Week* would also, quite reasonably, evaluate the books on behalf of their own primarily white audiences. Her work would, therefore, come to the attention of much of her readership via the filter of (generally positive) white judgment. In the late 1960s, however, Brooks became acquainted with the black power movement and its turn away from an integrationist politics as well as with the black arts movement and its emphasis on producing works specifically about African American life for specifically African American audiences. These movements gave her a framework for rereading the terms of the white approval she had enjoyed.

Poet Paul Engle wrote for the *Chicago Tribune* Sunday Books section one of the first reviews of Brooks's first book, her 1945 *A Street in Bronzeville*. Praising especially "Gay Chaps at the Bar," a series of poems about African American soldiers in World War II, Engle wrote: "They are the most controlled, the most intense poems in the book. And finest of all, they can be read for what they are and not, as the publishers want us to believe, as Negro poems. For they should no more be called Negro poetry than the poems of Robert Frost should be called white poetry. They are handsome and real and genuine poems by a civilized American citizen" (11).

The poems in the "Gay Chaps at the Bar" sequence are indeed "controlled" and "intense," and they are "handsome and real and genuine poems by a civilized American citizen" most certainly, but they are also a vivid depiction—

derived from letters sent her by male friends in the military—of a specifically African American experience of World War II.[1] Engle's acceptance demands that he be able to bleach out the African American references as he reads. He would include her in the canon of modern American poets right along with Frost but suggests that she fits so well already that the subject matter she might add to that canon—urban African American life—may be safely ignored. He is, furthermore, pleased that he can read the poems apolitically: "Miss Brooks is the first Negro poet to write wholly out of a deep and imaginative talent, without relying on the fact of color to draw sympathy and interest. Her poems would be finely lyrical and delightfully witty without the fact of color ever being mentioned." Indeed they would be. Engle, however, explicitly praises the suppression of racial politics and then goes on to assure readers they can safely ignore those hints of it that remain: "The finest praise that can be given the book is that it would be a superb volume of poetry in any year by any person of any color" (11). Henry Taylor has perceptively commented on Engle's review: "There is no reason to doubt Engle's sincere admiration of Brooks' work or the honesty of his conviction that race should not be the issue that it is, but it is hard to get away from the hint of exclusiveness, the suggestion that Brooks is a fine poet not regardless of her color, but in spite of it" (267). As Taylor suggests, Engle praises Brooks for transcending African American culture, implicitly treating it as a problem *to be* transcended rather than as a rich ground for a writer to work. Furthermore, it seems important for Engle to be able to ignore any suggestions of racially specific content. Glad as Brooks was to receive such a strong review at the start of her career, African American life was her subject matter, and in a couple decades that whiff of condescension toward it would come to offend her.

Stanley Kunitz, in a 1950 review in *Poetry*, likewise praised Brooks's second collection, the Pulitzer Prize–winning *Annie Allen*, for devotion to craft and suppression of racial politics: "There is in her work a becoming modesty. Though the materials of her art are largely derived from the conditions of her life in a Negro urban milieu, she uses these incendiary materials naturally for their intrinsic value without straining for shock or for depth without pretending to speak for a people. . . . I have been impressed by how little of the energy that should go into the building of the work has been diverted to the defense of the life" (52). Unlike Engle, Kunitz acknowledges "her life in a Negro urban milieu" as valuable material for the poetry, material with an "intrinsic value" of its own. And, rather than ignoring the implicit racial politics of that milieu, Kunitz further acknowledges that it is potentially "incendiary," that there is reason to fear that Brooks's subject matter could fan some passionate flames. He nonetheless praises her good taste in not exploring the political implications that might lead her to political conclusions. The focus remains individual, on Annie and other characters, not, Kunitz seems grateful to see, on any generalizations about how American racial politics in general has shaped these individual lives.

Kunitz praises Brooks not for racial indifference, as Engle does, but for political evasiveness, putting her energy into the aesthetic task of "building the work" of her poetry, rather than the rhetorical and political task of a "defense of the life" of African Americans against racist hostility.

Yet another white poet, Louis Simpson, recognizes, as does Kunitz, the African American cultural base of Brooks's work, but then, rather outrageously, he dismisses it as not at all a valid subject matter for poetry: "I am not sure it is possible for a Negro to write well without making us aware he is a Negro; on the other hand, if being a Negro is the only subject, the writing is not important" (25). This notorious remark appeared in his (once more, generally positive) review of Brooks's 1963 *Selected Poems*. The *us* is clearly white readers of the *New York Herald Tribune Book Week*. Of a black readership he is either unconcerned or unaware, as he is also of the range of African American literature. For he praises Brooks's singular achievement thus: "Miss Brooks must have had a devil of a time trying to write poetry in the United States, where there has been practically no Negro poetry worth talking about" (L. Simpson 25). So much for—well, you can write your own list, but, just to start, I'd like to include Langston Hughes, Sterling Brown, Jean Toomer, Richard Wright, Margaret Walker, Melvin Tolson, and Robert Hayden. Simpson either had little acquaintance with such writers or simply did not value their work. Since Simpson was writing, however, before the days of canon reform—before the days when the curriculum and the major anthologies, publishers' lists and their publicity organs, came not only to include to a greater extent but also to promote the works of African American writers, before, that is, the time that the works of African American writers were considered to count as a significant part of American literature—his opportunities to become acquainted with those traditions had been rather limited. My own literary education later in the twentieth century, on the other hand, introduced me to and taught me to value the traditions of African American literature. That I can so readily rattle off a list of prominent African American poets demonstrates that, clearly, there has been progress.

When Simpson's remarks were reprinted in 1996 in a collection of reviews of and essays on Brooks's work, Simpson took, as he says, the "opportunity to set the record straight." He wanted to clarify that, although his remarks were later interpreted as racist, they were, when he wrote them in 1963, neither intended nor, so far as he could tell, received as racist. He lets us know, in fact, "When I published this review, Ms. Brooks wrote me to thank me for it." And, regarding the crucial claim that, "if being a Negro is the only subject, the writing is not important," he elaborates, "I did not mean to suggest that black writers should not speak of their blackness—only that they should write about other things as well" (in S. Wright 23). Simpson thus defends what he wrote some thirty years before but restates it in a more moderate form, not that writing about African American life is unimportant but that African American writers—like any writers—should not limit themselves to a single topic. Given an opportunity to reflect on statements he made in a different historical context, he defends his integrity; what he wrote in 1963, despite all intervening historical change in racial consciousness, he stands by still in 1996. He misses the opportunity to see his 1963 comments as historically conditioned by racist assumptions and a limited awareness that was, at that time, invisible to him. He misses the opportunity to reflect on ways that his own awareness has expanded and changed in the course of three decades.

Simpson did not see his own remarks as racist, any more than Engle or Kunitz saw any racism, any devaluing of African American culture or experience, in their own remarks. They wrote at a time when progressive thought favored integration, and the struggle against the histories of segregation and of scientific racism demanded an emphasis on the common humanity of all peoples. Emphasizing and valuing difference, one ran the risk of justifying segregation, the preservation of separate traditions via separate and, in notorious practice, unequal institutions. In Brooks these reviewers found a fine example of a modernist they could claim transcended race. This finding, this aesthetic judgment, was consistent, then, with the integrationist position: they did not have to treat the work of this African American writer any differently from the work of any white writers. In 1950 Brooks was given the Pulitzer Prize for Poetry for her collection *Annie Allen*: the literary establishment could thus present Brooks as definitive evidence that African American writers, if given a chance, could meet the same cultural standards set for white writers. Her Pulitzer could stand as witness that integration—judge all by the same standards, bar none from consideration on grounds of race—could work.[2]

Color blindness was a corollary of this approach. Whatever called attention to racial difference, rather than common humanity, was to be downplayed. Simpson simply stated more bluntly what other reviewers had been saying more subtly in their praise of Brooks's work. They praised her for achieving universal cultural values, when those universals were actually a projection of their own values, those of the mid-twentieth-century white liberal American literati. They praised her for addressing their own concerns and found they could either neglect or dismiss elements in her work that addressed other (specifically African American) concerns not their own.

In the late 1960s, with the rise of the black power and black arts movements, this blind spot would become visible, cultural difference would become valued, and (contrary to Simpson), when being black was the subject, the writing would become especially important. Historical progress, in the form of recognition of the value of cultural diversity and an acceptance (as opposed to a denial) of difference, made it possible to become aware of that blind spot. It became possible to see the unthought, never quite escapable racism in remarks that had been, at the time of their publication, neither intended nor received as racist. Lacking the insights and concerns of a later day, even the most progressive-minded writers from a different cultural moment—such as Engle, Kunitz, and Simpson—can sometimes, unfortunately, come off looking wrongheaded. This is why Simpson's failure to reconsider, rather than defend, his earlier remarks is especially troubling. If the unthought racist assumptions of the past become obvious today, then the unthought racism of today is likely to become equally obvious to the next generation. White critics of African American literature have a special responsibility to recognize their place in that historical process, to recognize with humility the liability of their criticism to such historical reconsideration.

By the late 1960s Brooks had become aware that her work was received differently by African American and white audiences. In 1967 she felt the contrast with particular strength when, soon after being warmly received for a reading at "white white white South Dakota State College," she found herself merely "coldly Respected" by the audience for a writers' conference at predominantly African American Fisk University (Brooks, *Report* 84). Upon returning home to Chicago, she then began to encounter a range of audiences for poetry that she had not previously considered. She was invited to lead a workshop for gang members interested in writing poetry. That first workshop experience led her to start another informal poetry workshop for African American college students (193–194). One day her workshop students took her to a neighborhood bar, where they then gave an impromptu poetry reading. Recounting this story to an interviewer, Brooks said: "The poets started reading, and before we knew it, people had turned around on their bar stools, with their drinks behind them, and were listening. Then they applauded. And I thought that was a wonderful thing, something new. I want to write poetry—and it won't be Ezra Pound poetry, as you can imagine—that will be exciting to such people. And I don't see why it can't be 'good' poetry, putting quotes around 'good.'" (152–153). Gang members and tavern patrons who liked poetry: here was an audience she realized she had neglected in addressing a literary elite who responded especially to the modernist difficulty of her own "Ezra Pound poetry." For the particularly complex *Annie Allen*, in fact, they had given her the Pulitzer Prize. Don L. Lee, however, commented: "*Annie Allen* important? Yes. Read by blacks? No. *Annie Allen* more so than *A Street in Bronzeville* seems to have been written for whites" (17).

Beginning with *Riot* (1969), then, Brooks published new work only with African American–run publishers. Although her new publishers were small and thus lacked the resources to distribute and promote her books as widely as her old, large, commercial publisher could, they focused their resources on the primarily African American institutions, communities, and readers that Brooks most wanted to address. And she wanted to support and encourage African American cultural institutions. The opportunity to sell the work of an already well-known writer would be a great boost for a small, financially struggling publisher. After she had begun publishing with Haki R. Madhubuti's Third World Press, she explained in an interview, "I couldn't possibly think of going back to any white publisher. I'll always be with a black publisher and if Third World Press discontinues its operations, though it doesn't seem to have any prospects of that, I shall publish my own work. I will never go back to a white press. But I left them, as you probably know, because I wanted to encourage the Black publishers who at that time needed clients" (Brown and Zorn 54). Because her new publishers had more limited resources for printing, distributing, and publicizing her work and because they would focus those more limited resources primarily within African American communities, it became harder than it had been when Harper and Row was her publisher for much of her old audience to obtain—or even learn about—her new work. Since her new work was now available only through a specifically African American publishing context, it would now be more difficult than it had been to dismiss or diminish the specifically African American dimension of her work. In fact, she entitled her 1987 collected works *Blacks*, thus encouraging a reassessment of all her work, back to the 1940s, in terms of her later, more militant cultural identification. The new publishing context would now make it difficult for white critics to make the sort of remarks that had so annoyed Brooks—in part because they would now be less likely than before even to see or learn about such new work.

Yet I have read it. Although the 1963 Harper *Selected Poems* remains the most widely available of Brooks's work in major bookstores, her other, later, small press works have found their way onto my shelves. Why, however, read and write about Brooks at all, rather than heed her warning and respect the roadblocks she set up to slow my approach to her work? Why not set the book down and turn to writers who would not accuse me of colonizing their cultural productions?

As an undergraduate, I heard her when she spoke at my college, and I was charmed by the warmth and wit of her grandmotherly performance style, her playfulness with language, the emotional depth of her poetry, and (not least for a white suburban kid) the vision of African American urban life. So, I began to read, enjoy, and learn from her books. Later, in graduate school, for a seminar on contemporary American poetry, I began to write about her. Coming across some of the warnings quoted earlier, I learned that this writer I had come to admire had dismissed in advance anything I might say about her. What could I do? Well, for purposes of the seminar paper I went ahead and wrote anyway, hoping that, with enough research and self-consciousness, I might produce some valuable ideas even from across the cultural divide my author had, in the late 1960s and early 1970s, considered so impassible.

Over the years since then, the power of Brooks's work has repeatedly drawn me back to it, and, despite her warnings that I lack "the exceptional Doctorate which can be conferred only upon those with the proper properties of bitter birth and intrinsic sorrow," I have, in admiration, defied her by continuing to write and publish my thoughts on her poetry. I still rely on research and self-consciousness. In fact, continuing to write about Brooks has deepened that self-consciousness, made me more aware of myself as a specifically white reader in a specific historical moment, someone who brings to *Blacks*, or indeed to any book by any writer, a particular ethnic consciousness and frame of reference. Brooks's rejection of white critics emerged out of the concerns of a specific historical moment as well, but, if I continue to take that rejection seriously, then I have reason to subject myself and my criticism to a rigorous historical judgment.

To help me maintain that self-consciousness, I have the example of the earlier critics who did not see their own whiteness as a racial category. Of course, transported into a different cultural context or surviving into a different historical moment, anyone's work (not just that of mid-twentieth-century white liberals) can be made to appear silly in the light of still more enlightened insights and concerns. Writing about Brooks in the early twenty-first century, I leave myself open to a similar critique in the next generation (or perhaps even sooner). What I publish remains in the archive, available for the scrutiny of other scholars at other times and places, available too for the sort of invidious recontextualizing I have performed here on the writings of others. People who read my work in these other contexts will no doubt see with clarity the unconscious assumptions of my circumstances and historical moment, the shutters and distortions on what appears to me a clear, clean window. Some future scholar may see fit to tease out subtle racism or, as I do with Simpson, just quote a line that makes it, in a new or different setting, seem quite manifest.

None of us can control future uses of our writings or ideas. Once they are published, they become available for reinscription. Nor are any of us, of course, fully aware of the cultural assumptions, the ideological underlayer, of our own works. Readers in other times and places will see them much more clearly than we see them ourselves (notwithstanding the persistent unwillingness or inability of Louis Simpson, prize-winning poet and otherwise a writer of considerable insight and imagination, to see any racism in his review). But, if we see our criticism historically, we must recognize that, just as we have learned to see the ideologies that circumscribe works from the past, so too our own limitations will eventually become legible also. White critics writing about African American literature have a particular responsibility to be aware of the history of both overt and unconscious racism. We must also, however, have the humility to admit that that history is not yet ended and that we still work within it.

Like all critics, of course, I write because I consider my ideas worthwhile. But, when I write about Brooks, I remember her warning and recognize that I too may someday be held up as a bad example. What I write may turn out to have some lasting value in helping readers understand more richly one of twentieth-century American literature's most dazzling poets. But what I write may also simply illustrate my own cultural moment's particular weaknesses. My hope, in that case, is to provide a valuable provocation, a springboard for someone else's stronger ideas.

## NOTES

I would like to thank my colleagues Edwina Jordan, James Pearce, Kip Strasma, and Deborah Wilson for their critiques, insights, and advice as I prepared this essay.

1. Ann Folwell Stanford offers a particularly vivid reading of the quite strong racial politics of both "Gay Chaps at the Bar" and "Negro Hero," another World War II poem in *A Street in Bronzeville* ("Dialectics of Desire").
2. B. J. Bolden illuminates this debate among mid-twentieth-century African American writers, some of whom argued that, rather than address primarily an African American audience, they should try to reach larger, mainstream audiences by mainly addressing issues that were not obviously or specifically African American (*Urban Rage* 59–71).

# Truth and Talent in Interpreting Ethnic American Autobiography

## From White to Black and Beyond

KIMBERLY RAE CONNOR

From my current perch at the University of San Francisco it is impossible for me to address the role white academics play in contributing to African American scholarship in the same way I would have when I first began my study of African American literature at the University of Virginia in the early 1980s. Consider the following seasonal scenario:

> Walking my son to school for the first day of classes, within a block of our home my Vietnamese neighbors and I cross paths with worshippers at a Filipino Catholic Church that is shared by a Korean Presbyterian congregation. Along the way I pass Ramallah Hall, where later I am to meet an Arab Muslim colleague with whom I work in an interfaith movement. Every Halloween my son not only chooses a costume for trick-or-treating, he also creates a Hispanic-inspired Day of the Dead altar. On Indigenous Peoples' Day / Columbus Day he could watch the local Italian parade or go to an Ohlone pow-wow at the Presidio—originally a Native American village, then a military base, and now a national park—where on New Year's Eve we participated in a peace march led by a Japanese Buddhist monk and afterward shared a Sabbath meal with Russian Jewish acquaintances. On Lunar New Year my son accepts red envelopes from Chinese friends, while in the spring we join other families, some with two mommies and two daddies, at the Gay Pride festivities. And any time of year when we are feeling the need for special spiritual uplift, my son and I go to the St. John Coltrane African Orthodox Church, where his best friend from school is the bishop's granddaughter, and we enjoy three hours of jazz and a liturgy sung to "A Love Supreme."

So, to me, in this setting, issues surrounding racial representation are no longer just black and white.

This ambient ethnic diversity that is my son's unconscious entitlement, the multiculturalism that is his norm, was not available to me when I was growing up and being educated. Like many whites of my generation, I had to be an active agent in coloring my world, and this effort alone, however well intentioned, exposes me to charges of turning ethnicity into a commodity for my own benefit. Moreover, I suspect that nearly every white academic who responded to the call of multiculturalism as I did can identify an episode in her life when she had an intentional or accidental conversion experience, a "black like me" moment that awakened her to the promise of ethnic inclusion but brought with it a kind of shame for having so long occupied the condition James Baldwin calls "willed innocence." The challenge for most of us who share this context is what to do after the moment of conversion. How do we move from an appreciation of ethnicity as inspired by our imagination to a participation in ethnic discourse by way of our intellect? How do we will knowledge?

White academics accept that it is imperative to be informed about American ethnic cultures, but willing knowledge is complicated because we don't always know what we don't know. We are inspired but unsure about how to participate. Much of the racial history to which we have been exposed remains unprocessed by society at large and among the communities we inhabit. We inherit mythic assumptions about race that get idiosyncratically inflected by our own existential encounters as citizens, scholars, and teachers. While we can deepen our historical knowledge and expand our social contacts with ethnicity, there is no final racial arbiter on our intentions other than our own consciences. We must find affirmation on our own terms rather than seeking validation from people of color who are under no imperative to grant it; otherwise, we simply reinscribe paradigms of authority. And the validation on our production that is left up to the academy still bears all the problems that beset the larger social context. Ultimately, our *realness*—the current hip-hop measure of value—in intention or production is evaluated by a complex sampling of inherited mythic, acquired historical, and lived existential standards.

Because there is no simple standard for assessment, I turn to my authors for clarity. The possessive pronoun is intentional for, while I know I cannot *represent* ethnic American cultures, I do believe I can *interpret* them. I can interpret them because American ethnic writers intended their work to be evocative, to call for readers' responses. While it was African American literature that first called to me, this literature also led me to listen to other ethnic voices. The marvelous complications African American literature presented to my interpretative posture multiplied when I moved beyond a black-white paradigm. Going from white to black to beyond, I realized that all literary production is more than product. It is process, an agreement between the writer and the reader that is not static but dynamic. The relationship is an ongoing interpretative act that today necessitates the creative collaboration of many ethnic American perspectives.

To illustrate the dynamics of this relationship and the ways in which I have come to understand the role I play in African American scholarship—as an interpreter, not a representative of ethnicity—I want to relate a story that emerged from the laboratory of the classroom but took me deep into my own conscience. I hope this story will help untangle the mythic, historical, and existential strands that combine to weave our ethnic sensibilities. I also hope my interpretative example will demonstrate how white scholars, in addition to benefiting from, can also contribute to multicultural understanding.

Although she claimed in a letter to Amy Post in 1853, while she was writing *Incidents in the Life a Slave Girl*, that she could only deliver "truth but not talent" (236), most readers would now agree that Harriet Jacobs succeeded in providing both. The same assessment, however, is seldom applied to Monica Sone's 1953 autobiography, *Nisei Daughter*, a text that has not assumed the canonical status that Jacobs's autobiography enjoys. One of the few Nisei autobiographies that emerged not long after World War II and described the internment of Japanese Americans, Sone's book, like Jacobs's, is very important in documenting a shameful episode in American history and providing us access to a firsthand account. But, when presented in the context of ethnic studies and literature, Sone's autobiography disappoints scholars, teachers, and students alike. Of the little scholarship that has been done on *Nisei Daughter*, most critics take it at face value as a classic example of assimilationist writing while lamenting that the author was not more progressive in her ethnic stance or more critical in her social politics. They find neither truth nor talent in Sone's writing.

I recently taught *Nisei Daughter* as part of a course on ethnic American autobiography. With a solid background in autobiographical and African American literary scholarship and instruction, I felt confident that I could expand my repertoire to include a broader array of texts that reflected the diversity of my students in the San Francisco Bay Area. So, I tried to create a syllabus that was representative and balanced, including along with Sone's Japanese American autobiography one by an African American (Richard Wright's *Black Boy*), a Mexican American (Richard Rodriguez's *Hunger of Memory*), a Chinese American (Maxine Hong Kingston's *The Woman Warrior*) and a Native American (N. Scott Momaday's *The Way to Rainy Mountain*). I also did homework in current ethnic theory to broaden my scope of the issues and to find concepts and categories that crossed ethnic boundaries. All these elements combined, I assumed I was ready to teach.

After giving the students an overview of ethnic and autobiographical theory, I began with the slam-dunk of Richard Wright. The raw urgency and powerful descriptions in his text immediately captivated students. Although challenged by Kingston's text, her experimental forms and dramatic episodes also moved the students. Students admired Rodriguez's text for its lyrical writing and were stimulated by his refusal to submit to ethnic victimization. And Momoday's text gently ushered them into a profound appreciation for a native way of seeing the world. But Monica Sone's text, unlike any of the others, absolutely perplexed them. The text seemed to possess none of the traits of the other autobiographies that were so evocative for the students. They found it disappointing, uninspiring, trite, and of a wholly different order than the one they came to reserve for *real* ethnic literature.

I chose the text because I admired it but primarily because it satisfied my diversity criteria. Had I gone through the customary list of attributes ascribed to ethnic autobiographies, however, Sone's text would have emerged as my students perceived it: as ethnically incorrect. Although all the texts I taught were twentieth-century works, hers was the only one that was not written by a professional writer or by one who sought to establish a literary reputation. In terms of autobiographical agency or where one locates the factors that shape experience, Sone is coy in attributing her experience—positively or negatively—to her ethnicity. Likewise, the issue of motivation that establishes a political, social, and/or ethnic agenda is largely absent in Sone's text. We do not get any specific indication of what prompted her to write her autobiography. Regarding truthfulness in autobiography, Sone's text is also problematic. Her language is simple and unadorned, and seldom does she delve into any analysis of events. She avoids describing harsh and difficult moments; rather, she renders them discreetly, in the plainest of descriptions without emotional urgency. Finally, unlike the other writers we encountered in this class, Sone does not appear to be concerned with establishing her character as an ethnic American but, rather, seems interested only in creating a character who exhibits some ethnic traits.

Yet, even after using these standards of assessment for which Sone's text came up wanting, I still liked the book very much. I was convinced I could find a way to make my students like it, too. But first I had to figure out just why I liked it for some reason other than to justify my choice. In other words, Sone's autobiography presented me with a unique challenge that in some ways is characteristic of the dilemma faced by outsiders to the ethnic traditions they wish to present. How do we articulate our appreciation of an ethnic encounter that goes beyond satisfying contemporary diversity criteria? How do we responsibly present and provide instruction in ethnic literature that respects it not simply as an ethnic artifact but as a noteworthy literary contribution that is reflective of its time and place, even if it is not as artistically and ethnically salient in our own time and place?

Autobiographical theory wasn't helping me, and neither was ethnic theory. *Nisei Daughter* broadly fit the criteria for inclusion in an ethnic autobiography course. It dramatized the temporal and historical qualities of human experience that involve encounters with race or ethnicity. It depended on a concept of character (or some functional equivalent) that is part of but also distinct from ethnicity or race. But what Sone's text did not seem to negotiate as well or as obviously as the other texts was the shift from life (bios) to self (autos) that has become the hallmark of contemporary ethnic American autobiography. Sone's detachment and straightforward method of storytelling persuaded my students that she was lacking an appropriate ethnic consciousness and unable to represent her ethnicity with authenticity.

It was precisely this challenge to her ethnic authenticity, however, that made me finally realize why Sone's autobiography resonated so deeply with me. I was drawn to the text because it amplified aspects of my own essential experience as an outsider to American ethnic experience. Promoting Sone's ethnic value for my students became symbolic of how I tried as a white person to interpret ethnicity with authenticity. The struggle I had to articulate for my students the qualities that make Sone's book so remarkable came to represent my own struggle as a white person to establish an ethnic consciousness that was authentic without being apologetic.

Yet what enabled me to articulate both the struggle and the appreciation was the fact that I had acquired an understanding of ethnic experience by way of my long study of African American culture. My dedicated immersion in many things African American had shaped my ethnic consciousness and perceptions in ways that I had not even realized until confronted with Sone's text. In other words, my knowledge of African American texts passed on to me more than a body of knowledge; it bequeathed to me an unconscious grammar that gave me a vocabulary and sensibility to extend my interpretative range. A Filipino/Latino colleague of mine once remarked, in a moment of epiphany after he had delivered a paper at a conference, that all our work as academics is, at bottom, autobiographical. As I took stock of my own career, I admitted to myself the truth of what he said and began to discern how I had applied my talent to expressing that truth, how I had, unwittingly, made the movement from bios to autos. Monica Sone and Harriet Jacobs helped me to get there.

In the nearly fifteen years since I finished graduate school, the politics of identity and racial representation have shaped all aspects of my career and, in many respects, my very identity. I began as an earnest white person who chose African American culture as the topic of her scholarship not because it was an expedient or even clever choice to advance my career. I chose it because the literature awoke in me an aspect of my soul and ignited my intellectual passion in a way that none of my other literary studies had achieved. Indeed, professionally speaking, my choice was not wise. While my scholarship was welcome in the invisible world of publishing that was eager for academic work on black topics, it was impossible for me, in the early 1990s, to be hired to present African American culture visibly as an instructor.

In an essay published early in my career, I explored issues that surrounded this dilemma, trying to find a detached, scholarly way to understand and accept what I was feeling in a very deep, personal way. At the time I was living in central Virginia, where racial experiences and issues were neatly and rigidly divided between black and white. This binary distinction made it easier for me to achieve some control over my analysis. I knew I was white, not black, but I also knew, like every Southerner, that racial dynamics had shaped my identity. Informed also by the other discipline in which I am trained, religious studies, I was aware of the difference between being an adherent and an observer and how these two perspectives worked in collaboration and competition in drawing a picture of cultural experience. So, in my work, as in my life, I decided I could still find ways to bring African American topics to bear on whatever it was I had been hired to teach. As I concluded in my essay, jazz would be the metaphor for how I improvised a career in African American studies (Connor, "Can You Play?").

While I bounced around the academic world teaching everything from composition to world religions, I continued my scholarship on African American culture and in this way developed a modest reputation from my published work. This scholarship protected me from isolation and gradually led to my slow reintroduction to the academy. When I finally landed a tenure-track job, it was in a field that aptly described my eclectic experience: interdisciplinary studies. Back from the margins and to the center, I revisited my proximity to racial representation in another essay that explored the issue in broader ethnic terms, reflecting in part my new situation in the diverse San Francisco Bay Area and also describing the diminished intensity and willed control I had obtained through conscious self-reflection (Connor, "Teaching").

Previously, my consideration of the role white scholars play in African American academics was shaped by no single concept but, rather, constituted a series of comments, queries, and observations, informed by examples drawn from family history, popular culture, and current social debates. The second time I visited the issue, however, I turned to a classic, to Aristotle, and found in his rhetoric a more objective model for cross-ethnic discourse and conduct. I also applied principles of this rhetoric to the interpretation of a short story by an African American writer whose narrative explored what she called the "come and be black for me" phenomenon. In some ways this exercise became indicative of my own "come and be black" or "come and be white" for me moments, and I came to value the significance of using ancient principles to interpret a contemporary ethnic text while also drawing on my own culturally derived experience of working and living within ethnic categories (Connor, "Teaching").

Despite my achievements and my willed control notwithstanding, the issue of racial representation still informs nearly every aspect of my professional identity. It also almost always arises in ironic ways. It comes up when I am challenged by conservative colleagues at my home institution for the content of my courses and I find myself in a defensive posture, feeling like the only black person in the room, asserting the relevance of African American studies, but also when I am confronted by a colleague of color who claims my courses lack diversity. It surfaces in the classroom when some black students wonder why I am teaching about slavery (haven't we had enough reminders?) or when another African American student (well, her father is black, her mother is white, is she really black?) tells me she wants to be me—to know what I know and do what I do—after she takes a course I taught in African American literature. It emerges in professional gatherings when the under- or nonexistent representation of African American voices positions me as the authority on black topics or when I am excluded from panels on black topics because I am white. It arises in conversation with African American colleagues at other universities who lament the low standards of achievement set by their students of color while others complain about the lack of attention given to minority recruitment of students and faculty. It appears when a graduate student, also white, contacts me after reading my book and asks for help not just in articulating her own treatment of the slave narrative tradition but seeks advice about how radical she can be in stretching racial categories. And, while I am gratified that my work has never been rejected by publishers because of my being white, my racial status has figured negatively in the reviews my books have received, even though my books have won awards, been acquired by university libraries, and been adopted and recommended for course use.

Yet where I really live with this issue of racial representation and how I negotiate my responsibility to the African American tradition is not in any public sphere but in the private world of my scholarship, where the irony becomes autobiographical. There is no doubt in my mind that all my scholarship, however academically sound and original, is motivated by my own praxis, my own positionality, my own need to make sense of the life I have chosen that prioritizes the African American experience as exemplary.

I explored conversion as a trope in African American female-authored texts because I was trying to understand my own conversion to the literature, how the narratives of these women whose lives were so remote to mine spoke to me with more clarity and meaning than any I had ever read. I investigated the liberating aspects of the slave narrative tradition in a variety of cultural modes because I wanted to imagine my own participation in that tradition as a partner in expressing and achieving liberation. I researched evidence of Africanisms in slave narratives to illustrate how these retentions resisted the assimilation of the dominant culture I represented. I identified ritual movement and sacred spaces in Gloria Naylor's fiction to show how she creates a place for readers like me to enter into black experience. I even forayed into gay autobiography, finding a parallel between the desire to establish a "common geography of the mind" that Paul Monette articulates in his AIDS narratives and my own search for a shared ground of meaning.

Most striking to me was when I investigated the complicated life of John Brown through his portrayal in Russell Banks's novel *Cloudsplitter*. I was drawn not just to the character of Brown as a model for white behavior and thought but to the white novelist himself who chose Brown as a vehicle for understanding the United States' racial dilemma. Confronting the painful aspects of Brown's intense Negro identification, tropes of exoticized minstrelsy, on the one hand, and demure abolitionism, on the other hand, indicted my own position. In all my scholarship my self became my text, and I used my acquired talent to learn the truth about my own ethnically challenged life.

This blend of truth and talent—using one's talent to uncover some truth, if only about oneself—is where I ended up in trying to explain my strong attraction to Monica Sone's autobiography. In complicated and indirect ways my choice as a white American to specialize in African American literature influenced my intense response to the life of a Japanese American. Sone's *Nisei Daughter* at once reminded me of my polite, cautious self *and* the alert, inspired self I found when I read Harriet Jacobs's *Incidents in the Life of a Slave Girl*. Because these women shared qualities with each other that both transcended and extended an American ethnic portrait, my dual identification with them positioned me as a link in an ethnic chain of narration.

I was able to name truth and talent as the qualities others neglected to appreciate in Sone's text because I had already extensively researched Jacobs's text. I easily recalled Jacobs's assessment of her own work because it so aptly described my encounter with Sone. Thus, I began comparing the narratives of Jacobs and Sone. In so doing, I noticed that, for nearly every literary or ethnic characteristic I attributed to *Nisei Daughter*, there was a parallel to *Incidents in the Life of a Slave Girl* and, in some respects, a parallel to my own academic career of encountering ethnicity.

Like Jacobs, Monica Sone did not consider herself a writer and made no pretensions to literary aspirations. Furthermore, Sone employs writing strategies similar to the ones Jacobs employs, and both are ironically inflected in ways that honor their ethnicities. The problems my students had with *Nisei Daughter* I could now attribute to the fact that we were holding Sone's text up to a contemporary standard of ethnic identification and aesthetic accomplishment, rather than comparing her work to one that was a more accurate example of the proximity of reflection and experience that typically characterizes an autobiography. And by this I do not mean how close she is to the experience she relates but how close she is to the ethnic moment that her autobiography comes to epitomize.

When Sone wrote her book, she had more in common with Harriet Jacobs than she did with other ethnic writers of her own time. The texts to which I initially compared her work when I created my syllabus shared with *Nisei Daughter* a proximity to the racial humiliations and ethnic conflicts that their authors experienced and described. But they all also were written in a context of heightened ethnic consciousness, when hyphenated terms positioned them culturally and politically as representing a specific ethnic constituency that was asserting itself in a larger social consciousness.

Teaching *Nisei Daughter*, therefore, forced me to consider a related set of issues that I had neglected to appreciate as interdependent when presenting an ethnic autobiography. I had to contextualize the ethnicity of the text and the author while also showing how that historical context shaped the literary form the autobiography would take. I had to drop my contemporary standards and locate the standards that made sense to the author at the time she was writing. Considering my own autobiography in much the same way, I had to contextualize my personal and professional encounters with racial politics and ethnic identity as indicative of the moment I occupied in our social history, not as a judgment on me as a white person or an academic.

When Jacobs wrote *Incidents in the Life of a Slave Girl*, there was no common usage of the term *African American* or a distinctly racialized identity expressed on the part of African Americans. Indeed, the challenge at the time was to convince the dominant culture of the humanity of people of African descent, and this necessity took priority over the development of a specific ethnic assertion. So, too, when Sone wrote *Nisei Daughter*, postwar, anti-Japanese sentiment was still high, and Nikei were working toward being accepted simply as American citizens and to avoid the perception that they were treasonous others. Likewise, there was no common usage of the term *Japanese American*. Her community identified itself in ethnic terms that derived from its members' generational order. Sone's parents were Issei, the first immigrants, and their children, the Nisei, were the first American-born generation. The irony this presents the American ethnic situation is that these terms themselves explicitly suggest a proud ethnic orientation and affirmation, yet, because they do so outside of the parameters of a more politicized ethnic consciousness, they seem to denote for many a kind of naïveté. My own ethnic autobiography is similar, for I chose African American studies as my academic subject in a naive state that did not fully register the racial dynamics of my choice nor consider deeply the implications of my own racial status.

Although neither Jacobs nor Sone sought to establish a literary reputation or to conform to a prevailing ethnic ideology, both writers understood the power of language to shape human responses. Both women, having recently endured and escaped confinement and the confiscation of or denial of reading materials and opportunities, nonetheless affirm the influence writing can have not just by committing their own lives to paper but also by explicitly citing culturally significant writings in their texts. Jacobs peppers her story with biblical quotes familiar to her family, and Sone includes Japanese poetry that her mother both read and wrote. So, too, had I chosen a kind of ethnic professional identity not in a calculated attempt to advance my career but because I had a passion for African American topics and was moved by the language of African American writers and wished to move others to appreciate the power and beauty of this literature.

Both authors are highly conscious of a need to reach a broad audience while also maintaining a degree of privacy and control over the stories of their own racially shaped lives. Jacobs published under the pseudonym Linda Brent and Sone under her middle Anglo name, Monica, rather than her first Japanese name, Kazuko. Both women devote most of their texts to their adolescent experiences and tell us little about their adult lives. And both women wrote at times when the mere act of writing was deemed not just suspicious but dangerous to the dominant culture. Publications by former slaves could imperil fugitives and were seen as libelous by much of the American population, just as Issei and Nisei writing was viewed as treasonous and censored during the World War II era. Likewise, I wished to reach a broad audience of students in order to demonstrate to them that, no matter my ethnicity or theirs, ethnic literature had something important to offer all of us. I did not intend to out myself as white or to color myself as representative of a certain ethnicity.

As Jacobs often employs the trope of veiling to protect aspects of her and her family's identity in recognition of their perilous status in the antebellum South, so does Sone apply masking, a technique that distances her from the protagonist she creates but recognizes the sentiments of her family and her community's imperative that strongly encouraged assimilation in order to avoid racism. Jacobs's use of a veiling trope was employed by many former slave narrators and was an acceptable practice that tied her work to a larger ethnic genre and established her racial voice. Likewise, Sone's masking and her reluctance to speak critically reflect a Japanese decorum of saving face that links her to a larger ethnic tradition and mode of response. These techniques of veiling and masking, moreover, are ripe with possibilities for ironic application in describing the condition of minority women in the United States. The veil I wore or the mask I put on was my scholarship, devoting myself to the intellectual integrity and academic credibility of my work, which I assumed would protect me from charges of ethnic insincerity or hide me from claims of inordinate appropriation.

Jacobs extends the ironic potential of veiling by employing the conventions of a sentimental novel to tell her story, a strategy designed to appeal to her audience of uninformed but well-intentioned Northern white women, who were unaware of how she was exploiting the genre to achieve her aim. The irony of her approach is that, even though she demonstrates herself as an ideal mother for whom "every trial I endured, every sacrifice I made for their sakes"

(Jacobs 89), she does so under a system that denies her the legal protections and customary privileges of parenthood. Likewise, Sone's masked text resembles a young adult novel, shaped and stylized so that uninformed readers could easily understand and learn from the events she relates and appreciate how as she matured she became "a whole person instead of a sadly split personality. The Japanese and the American parts of me were now blended into one" (238). The irony of her approach lies in the fact that, although she relates a familiar adolescent tale, she does so while describing how she was robbed of her own adolescent development and American rights of citizenship. In a similar fashion I found subtle ways to blend African American topics and examples into my traditional courses, using conventional structures to introduce the ironic complications presented by an ethnic perspective.

But, despite the ironic use of these conventions, which to some still suggest a lack of ethnic integrity and aesthetic accomplishment, Jacobs and Sone also find ingenious ways to assert and celebrate their ethnicity while also accomplishing impressive literary feats. Both include among their stories events of cultural significance within their family life but also of significance to the ethnic group with which they identify. Jacobs and Sone deftly and inconspicuously weave folkways into their narratives that demonstrate the retention of African and Japanese sensibilities. Jacobs relates worship patterns that match African practices, a Johnkannaus festival whose ritual elements derive from African forms, examples of medicinal treatments that have origins in African sympathetic magic, and she describes symbols and rituals that are related to African ancestor worship and reverence as functional in her own community's life. Likewise, Sone portrays the Japanese decorum of her social encounters and her school's regime, and her spare prose becomes lush when describing Japanese-style meals and picnics, when she details the Japanese ornamental aspects of her home, and when she provides accounts of rituals such as weddings and tea parties in which behavior is strictly stylized. So, too, I revealed my ethnicity as a white person in indirect but specific ways: when I used public occasions to speak about African American culture, when I would offer a course on the topic to unsuspecting students who assumed I was black, and when I would eventually disclose, in my scholarship, my whiteness as a way of orienting or commenting on my interpretative approach.

Each author opens up her autobiography with a stunning admission. Jacobs's first sentence claims, "I was born a slave; but I never knew it till six years of happy childhood had passed away" (5). Similarly, Sone writes in her first sentences, "The first five years of my life I lived in amoebic bliss. . . . One day when I was a happy six-year-old, I made the shocking discovery that I had Japanese blood" (3) These comments are ironically rendered in the mood of a "shocking discovery," but the real shock is the eventual humiliations each woman will suffer. Moreover, this shock technique establishes the origins not only of the journey the protagonists will take in their movements from innocence to experience but also the one readers will take. The narrators' movement from astonishment to disillusionment and eventual reconciliation anticipates the response of innocent readers. Far from establishing a racial polarity between the authors and their audiences, this technique creates a kind of intimacy and slowly ushers the reader into an appreciation and understanding of living a life shaped by racial and ethnic influences. I took a similar path toward a consciousness of racial forces that were shaping my academic experience, recorded most specifically in the essays I wrote about the issue at distinct phases of my career: from astonishment to disillusionment to, now, reconciliation.

Their rhetorical strategies indicate that, whatever Jacobs and Sone wanted to communicate about their experiences as African American and Japanese American women, they also wanted to do so in a way that represented racialized women in general, not themselves in particular. Just as Jacobs serves for her readers as a model mother, so Sone serves for her readers as a model American. The tropes that each writer establishes and the roles that each protagonist plays do not exclude or deny the ethnicities of the authors. Rather, they relegate them to a lesser order of significance in relation to the larger points they wish to make, about the basic human aspects of their identities, that will reach an audience that needs to be informed and persuaded about the experiences of ethnic Americans at that moment in history. And in that moment both deliberately pay homage to their ethnic origins while finding ways to transform their captive situations, as general victims of slavery and racism and as specific victims of confinement—Jacobs's seven years in the attic, Sone's year in an internment camp—into sites of liberation. While it would be hubristic to match my own experiences with those of Sone and Jacobs, I have, to some degree, achieved my own freedom in academic terms with the institutionalization of my status as a scholar and a teacher who finally found her place and assumed the role she was intended to play at this moment in our society's history.

Comparing the works of Jacobs and Sone taught me once again about the responsibility I have as an instructor in ethnic American literature to present both truth and talent as constituent elements in the texts I am charged to interpret. How I ascertain elements of truth and achievements of talent depends on my willingness to enter that moment in history as each writer did in her stunning overture—with shock and openness to discovery—and to proceed from that moment in reconciliation. Both Jacobs and Sone had to reject, to some degree, a familiar ethnic norm in order to survive. Each leaves the site of her ethnic affirmation to establish an identity elsewhere. Sone leaves her family in the camps to attend college, and Jacobs leaves her family in the South to achieve emancipation. So, too, did I have to leave my entitled, white, contemporary perch and travel back to those times when women of color had to make difficult choices. As their restrictions in slavery and internment led to a complicated diaspora of their ethnic communities, so goes the irony that from that diaspora I should need to return to the times when ethnic identification was assumed, if not proclaimed.

In 1979 Monica Sone wrote an introduction for a new edition of *Nisei Daughter.* In it she registers in her simple prose recognition of the legal and ethical dimensions of the Japanese American internment experience, but she does not demonstrate any new ethnic consciousness. She remains not a Japanese American but a Nisei daughter. Yet 1979 is when Japanese Americans began a formal movement to seek reparations and an apology for their internment. By acknowledging this movement, which was inspired by the Southern black civil rights movement, Sone's subtle gesture provides certain symmetry to the life of Harriet Jacobs, whose writing contributed to abolitionism, the original civil rights movement in American history. This gesture also directs us to consider the ways in which ethnic sensibilities in the United States are creatively informed and joined.

Would Harriet Jacobs have retained the same authorial posture had she been given the opportunity, like Sone, to revisit her autobiography twenty-six years later? As Sone had put her book behind her and continued her life as a counselor, Jacobs took on a career not with the literati but with Quakers, doing relief work for former slaves. After reading *Nisei Daughter*, I am inclined to think Jacobs would have finally been able to admit that she had given us both truth and talent and said no more. Jacobs and Sone both appreciated the irony that their books, by being so reflective of their times, were also prescient of later times. The challenge for us, as instructors, is to help our students to see that their uncontested ethnic pride was made possible because of what was accomplished by slave mothers and Nisei daughters.

And the challenge for me, as a teacher whose scholarship is always, to some degree, autobiographical, is to remember that I chose to engage, in academic ways, the ethnic American experience because of the ways in which it completed my identity. As a white, twenty-first-century academic, my own racial referentiality is best illustrated by how I encountered a twentieth-century Japanese American text and interpreted it through the lens of a nineteenth-century African American text. In my academic work, both teaching and writing, I am constantly discerning not only what it means to be the other but also, in the process, what it means to be me. My way of proceeding is not my own but is my individual inflection on a collective, multiethnic experience that demonstrates daily that the way to change the world is to start by changing oneself. I learned from the dignified detachment of both Sone and Jacobs that, while we may not always be able to represent ethnicity, we must interpret it if we are ever to find our place not just in the academy but also in the world. As I connected the links in a chain of ethnic narration from Harriet Jacobs to Monica Sone, I found my place in that chain and, I hope, made a place for my students and my son. When my talent met truth, I did not cease to be white, nor did I acquire a new ethnic identity. I simply became me.

# WORKS CITED


Abel, Elizabeth. "Black Writing, White Reading: Race and the Politics of Feminist Interpretation." *Critical Inquiry* 12 (Spring 1993): 470–498.

Abrahams, Peter. "Conflict of Cultures in Africa." *International Affairs* 30 (1954): 304–312.

———. *The Coyaba Chronicles: Reflections on the Black Experience in the 20th Century.* Cape Town: David Philip, 2000.

———. *Tell Freedom.* London: Faber and Faber, 1954.

———. *The View from Coyaba.* London: Faber and Faber, 1985.

Adorno, Theodor. "Commitment." *Aesthetics and Politics.* Comp. Ernst Bloch et al. London: New Left Books, 1977. 177–195.

Aidoo, Ama Ata. *Our Sister Killjoy.* New York: Longman, 1977.

Alcoff, Linda Martin. "The Problem of Speaking for Others." *Who Can Speak? Authority and Critical Identity.* Ed. Judith Roof and Robyn Wiegman. Urbana: U of Illinois P, 1995. 97–119.

Alcott, Louisa May. *Little Women.* 1868. New York: Modern Library, 2000.

Allen, Dennis. "Lesbian and Gay Studies: A Consumer's Guide." *Genders 26: The Gay 90s.* Ed. Thomas Foster, Carol Siegel, and Ellen E. Berry. New York: NYU Press, 1997. 23–50.

Andrews, William L. "Chesnutt's Patesville: The Presence and Influence of the Past in *The House behind the Cedars* ." *CLA Journal* 15 (March 1972): 284–294.

———. *The Literary Career of Charles W. Chesnutt.* Baton Rouge: Louisiana State UP, 1980.

———. *To Tell a Free Story: The First Century of Afro-American Autobiography, 1760–1865.* Urbana: U of Illinois P, 1986.

Andrews, William L., Frances Smith Foster, and Trudier Harris, eds. *The Oxford Companion to African American Literature.* New York: Oxford UP, 1997.

Angelou, Maya. *I Know Why the Caged Bird Sings.* New York: Bantam Books, 1996.

Appiah, Kwame Anthony, and Henry Louis Gates Jr. "Editors' Introduction: Multiplying Identities." *Identities.* Ed. Kwame Anthony Appiah and Henry Louis Gates Jr. Chicago: U of Chicago P, 1995. 1–7.

Awkward, Michael. *Negotiating Difference: Race, Gender, and the Politics of Positionality.* Chicago: U of Chicago P, 1995.

———. "Negotiations of Power: White Critics, Black Texts, and the Self-Referential Impulse." *American Literary History* 2.4 (Winter 1990): 581–606.

Baker, Houston A., Jr. *Long Black Song: Essays in Black American Literature and Culture.* Charlottesville: UP of Virginia, 1990.

———. *Workings of the Spirit: The Poetics of Afro-American Women's Writing.* Chicago: U of Chicago P, 1991.

Baker, Houston A., Jr., and Patricia Redmond. *Afro-American Literary Study in the 1990s.* Chicago: U of Chicago P, 1989.

Baldwin, James. "Black English: A Dishonest Argument." *Black English and the Education of Black Children and Youth.* Ed. Geneva Smitherman. Detroit: Wayne State UP, 1981. 54–60.

——. *The Fire Next Time.* New York: Vintage, 1993.

Banks, James A. *Multicultural Education, Transformative Knowledge, and Action: Historical and Contemporary Perspectives.* New York: Teacher's College Press, 1996.

Barksdale, Richard, and Keneth Kinnamon, eds. *Black Writers of America: A Comprehensive Anthology.* New York: Macmillan, 1972.

Bataille, George. *Visions of Excess: Selected Works, 1927–1939.* Ed. Allan Stoekl. Minneapolis: U of Minnesota P, 1985. 137–160.

Batukezanga, Zamenga. *Carte Postale.* Kinshasa: Saint-Paul Afrique, 1974.

Bell, Roseann P., Bettye J. Parker, and Beverly Guy-Sheftall, eds. *Sturdy Black Bridges: Visions of Black Women in Literature.* New York: Anchor Books, 1979.

Benston, Kimberly W. *Performing Blackness: Enactments of African-American Modernism.* London: Routledge, 2000.

Bentley, Eric. "Must I Side with Blacks or Whites?" *The Theatre of Black Americans, Vol. 2.* Ed. Errol Hill. New Jersey: Prentice-Hall, 1980. 336–340.

Berlant, Lauren, and Michael Warner. "What Does Queer Commentary Teach Us about X?" *PMLA* 110.3 (Fall 1995): 343–349.

Berlin, James. *Writing Instruction in Nineteenth-Century American Colleges.* Carbondale: Southern Illinois UP, 1984.

Bhabha, Homi K. "Postcolonial Criticism." *Postcolonialism: Critical Concepts in Literary and Cultural Studies: I.* Ed. Diana Brydon. London: Routledge, 2000. 105–133.

Bleich, David. "Reading as Membership." *ADE Bulletin* 102 (Fall 1992): 6–10.

Bohannan, Laura. "Shakespeare in the Bush." *Natural History* 75 (1966): 28–33.

Bolden, B. J. *Urban Rage in Bronzeville: Social Commentary in the Poetry of Gwendolyn Brooks.* Chicago: Third World, 1999.

Bow, Leslie. "'For Every Gesture of Loyalty, There Doesn't Have to Be a Betrayal': Asian American Criticism and the Politics of Locality." *Who Can Speak? Authority and Critical Identity.* Ed. Judith Roof and Robyn Wiegman. Urbana: U of Illinois P, 1995. 30–55.

Brooks, Gwendolyn. *Blacks.* Chicago: David Company, 1987.

——. *Report from Part One.* Detroit: Broadside, 1972.

Brown, Martha H., and Marilyn Zorn. "GLR Interview: Gwendolyn Brooks." *Great Lakes Review* 6.1 (1979): 48–55.

Brown, Sterling A., Arthur P. Davis, and Ulysses Lee, eds. *The Negro Caravan: Writings by American Negroes.* New York: Dryden, 1941.

Brown, William Wells. *Clotel; or the President's Daughter: A Narrative of Slave Life in the United States.* 1853. Boston: Bedford/St. Martin's Press, 1999.

Butler, Octavia. *Kindred.* Boston: Beacon P, 1988.

Cade, Toni. *The Black Woman: An Anthology.* New York: New American Library, 1970.

Callahan, John F. *In the African American Grain: Call-and-Response in Twentieth-Century Black Fiction.* 2d ed. Middletown, CT: Wesleyan UP, 1990.

Castronovo, Russ. *Necro Citizenship: Death, Eroticism, and the Public Sphere in the Nineteenth-Century United States.* Durham: Duke UP, 2001.

Chesnutt, Charles W. "Baxter's Procrustes." *Black Voices.* Ed. Abraham Chapman. New York: Mentor, 1968. 52–62.

——. "Post-Bellum-Pre-Harlem." *Crisis* 40 (June 1931): 193–194.

Chinweizu, Onuwuchekwa Jemie, and Ihechukwu Madubuike. *Toward the Decolonization of African Literature.* Washington, DC: Howard UP, 1983.

Chiwengo, Ngwarsungu. "Richard Wright's Africa." *Richard Wright's Travel Writings.* Ed. Virginia Whately Smith. Jackson: UP of Mississippi, 2001. 20–44.

Christian, Barbara T. *Black Women Novelists: The Development of a Tradition, 1892–1976.* Westport, CT: Greenwood, 1980.

———. "The Highs and the Lows of Black Feminist Criticism." *Reading Black, Reading Feminist: A Critical Anthology.* Ed. Henry Louis Gates Jr. New York: Meridian, 1990. 44–51.

———. "The Race for Theory." *Gender and Theory: Dialogues on Feminist Criticism.* Ed. Linda Kauffman. Oxford: Basil Blackwell, 1989. 225–237.

———. "Response to 'Black Women's Texts.'" *NWSA Journal* 1.1 (1988): 32–36.

Clarke, Lewis, and Milton Clarke. *Narratives of the Sufferings of Lewis and Milton Clarke, Sons of a Soldier of the Revolution, during a Captivity of More than Twenty Years among the Slaveholders of Kentucky, One of the So Called Christian States of North America.* Boston: Bela Marsh, 1846.

Cole, Johnetta B. *Conversations: Straight Talk with America's Sister President.* New York: Doubleday, 1993.

Coleman, Beth. "Pimp Notes on Autonomy." *Everything but the Burden: What White People Are Taking from Black Culture.* Ed. Greg Tate. New York: Broadway Books, 2003. 68–80.

Cone, James H. *A Black Theology of Liberation.* 2d. ed. Maryknoll, NY: Orbis, 1990.

Connor, Kimberly Rae. "Can You Play? The Reconstruction of Instruction." *Cross Currents* 45 (Fall 1995): 368–379.

———. "Teaching in the Global Village: Notes towards a Religious Studies Rhetoric." *Teaching Theology and Religion* 6.1 (2003): 18–23.

Connors, Robert. "Women's Reclamation of Rhetoric in Nineteenth-Century America." *Feminine Principles and Women's Experience in American Composition and Rhetoric.* Ed. Louise Wetherbee Phelps and Janet Emig. Pittsburgh: U of Pittsburgh P, 1995. 67–90.

Cooper, Anna Julia. "Womanhood a Vital Element in the Progress and Regeneration of a Race." *A Voice from the South. By a Black Woman of the South.* 1892. New York: Oxford UP, 1988. 9–47.

Cose, Ellis. "The Black Gender Gap." *Newsweek* 3 March 2003: 48–51.

Davis, Lennard J. *Enforcing Normalcy: Disability, Deafness and the Body.* London: Verso, 1995.

Davis, Rebecca Harding. *Life in the Iron Mills.* Life in the Iron Mills *and Other Stories.* Ed. Tillie Olsen. New York: The Feminist Press, 1985. 11–66.

Dean, Jodi. *Solidarity of Strangers: Feminism after Identity Politics.* Berkeley: U of California P, 1996.

Diop, Birago. "Breaths." *The Norton Anthology of World Literature, Volume F.* Ed. Sarah Lawell et al. New York: Norton, 2002. 2489.

Douglass, Frederick. *Narrative of the Life of Frederick Douglass, an American Slave, Written by Himself.* 1844. New York: Penguin, 1982.

DuBois, W.E.B. *The Souls of Black Folk.* New York: Bantam, 1989.

DuCille, Ann. "The Occult of True Black Womanhood: Critical Demeanor and Black Feminist Studies." *Female Subjects in Black and White: Race, Psychoanalysis, Feminism.* Ed. Elizabeth Abel, Barbara Christian, and Helene Morgan. Berkeley: U of California P, 1997. 21–56.

Dyer, Richard. *White.* New York: Routledge, 1997.

Dyson, Michael. "Contesting Racial Amnesia: From Identity Politics towards Post-Multiculturalism." *Higher Education under Fire.* Ed. Michael Bérubé and Cary Nelson. New York: Routledge, 1995. 336–343.

Eddy, Charmaine. "The Black and White of Race." *Canadian Review of American Studies* 28.1 (1998): 79–104.

Edmundson, Mark. *Teacher.* New York: Random House, 2002.

Eldred, Janet Carey, and Peter Mortensen. *Imagining Rhetoric: Composing Women of the Early United States.* Pittsburgh: U of Pittsburgh P, 2002.

Ellison, Ralph. "The Art of Fiction." *Shadow and Act.* New York: Random House, 1953. 167–183.

——. "Change the Joke and Slip the Yoke." *Shadow and Act.* New York: Random House, 1972. 45–59.

——. *Invisible Man.* New York: Vintage Books, 1990.

——. "The World and the Jug." *Shadow and Act.* New York: Random House, 1953. 107–143.

Engle, Paul. "Chicago Can Take Pride in New, Young Voice in Poetry." *Chicago Tribune* 26 August 1945, Books sec. 11.

Estes, Thomas H., Carol J. Gutman, and Elise K. Harrison. "Cultural Literacy: What Every Educator Needs to Know." *Educational Leadership* 46.1 (1988): 14–17.

Farnham, Christie. "The Discipline of History and the Demands of Identity Politics." *Teaching What You're Not: Identity Politics in Higher Education.* Ed. Katherine J. Mayberry. New York: New York UP, 1996. 107–130.

Favor, J. Martin. *Authentic Blackness: The Folk in the New Negro Renaissance.* Durham: Duke UP, 1999.

"Findings from the MLA Surveys of PhD Placement. 1977–1997." 10 June 2003. Modern Language Association. <http://www.mla.org/jil_phd_survey_t10>.

Fletcher, Tom. *100 Years of the Negro in Show Business.* New York: Da Capo, 1984.

Foreman, P. Gabrielle. "Who's Your Mamma? 'White' Mulatta Genealogies, Early Photography, and Anti-Passing Narratives of Slavery and Freedom." *American Literary History* 14.3 (Fall 2002): 505–539.

Fuller, Hoyt. "Introduction: Towards a Black Aesthetic." *The Black Aesthetic.* Ed. Addison Gayle Jr. New York: Doubleday, 1971. 3–12.

Gallagher, Charles A. "White Construction in the University." *Privilege.* Ed. Michael S. Kimmel and Abby L. Ferber. Boulder, CO: Westview P, 2003. 299–318.

Gallop, Jane. *Around 1981: Academic Feminist Literary Theory.* New York: Routledge, 1992.

Garland, Phyl. "Gwendolyn Brooks: Poet Laureate." *Ebony* July 1968: 48–56.

Garvey, John, and Noel Ignatiev. "Toward a New Abolitionism: A *Race Traitor* Manifesto." *Whiteness: A Critical Reader.* Ed. Mike Hill. New York: New York UP, 1997. 346–349.

Gates, Henry Louis, Jr. *Black Theory and Literary Theory.* New York: Methuen, 1984.

——. *Figures in Black: Words, Signs, and the "Racial Self."* New York: Oxford UP, 1987.

——. Intro. *Voices in Black and White: Writings on Race in America from Harper's Magazine.* Ed. Katherine Whittemore and Gerald Marzorati. New York: Franklin Square P, 1993. vii–xvi.

——. "The King of Cats." *New Yorker* 8 April 1996: 70–81.

——. *Loose Canons: Notes on the Culture Wars.* New York: Oxford UP, 1992.

Gates, Henry Louis, Jr., and Nellie Y. McKay, gen. eds. *The Norton Anthology of African American Literature.* New York: Norton, 1996.

Gatewood, Willard B. "Aristocrats of Color: The Educated Black Elite of the Post-Reconstruction Era." *Journal of Blacks in Higher Education* 29 (Fall 2000): 112–118.

Gayle, Addison. *Black Expression: Essays by and about Black Americans in the Creative Arts.* New York: Waybright and Tally, 1969.

Gerschick, Thomas J. "Should and Can a White, Heterosexual Middle-Class Man Teach Students about Social Inequality and Oppression? One Person's Experience and Reflections." *Multicultural Teaching in the University.* Ed. David Schoem, Linda Frankel, Ximena Zuniga, and Edith A. Lewis. Westport, CT: Praeger, 1993. 200–207.

Giddings, Louise R. "Beyond E. D. Hirsch and Cultural Literacy: Thinking Skills for Cultural Awareness." *Community Review* 16 (1998): 109–118.

Gilroy, Paul. *Against Race: Imagining Political Culture beyond the Color Line.* Cambridge: Harvard UP, 2000.

———. *The Black Atlantic.* Cambridge: Harvard UP, 1993.

Giroux, Henry A. "Literacy, Pedagogy, and the Politics of Difference." *College Literature* 19.1 (1992): 1–11.

Gĩtĩtĩ, Gĩtahi. "Menaced by Resistance: The Black Teacher in the Mainly White School/ Classroom." *Race in the College Classroom: Pedagogy and Politics.* Ed. Bonnie TuSmith and Maureen T. Reddy. New Brunswick: Rutgers UP, 2002. 176–188.

Goldman, Anne E. "'I Made the Ink': (Literary) Production and Reproduction in *Dessa Rose* and *Beloved.*" *Feminist Studies* 16.2 (Summer 1990): 313–331.

Gonsalves, Lisa M. "Making Connections: Addressing the Pitfalls of White Faculty / Black Male Student Communication." *College Composition and Communication* 53.3 (February 2002): 435–465.

Gordon, Lewis. "Critical Reflections on Three Popular Tropes in the Studies of Whiteness." *What White Looks Like.* Ed. George Yancy. New York: Routledge, 2004. 173–193.

Gossett, Thomas F. *Uncle Tom's Cabin and American Culture.* Dallas: Southern Methodist UP, 1985.

Graff, Gerald. *Professing Literature.* Chicago: U of Chicago P, 1987.

Griffin, Gail B. "Speaking of Whiteness: Disrupting White Innocence." *Journal of the Midwest Modern Language Association* 31.3 (Spring 1998): 3–14.

Griffith, Cyril E. *The African Dream: Martin R. Delany and the Emergence of Pan-African Thought.* University Park: Pennsylvania State UP, 1975.

Griffiths, Gareth. "The Myth of Authenticity." *The Post-Colonial Studies Reader.* Ed. Bill Ashcroft, Gareth Griffiths, and Helen Tiffin. London: Routledge, 1995. 237–241.

Gwin, Minrose C. "A Theory of Black Women's Texts and White Women's Readings, or . . . the Necessity of Being Other." *NWSA Journal* 1.1 (1988): 21–31.

Hall, Stuart. "Introduction: Who Needs 'Identity'?" *Questions of Identity.* Ed. Stuart Hall and Paul Du Gay. London: Sage, 1996. 1–17.

Harris, Joel Chandler. "Free Joe and the Rest of the World." *The Heath Anthology of American Literature, Vol 2.* Ed. Paul Lauter et al. Lexington, MA: D. C. Heath, 1994. 340–347.

Hartman, Geoffrey. *Scars of the Spirit: The Struggle against Inauthenticity.* New York: Palgrave Macmillan, 2002.

Hartman, Saidiya V. *Scenes of Subjection: Terror, Slavery, and Self-Making in Nineteenth-Century America.* New York: Oxford UP, 1997.

Hawthorne, Nathaniel. *The Blithedale Romance.* New York: Penguin, 1986.

Henderson, Peter H., Julie E. Clarke, and Mary A. Reynolds. *Summary Report 1995: Doctorate Recipients from United States Universities.* Washington, DC: National Academy P, 1996.

Henderson, Stephen. "Introduction: The Forms of Things Unknown." *Understanding the New Black Poetry: Black Speech and Black Music* as *Poetic References.* New York: William Morrow, 1973. 3–69.

Hennessy, Rosemary. "Queer Theory, Left Politics." *Rethinking Marxism* 7.3 (Fall 1994): 85–111.

Hill, Herbert, ed. *Soon, One Morning: New Writing by American Negroes, 1940-1962.* New York: Knopf, 1963.

Hill, Mike. *After Whiteness: Unmaking an American Majority.* New York: New York UP, 2004.

Hirsch, E. D., Jr. *Cultural Literacy: What Every American Needs to Know*. Boston: Houghton Mifflin, 1987.

Hoffer, Thomas B., et al. *Doctorate Recipients from United States Universities: Summary Report 2002*. Chicago: National Opinion Research Center, 2003.

Holly, James Theodore. "In Memoriam." *African Methodist Episcopal Church Review* 3 (1886): 117–125.

hooks, bell. *Black Looks: Race and Representation*. Boston: South End P, 1992.

———. *Teaching to Transgress: Education as the Practice of Freedom*. New York: Routledge, 1994.

Hopkins, Pauline. *Contending Forces*. 1900. New York: Oxford UP, 1988.

———. *Of One Blood*. 1903. New York: Oxford UP, 1988.

Hughes, Langston. *The Collected Poems of Langston Hughes*. Ed. Arnold Rampersad. New York: Knopf, 1994.

Hughes, Langston, and Milton Meltzer. *Black Magic: A Pictorial History of the Negro in American Entertainment*. Englewood Cliffs, NJ: Prentice-Hall, 1968.

Hurston, Zora Neale. *Their Eyes Were Watching God*. New York: HarperCollins, 1998.

Ignatiev, Noel. *How the Irish Became White*. New York: Routledge, 1995.

Jacobs, Harriet A. *Incidents in the Life of a Slave Girl*. Ed. Jean Fagan Yellin. Cambridge: Harvard UP, 1987.

Jacobson, Matthew Frye. *Whiteness of a Different Color: European Immigrants and the Alchemy of Race*. Cambridge: Harvard UP, 1998.

James, Joy. "The Academic Addict." *What White Looks Like*. Ed. George Yancy. New York: Routledge, 2004. 263–268.

Jefferson, Thomas. *Notes on the State of Virginia. The Heath Anthology of American Literature, Vol. 1*. Ed. Paul Lauter et al. 4th ed. Boston: Houghton Mifflin, 2002. 975–991.

Johnson, Barbara. "Metaphor, Metonymy and Voice in *Their Eyes Were Watching God*." *Black Literature and Literary Theory*. Ed. Henry Louis Gates Jr. New York: Methuen, 1984. 205–219.

———. *A World of Difference*. Baltimore: Johns Hopkins UP, 1987.

Johnson, Charles. *Middle Passage*. New York: Penguin, 1990.

Johnson, James Weldon. *The Autobiography of an Ex-Coloured Man*. New York: Random House, 1989.

Johnson, James Weldon, and J. Rosamond Johnson. *The Books of American Negro Spirituals*. New York: Arno Press, 1969.

Jones, Hettie. *How I Became Hettie Jones*. New York: Grove, 1990.

Jordan, June. "The Difficult Miracle of Black Poetry in America; or, Something like a Sonnet for Phillis Wheatley." *Massachusetts Review: A Quarterly of Literature, the Arts and Public Affairs* 27 (1986): 252–262.

Judy, R. A. T. "On the Question of Nigga Authenticity." *Boundary 2* 1.3 (Fall 1994): 211–230.

Kaplan, Carla. "The Erotics of Talk: 'That Oldest Human Longing' in *Their Eyes Were Watching God*." *American Literature* 67 (March 1995): 115–142.

Kelley-Hawkins, Emma Dunham. *Megda*. 1891. New York: Oxford UP, 1988.

———. *Four Girls at Cottage City*. 1898. New York: Oxford UP, 1988.

Kolchin, Peter. "Whiteness Studies: The New History of Race in America." *Journal of American History* 89 (2002): 154–173.

Kubitschek, Missy Dehn. *Claiming the Heritage: African-American Women Novelists and History*. Jackson: UP of Mississippi, 1991.

Kumar, Nita N. "Patriotic Past and Needy Present: Can the Native Be Postcolonial?" *Critical Theory Textual Application*. Ed. Shormishtha Panja. New Delhi: Worldview, 2002. 314–326.

Kunitz, Stanley. "Bronze by Gold." *Poetry* April 1950: 52–56.

Lakritz, Andrew. "Identification and Difference: Structures of Privilege in Cultural Criticism." *Who Can Speak? Authority and Critical Identity*. Ed. Judith Roof and Robyn Wiegman. Urbana: U of Illinois P, 1995. 3–29.

Lee, Don L. "Gwendolyn Brooks: Beyond the Wordmaker—The Making of an African Poet." *Report from Part One*. By Gwendolyn Brooks. Detroit: Broadside, 1972. 13–30.

Levi, Primo. *I sommersi e i salvati*. 1986. Torino: Einaudi, 1991.

———. *Se questo è un uomo*. 1947. Torino: Einaudi, 1975.

Levin, Amy K. *Africanism and Authenticity in African-American Women's Novels*. Gainesville: UP of Florida, 2003.

Levine, Robert S. "Commentary: Critical Disruptions." *American Literary History* 14.3 (Fall 2002): 540–550.

———. *Martin Delany, Frederick Douglass, and the Politics of Representative Identity*. Chapel Hill: U of North Carolina P, 1997.

———, ed. *Martin R. Delany: A Documentary Reader*. Chapel Hill: U of North Carolina P, 2003.

Lipsitz, George. *The Possessive Investment in Whiteness: How White People Profit from Identity Politics*. Philadelphia: Temple UP, 1998.

Long, Lisa A. "A Relative Pain: The Rape of History in Octavia Butler's *Kindred* and Phyllis Alesia Perry's *Stigmata*." *College English* 64.4 (March 2002): 459–483.

Longino, Helen. "Subjects, Power, and Knowledge: Description and Prescription in Feminist Philosophies of Science." *Feminist Epistemologies*. Ed. Linda Alcoff and Elizabeth Potter. New York: Routledge, 1993. 101–120.

Lorde, Audre. "The Master's Tools Will Never Dismantle the Master's House." *Sister Outsider*. Trumansburg, NY: Crossing P, 1984. 110–113.

"The Lost Museum Archive: What Is It? Portraits by Matthew Brady." Meserve Collection, National Portrait Gallery, Smithsonian. 30 December 2003 <http://chnm.gmu.edu/lostmuseum/lm/131>.

Lucas, Sam. "Carve Dat Possum." New York: John F. Perry & Co., 1875.

Maran, René. *Batouala*. New York: Thomas Seltzer, 1922.

Mattison, Hiram. *Louisa Picquet, the Octoroon: A Tale of Southern Slave Life. Collected Black Women's Narratives*. Ed. Anthony Barthelmy. New York: Oxford UP, 1988.

Mayberry, Katherine J. "Introduction: Identity Politics in the College Classroom." *Teaching What You're Not: Identity Politics in Higher Education*. Ed. Katherine J. Mayberry. New York: New York UP, 1996. 1–19.

Mayberry, Katherine J., ed. *Teaching What You're Not: Identity Politics in Higher Education*. New York: New York UP, 1996.

McDowell, Deborah E. "Boundaries: Or Distant Relations and Close Kin." *Afro-American Literary Study in the 1990s*. Ed. Houston A. Baker Jr. and Patricia Redmond. Chicago: U of Chicago P, 1989. 51–70.

———. "New Directions in Black Feminist Criticism." *The New Feminist Criticism*. Ed. Elaine Showalter. New York: Pantheon, 1985. 186–199.

McIntosh, Peggy. "White Privilege: Unpacking the Invisible Knapsack." *Race, Class, and Gender in the United States: An Integrated Study*. Ed. Paula S. Rothenberg. 5th ed. New York: Worth, 2001. 163–168.

McKay, Nellie Y. "Minority Faculty in [Mainstream White] Academia." *The Academic's Handbook.* Ed. A. Leigh Deneef, Craufurd D. Goodwin, and Ellen Stern McCrate. Durham: Duke UP, 1988. 46–60.

———. "Naming the Problem That Led to the Question 'Who Shall Teach African American Literature?'; or, Are We Ready to Disband the Wheatley Court?" *PMLA* 113.3 (May 1998): 359–369. Reprinted here, 17–26.

McKay, Nellie Y., and Kathryn Earle, eds. *Approaches to Teaching the Novels of Toni Morrison.* New York: Modern Language Association of America, 1997.

McKee, Patricia. *Producing American Races: Henry James, William Faulkner, Toni Morrison.* Durham: Duke UP, 1999.

McLeod, Kembrew. "Authenticity within Hip-Hop and Other Cultures Threatened with Assimilation." *Journal of Communication* 49.4 (Fall 1999): 134–150.

Mills, Charles W. *The Racial Contract.* Ithaca: Cornell UP, 1997.

Morrison, Toni. Afterword. *The Bluest Eye.* New York: Plume, 1994. 211–221.

———. *Beloved.* New York: Plume, 1987.

———. *The Bluest Eye.* New York: Washington Square P, 1970.

———. "An Interview with Toni Morrison." Interview with Nellie Y. McKay. *Contemporary Literature* 24 (1983): 413–429. Rpt. in *Conversations with Toni Morrison.* Ed. Danielle Taylor-Guthrie. Jackson: UP of Mississippi, 1994. 138–155.

———. *Playing in the Dark: Whiteness and the Literary Imagination.* Cambridge: Harvard UP, 1992.

———. *Song of Solomon.* New York: Holt, Rinehart and Winston, 1970.

———. *Sula.* New York: Knopf, 1973.

———. "Unspeakable Things Unspoken: The Afro-American Presence in American Literature." *Within the Circle: An Anthology of African American Literary Criticism from the Harlem Renaissance to the Present.* Ed. Angelyn Mitchell. Durham: Duke UP, 1994. 368–398.

Mufwene, Salikoko S. "Investigating Gullah: Difficulties in Ensuring 'Authenticity.'" *Language Variations in North American English.* Ed. A. Wayne Glowka and Donald M. Lance. New York: Modern Language Association of America, 1993. 178–190.

Murdy, Anne-Elizabeth. *Teach the Nation: Public School, Racial Uplift, and Women's Writing in the 1890s.* New York: Routledge, 2003.

Murray, Albert. *The Blue Devils of Nada: A Contemporary Approach to American Aesthetic Statement.* New York: Pantheon, 1996.

———. *From the Briarpatch File: On Context, Procedure, and American Identity.* New York: Pantheon, 2001.

———. Ralph Ellison Memorial Lecture. Tuskegee University, Alabama. 26 March 1999.

———. *Stomping the Blues.* New York: Da Capo, 1976.

Naylor, Gloria, *Mama Day.* New York: Vintage Contemporaries, 1993.

Neal, Larry. "The Ethos of the Blues." *Black Scholar* (Summer 1972): 42–48.

Nelson, Dana. *The Word in Black and White: Reading "Race" in American Literature, 1638–1867.* New York: Oxford UP, 1992.

Newman, Jay. *Inauthentic Culture and Its Philosophical Critics.* Montreal: McGill-Queen's UP, 1997.

Oates, Joyce Carol. *Them.* New York: Fawcett Crest, 1969.

Okihiro, Gary Y. *Margins and Mainstreams: Asians in American History and Culture.* Seattle: U of Washington P, 1994.

Pentony, Joseph F. "Cultural Literacy." *Adult Basic Education* 7.1 (1997): 39–45.

Perry, Phyllis Alesia. *Stigmata.* New York: Hyperion Press, 1998.

Peterson, Carla L. E-mail to Lisa A. Long. 6 October 2002.

——. "New Negro Modernity." *Women's Experience of Modernity, 1875–1945*. Ed. Ann Ardis and Leslie W. Lewis. Baltimore: Johns Hopkins UP, 2003. 111–129.

Phelan, Shane. *Getting Specific: Postmodern Lesbian Politics*. Minneapolis: U of Minnesota P, 1994.

Pierce-Baker, Charlotte. *Surviving the Silence: Black Women's Stories of Rape*. New York: Norton, 1998.

Portelli, Alessandro. *The Battle of Valle Giulia: Oral History and the Art of Dialogue*. Madison: U of Wisconsin P, 1997.

——. *Bianchi e neri nella letteratura americana. La dialettica dell'identità*. Bari: Laterza, 1975.

——. "Blood, Milk, and Ink: A Reading of *Beloved*." *"Beloved, she's mine": Essais sur* Beloved *de Toni Morrison*. Ed. G. Fabre and C. Raynaud. Paris: Cetanla, 1993. 109–114.

——. *Canoni americani. Oralità, letteratura, cinema, musica*. Rome: Donzelli, 2004.

——. "Cultura poetica afro-americana." *Studi Americani* 14 (1968 [issued in 1970]): 402–429.

——. *La linea del colore. Saggi sulla cultura afroamericana*. Rome: manifestolibri, 1993.

——. *L'America della contestazione*. Milan: Dischi del Sole, 1969.

——. "Padri e figlie, oralità e scrittura in *Beloved* di Toni Morrison." *Acoma* 5 (Fall 1995): 45–57.

——. "Su alcune forme e articolazioni del discorso razzista nella cultura di massa in Italia." *La Critica Sociologica* 89 (Spring 1989): 94–97.

——. *The Text and the Voice: Speaking, Writing, and Democracy in American Literature*. New York: Columbia UP, 1994.

——. "Tropes of the Talking Book: Olaudah Equiano between Three Worlds." *Palara. Publication of Afro-Latin American Research Association* 1 (Fall 1997): 55–65.

——. *Veleno di piombo sul muro. Le canzoni del Black Power* [*Lead Poison on the Wall: The Songs of Black Power*]. Bari: Laterza, 1969.

——. "Who Ain't a Slave? On the Universality of Frederick Douglass." *Regards croisés sur les afro-amèricains / Hommage a Michel Fabre [Cross Perspectives on African Americans / Celebrating Michel Fabre]*. Ed. Claude Julien. Tours: Presses de l'Université de Tours, 2003. 59–73.

——, ed. *Autobiografia di uno schiavo [Life and Times of Frederick Douglass]*. By Frederick Douglass. Rome: Savelli, 1974.

——, ed. *Libri parlanti. Scritture afroatlantiche*. Turin: Paravia Scriptorium, 1999.

——, ed. *Memorie di uno schiavo fuggiasco [Narrative of the Life of Frederick Douglass, An American Slave]*. By Frederick Douglass. Rome: manifestolibri, 1992.

——, ed. *Saggi sulla cultura afroamericana*. Rome: Bulzoni, 1979.

Powell, Timothy B., ed. *Beyond the Binary: Reconstructing Cultural Identity in a Multicultural Context*. New Brunswick: Rutgers UP, 1999.

——. *Ruthless Democracy: A Multicultural Interpretation of the American Renaissance*. Princeton: Princeton UP, 2000.

Reed, Ishmael. *Flight to Canada*. New York: Atheneum, 1989.

Reddy, Maureen T. *Crossing the Color Line: Race, Parenting, and Culture*. New Brunswick, NJ: Rutgers UP, 1997.

——. "Smashing the Rules of Racial Standing." *Race in the College Classroom: Pedagogy and Politics*. Ed. Bonnie TuSmith and Maureen T. Reddy. New Brunswick: Rutgers, UP, 2002. 51–61.

Riggs, Marlon, dir., prod., and writer. *Black Is . . . Black Ain't*. Videorecording. California Newsreel, 1995.

——, dir., prod., and writer. *Ethnic Notions*. Videorecording. California Newsreel, 1987.

Roediger, David. *Towards the Abolition of Whiteness: Essays on Race, Politics, and Working Class History.* New York: Verso, 1994.

———. *The Wages of Whiteness: Race and the Making of the American Working Class.* New York: Verso, 1991.

Roof, Judith. "Buckling Down and Knuckling Under: Discipline and Punish in Lesbian and Gay Studies." *Who Can Speak: Authority and Critical Identity.* Urbana: U of Illinois P, 1995. 180–192.

Roof, Judith, and Robyn Wiegman. "Introduction: Negotiating the Question." *Who Can Speak? Authority and Critical Identity.* Ed. Judith Roof and Robyn Wiegman. Urbana: U of Illinois P, 1995. ix–xi.

———, eds. *Who Can Speak? Authority and Critical Identity.* Urbana: U of Illinois P, 1995.

Rothenberg, Paula S., ed. *White Privilege: Essential Readings on the Other Side of Racism.* New York: Worth, 2002.

Rowell, Charles H. "An Interview with Larry Neal." *Callaloo* 6 (1985): 11–35.

Russo, Ann. *Taking Back Our Lives: A Call to Action for the Feminist Movement.* New York: Routledge, 2001.

Ryan, Susan M. *The Grammar of Good Intentions: Race and the Antebellum Culture of Benevolence.* Ithaca: Cornell UP, 2003.

*Sankofa.* Dir. Gerima Haile. United States / Ghana, 1993.

Scherman, Tony. "The Omni-American." *Conversations with Albert Murray.* Ed. Roberta S. Maguire. Jackson: UP of Mississippi, 1997. 122–136.

Shields, John, ed. *The Collected Works of Phillis Wheatley.* Schomburg Library of Nineteenth-Century Black Women Writers. Henry Louis Gates Jr., gen. ed. New York: Oxford UP, 1988.

Showalter, Elaine. "A Criticism of Our Own: Autonomy and Assimilation in Afro-American and Feminist Literary Theory." *The Future of Literary Theory.* Ed. Ralph Cohen. New York: Routledge, 1989. 347–369.

Siemerling, Winfried, and Katrin Schwenk, eds. *Cultural Difference and the Literary Text: Pluralism and the Limits of Authenticity in North American Literature.* Iowa City: U of Iowa P, 1996.

Simmons, Robert O., and Delores H. Thurgood. *Summary Report 1994: Doctorate Recipients from United States Universities.* Washington, DC: National Academy P, 1995.

Simpson, David. *Situatedness, or, Why We Keep Saying Where We're Coming From.* Durham: Duke UP, 2002.

Simpson, Louis. "Don't Take the Poem by the Horns." *Book Week* 27 October 1963: 6, 25.

Singh, Amritjit, and Peter Schmidt, eds. *Postcolonial Theory and the United States: Race, Ethnicity, and Literature.* Jackson: UP of Mississippi, 2000.

Smith, Barbara. "Toward a Black Feminist Criticism." *Conditions Two* 1.2 (1977): 25–44.

Smith, Valerie. "Black Feminist Theory and the Representation of the 'Other.'" *Changing Our Own Words: Essays on Criticism, Theory, and Writing by Black Women.* Ed. Cheryl A. Wall. New Brunswick: Rutgers UP, 1989. 38–57.

Smith, Virginia Whatley. "The Question of Comfort: The Impact of Race on/in the College Classroom." *Race in the College Classroom: Pedagogy and Politics.* Ed. Bonnie TuSmith and Maureen T. Reddy. New Brunswick: Rutgers UP, 2002. 153–166.

Sone, Monica. *Nisei Daughter.* Seattle: U of Washington P, 1979.

Sophocles. *Oedipus the King.* Trans. David Grene. *Sophocles* I. Ed. David Grene and Richard Latimore. Chicago: U of Chicago P, 1942.

Spivak, Gayatri C. *The Post-Colonial Critic: Interviews, Strategies, Dialogues.* Ed. Sarah Harasym. New York: Routledge, 1990.

Stanford, Ann Folwell. "Dialectics of Desire: War and the Resistive Voice in Gwendolyn Brooks's 'Negro Hero' and 'Gay Chaps at the Bar.'" *African American Review* 26 (1992): 197–211.

Staples, Robert. "The Illusion of Racial Equality: The Black American Dilemma." *Lure and Loathing: Essays on Race, Identity, and the Ambivalence of Assimilation.* Ed. Gerald Early. New York: Viking Penguin, 1993. 227–244.

Stowe, Harriet Beecher. *Dred: A Tale of the Great Dismal Swamp.* 1856. New York: Penguin, 2000.

Sundquist, Eric. *To Wake the Nations: Race in the Making of American Literature.* Cambridge: Harvard UP, 1993.

Takaki, Ronald. *A Different Mirror: A History of Multicultural America.* Boston: Little, Brown, 1993.

Tate, Claudia. *Psychoanalysis and Black Novels.* New York: Oxford UP, 1998.

Tate, Greg. "Introduction: Nigs R Us, or How Blackfolk Became Fetish Objects." *Everything but the Burden: What White People Are Taking from Black Culture.* Ed. Greg Tate. New York: Broadway Books, 2003. 1–14.

Taylor, Henry. "Gwendolyn Brooks: An Essential Sanity." *On Gwendolyn Brooks: Reliant Contemplation.* Ed. Stephen Wright Caldwell. Ann Arbor: U of Michigan P, 1996. 254–275.

Thomas, Kendall. "'Ain't Nothin' like the Real Thing': Black Masculinity, Gay Sexuality, and the Jargon of Authenticity." *Representing Black Men.* Ed. Marcellus Blount and George P. Cunningham. New York: Routledge, 1996. 55–69.

Thompson, Becky. *A Promise and a Way of Life: White Antiracist Activism.* Minneapolis: U of Minnesota P, 2001.

Thurgood, Delores H., and Julie E. Clarke. *Summary Report 1993: Doctorate Recipients from United States Universities.* Washington, DC: National Academy P, 1995.

Tompkins, Robert Farris. *Flash of the Spirit: African American Art and Philosophy.* New York: Random House, 1983.

Toomer, Jean. *Cane.* New York: Liveright, 1975.

Toth, Emily. "Women in Academia." *The Academic's Handbook.* Ed. A. Leigh Deneef, Craufurd D. Goodwin, and Ellen Stern McCrate. Durham: Duke UP, 1988. 36–45.

Trower, Cathy A., and Richard P. Chait. "Faculty Diversity: Too Little for Too Long." *Harvard Magazine* 104.4 (March–April 2002): 33–47. <http://www.harvard-magazine.com/on-line/030218.html>.

TuSmith, Bonnie, and Maureen T. Reddy, eds. *Race in the College Classroom: Pedagogy and Politics.* New Brunswick, NJ: Rutgers UP, 2002.

Twain. Mark. *Adventures of Huckleberry Finn.* Ed. Gerald Graff and James Phelan. New York: Bedford Books, 1995.

Walker, Alice. *The Color Purple.* New York: Washington Square P, 1982.

———. "In Search of Our Mothers' Gardens." *Ms.* May 1974: 64–70.

———. "In Search of Zora Neale Hurston." *Ms.* March 1975: 74+.

Warner, Michael. "The Mass Public and the Mass Subject." *The Phantom Public Sphere.* Ed. Bruce Robbins. Minneapolis: U of Minnesota P, 1993. 234–256.

Washington, Booker T. *Up from Slavery.* Ed. William L. Andrews. New York: Norton, 1996.

Washington, Mary Helen, ed. *Black-Eyed Susans: Classic Stories by and about Black Women.* New York: Anchor, 1975.

Washington, Robert E. *The Ideologies of African American Literature: From the Harlem Renaissance to the Black Nationalist Revolt.* Lanham: Rowman and Littlefield, 2001.

wa Thiong'o, Ngugi. "The Language of African Literature." *Colonial Discourse and Post-Colonial Theory.* Ed. Patrick Williams and Laura Chrisman. New York: Columbia UP, 1994. 435–456.

Watson, Donna J. "Scratching Heads: The Importance of Sensitivity in Analysis of 'Others.'" *Teaching What You're Not: Identity Politics in Higher Education.* Ed. Katherine J. Mayberry. New York: New York UP, 1996. 308–314.

Wheatley, Phillis. *Poems on Various Subjects, Religious and Moral.* London, 1773.

Wiegman, Robyn. *American Anatomies: Theorizing Race and Gender.* Durham: Duke UP, 1995.

———. "Whiteness and the Paradox of Particularity." *Boundary 2* 26.3 (Fall 1999): 115–147.

Williams, Gregory Howard. *Life on the Color Line: The True Story of a White Boy Who Discovered He Was Black.* New York: Dutton, 1995.

Wilson, Harnet E. *Our Nig; or, Sketches from the Life of a Free Black.* 1859. New York: Vintage, 1983.

"Women in the Profession, 2000." MLA Committee on the Status of Women in the Profession." *Profession 2000.* New York: MLA, 2000. 191–217.

Worsham, Toni. "From Cultural Literacy to Cultural Thoughtfulness." *Educational Leadership* 46.1 (1988): 20–21.

Wright, Richard. *Black Power.* New York: Harper, 1954.

Wright, Stephen Caldwell, ed. *On Gwendolyn Brooks: Reliant Contemplation.* Ann Arbor: U of Michigan P, 1996.

Yezierska, Anzia. *Bread Givers.* 1925. New York: Persea Books, 1975.

# NOTES ON CONTRIBUTORS

**WILLIAM L. ANDREWS** is E. Maynard Adams Professor of English and former Chair of the Department of English at the University of North Carolina–Chapel Hill. He is the author of *The Literary Career of Charles W. Chesnutt* (1980) and *To Tell a Free Story: The First Century of Afro-American Autobiography, 1760–1865* (1986). He is coeditor of *The Norton Anthology of African American Literature* (1997, 2003) and *The Oxford Companion to African American Literature* (1997) and general editor of *The Literature of the American South: A Norton Anthology* (1998) and "North American Slave Narratives, A Database and Electronic Text Library" <http://metalab.unc.edu/docsouth/neh/neh.html>.

**BARBARA A. BAKER** is Associate Professor of English at Tuskegee University in Alabama. She is the author of *The Blues Aesthetic and the Making of American Identity* (2003) and articles that explore African American musical forms in American literature, including "Jamming with Julius: Charles Chesnutt and Post-Bellum–Pre-Harlem Blues," forthcoming in *"Post-Bellum–Pre-Harlem": African American Literature and Culture, 1877–1919.* She is also the recipient of two grants from the National Endowment for the Humanities.

**DALE M. BAUER** is Professor of English and Women's Studies at the University of Illinois–Urbana-Champaign. Her book *Sex Expression and American Women* is forthcoming. She has also published books on Wharton, Gilman, and feminist dialogics.

**RUSS CASTRONOVO** is Jean Wall Bennett Professor of English and American Studies at the University of Wisconsin–Madison. He has written widely on African American literature, and his books, *Necro Citizenship: Death, Eroticism, and the Public Sphere in the Nineteenth-Century United States* (2001) and *Fathering the Nation: American Genealogies of Slavery and Freedom* (1995), include chapters on William Wells Brown, William and Ellen Craft, Frederick Douglass, Frances Harper, Harriet Jacobs, and Louisa Picquet. He is also coeditor, with Dana Nelson, of *Materializing Democracy: Toward a Revitalized Cultural Politics* (2002).

**NGWARSUNGU CHIWENGO**, Associate Professor of English, Director of the World Literature Program, and Acting Director of Black Studies at Creighton University, has published work on Anglophone and Francophone African, American, and African American literatures. She has taught both in the Congo and the United States. She is currently working on a book on Congolese literature and the body political and is completing work on a book on the South African novelist Peter Abrahams.

**KIMBERLY RAE CONNOR** is author of *Conversion and Visions in the Writings of African American Women* (1994) and *Imagining Grace: Liberating Theologies in the Slave Narrative Tradition* (2000) and many articles, reviews, and encyclopedia entries on topics related to African American religion and literature and multicultural pedagogy. Connor is also editor for the Academy Series, a joint publishing venture of the American Academy of Religion and Oxford University Press. She teaches at the University of San Francisco.

**JOHN ERNEST** is a Professor of English and Director of the African American Studies Minor at the University of New Hampshire (UNH). He received the Outstanding Assistant Professor Award in 1997, the UNH Diversity Support Coalition's Positive Change Award in 1998, the 2003–2004 Jean Brierley Award for Excellence in Teaching, and the New Hampshire Excellence in Education Award in 2004. His books include *Resistance and Reformation in Nineteenth-Century African-American Literature: Brown, Wilson, Jacobs, Delany, Douglass, and Harper* (1995) and *Liberation Historiography: African American Writers and the Challenge of History, 1794–1861* (2004).

**APRIL CONLEY KILINSKI** is a fifth-year doctoral student at the University of Tennessee. She is currently writing her dissertation entitled "Embodying History: Women, Representation, and Resistance in Southern African and Caribbean Literature." She has entries on African American authors forthcoming in the *Encyclopedia of the Harlem Renaissance* and in the *Encyclopedia of Ethnic American Literature.*

**NITA N. KUMAR** is Reader of English at Shyama Prasad Mukherji College, University of Delhi. Her recent publications include "The Logic of Retribution: Amiri Baraka's *Dutchman*" in *African American Review* (2003), "Black Arts Movement and Ntozake Shange's Choreopoem" in *Black Arts Quarterly* (2001), and many essays and reviews on African American and postcolonial literatures. She is also the recipient of a Mellon Fellowship at the Harry Ransom Humanities Research Center, University of Texas–Austin.

**AMANDA M. LAWRENCE** recently completed her doctorate at the University of Tennessee and is now Professor of English at Young Harris College. She has coauthored two textbooks for college writers and has published encyclopedia articles on numerous topics related to ethnic literatures. She is currently developing research on the development of the immigrant narrative across Jewish, African, Cuban, and Korean American literature for publication.

**ROBERT S. LEVINE** is Professor of English at the University of Maryland, College Park. His books include *Conspiracy and Romance: Studies in Brockden Brown, Cooper, Hawthorne, and Melville* (1989), *Martin Delany, Frederick Douglass, and the Politics of Representative Identity* (1997), and *Martin R. Delany: A Documentary Reader* (2003).

**LESLIE W. LEWIS** is Associate Professor of English and Director of American Studies at the College of Saint Rose. She coedited *Women's Experience of Modernity, 1875–1945* with Ann L. Ardis (2003). She is currently finishing a book entitled *Telling Narratives: African American Secrets and the American Psyche*.

**LISA A. LONG** is Associate Professor of English and Coordinator of the Gender and Women's Studies Program at North Central College. She is the author of *Rehabilitating Bodies: Health, History, and the American Civil War* (2003) and editor of the critical edition of Paul Laurence Dunbar's *The Fanatics* (2001) and has published numerous essays on African American literature and American women writers.

**BARBARA McCASKILL** is an Associate Professor of English at the University of Georgia. She is coeditor of the forthcoming book *"Post-Bellum–Pre-Harlem": African American Literature and Culture, 1877–1919* with Caroline Gebhard of Tuskegee University. She wrote the introduction for the University of Georgia Press edition of *Running a Thousand Miles for Freedom* (1999), the autobiography of the fugitive slaves William and Ellen Craft, and she is completing two books on the couple, *William and Ellen Craft in the Transatlantic World* and *New and Selected Essays on William and Ellen Craft*. She was a 2004–2005 residential fellow at the Radcliffe Institute for Advanced Study, Harvard University.

**NELLIE Y. McKAY** is Professor of English and Afro-American Studies at the University of Wisconsin–Madison. She is coeditor with Henry Louis Gates Jr. of the *Norton Anthology of African American Literature* (1996); author of *Jean Toomer, Artist: A Study of His Literary Life and Work, 1894–1936* (1984); editor of *Critical Essays on Toni Morrison* (1988); and coeditor of the Norton Critical

Edition of Harriet Jacobs's *Incidents in the Life of a Slave Girl* (2001), *Approaches to Teaching the Novels of Toni Morrison* (1997), and *Beloved: A Casebook* (1999). With Professor Stanlie James she is coediting the twentieth anniversary edition of *All the Women Are White, All the Blacks Are Men, but Some of Us Are Brave.*

**SABINE MEYER** recently received her doctorate in English and Feminist Studies from the University of Minnesota, Twin Cities. She is the General Education Program Coordinator for Rasmussen College in Eagan, Minnesota, where she teaches classes in American Literature, Popular Culture, and Film. Meyer has published on African American poets, lesbian vampire fiction, and queer parenting. Currently, she is completing a book project on the narration of deviance in recent "multicultural" American theory, fiction, and film.

**VENETRIA K. PATTON** is Director of the African American Studies and Research Center and Associate Professor of English at Purdue University. She is the author of *Women in Chains: The Legacy of Slavery in Black Women's Fiction* (2000), a *CHOICE 2000* Outstanding Academic Book, and the coeditor of *Double-Take: A Revisionist Harlem Renaissance Anthology* (2001). Her essays have appeared in black studies and women's studies journals as well as the recent essay collection *Postcolonial Perspectives on Women Writers from Africa, the Caribbean, and the U.S.*, edited by Martin Japtok (2003). Patton is pursuing several new research projects, including a book-length study on elders and ancestors in African American women's fiction.

**ALESSANDRO PORTELLI** teaches American Literature at the University of Rome "La sapienza" and is currently Advisor to the Mayor of Rome on historical memory. He was one of the founders of the Collegium for African American Research in Europe. Among his works published in English are *The Death of Luigi Trastulli and Other Stories: Form and Meaning in Oral History* (1991); *The Text and the Voice: Speaking, Writing, and Democracy in American Literature* (1994); *The Battle of Valle Giulia: Oral History and the Art of Dialogue* (1997); and *The Order Has Been Carried Out: History, Memory, and Meaning of a Nazi Massacre in Rome* (2003).

**JAMES D. SULLIVAN** is an Assistant Professor of English at Illinois Central College and the author of *On the Walls and in the Streets: American Poetry Broadsides from the 1960s* (1997).

# INDEX